The Forgotten World
of R. J. MacSween: a Life

By Stewart Donovan

Cape Breton University Press
Sydney, Nova Scotia

Cape Breton University Press recognizes the support of **NOVA SCOTIA**
the Province of Nova Scotia, through the Department of Tourism, Culture and Heritage
Tourism, Culture and Heritage. We are pleased to work in
partnership with the Culture Division to develop and promote our cultural resources for Nova Scotians.

Cover Design: Cathy MacLean, Pleasant Bay, NS
Layout: Mike Hunter, Louisbourg, NS
Cover photo: White Point, by Bill Danielson, Smelt Brook, NS.
Printing in Canada by Marquis Book Printing, Cap Ste Ignace, QC

Library and Archives Canada Cataloguing in Publication

Donovan, Stewart L. (Stewart Leo)
    The forgotten world of R.J. MacSween / Stewart Donovan.

Includes bibliographical references and index.
ISBN 978-1-897009-11-6

1. MacSween, R. J. 2. Poets, Canadian (English)--20th century--
Biography. 3. Authors, Canadian (English)--20th century--Biography.
4. Catholic Church--
Canada--Clergy--Biography. I. Title.

PS8575.S84Z57 2007   C811'.54   C2007-900806-2

Cape Breton University Press
PO Box 5300
Sydney, NS B1P 6L2 Canada

The Forgotten World
of R. J. MacSween: a Life

By Stewart Donovan

Cape Breton University Press
Sydney, Nova Scotia

Contents

$\mathcal{A}$cknowledgements

$\mathcal{M}$any people have contributed to the making of this story, no one more so than the group of former students and colleagues who surrounded and supported R. J. MacSween at *The Antigonish Review*. I am sad that George Sanderson, who died in November 2005, did not live to see the completion of this project. But I thank his widow, Gertrude Kearns Sanderson, along with Patrick Walsh, Sheldon Currie and James Taylor. In the MacSween family, I am indebted to Jessie (MacSween) Sutherland and her husband Art; Theresa (MacSween) Gallant and her husband Ivan; John MacEachern, Rod and Geraldine MacSween, Margaret MacSween and especially Dolores (MacSween) Crawford. Of friends, colleagues and former students the list is long: Mary MacKinnon, Jacqueline Walsh, Betty and Jack MacDonald, Leona MacDonald, Rev. Joe Marinelli, Katherine Chisholm, Rev. Frank MacNeil, Rev. Arthur Doyle, Rev. Malcolm MacDonell (former President of St. Francis Xavier University), Rev. C. H. Bauer, Rev. B. A. MacDonald, Sister Margaret MacDonell, CND; Kevin MacNeil, Effie and Jim Duggan, Margaret Drohan, Sister Helen Aboud, Rev. John Hector MacGregor, John Ross, Donald Gillis, Rev. B. M. Broderick, Rev. Hugh A. MacDonald, Kay Beaton, Freeman Whitty, Sister Madeline Connolly, Leo Furey, John Young, Sister Agnes Cordeau, Frances MacDonald, Lila Donovan, Oliva Dube, Alvin Donovan, Joe Coffey, Michael Dunphy, Barbara Donovan, Peter Sanger, David Conrad and John Donovan. Thanks to Norma Burke and Susan Parsons for transcribing interviews and to Kathleen MacKenzie, St. FX university archivist, for her help and expertise in the university records.

Many scholars have given advice, criticism and support: my brother, Ken Donovan of Fortress Louisbourg and CBU; Terry Whalen of Saint Mary's University; the late Fred Cogswell at University of New Brunswick; Alistair MacLeod of the University of Windsor; and James Cameron at St. FX. At my own St. Thomas University, thanks are due to William Spray, Robert Montario, Michael Clow, Rev. Jack Dolan, Trevor Sawler, Lorraine Nolan, Rev. George Martin (former President), Russ Hunt, Richard Kennedy, Tony Tremblay and Denis Desroches.

Some of the family, friends and colleagues of MacSween who helped, and whom I had hoped to please, are now deceased: his brothers Murdock and Michael MacSween (Father Mike), Rev. George Kehoe, Rev. E. Gatto, Ray Drohan and Msgr. Malcolm MacLellan (a former President of St. FX).

I would like to thank Dr. Daniel O'Brien, former president of St. Thomas University, for his support over the years and for the granting of a sabbatical leave on which much of this book was written. I would also like to thank Mike Hunter and the staff at Cape Breton University Press.

This book is dedicated to George Sanderson, Fenton Burke and Louis Dudek: three trusted friends and mentors who admired MacSween and encouraged the project.

Finally, I wish to acknowledge my partner and fellow traveller, Wanda Paul, for her support and encouragement.

*P*reface

I first met R. J. MacSween in 1974 when I took an undergraduate class from him in Modern British and American Literature at St. Francis Xavier University in Antigonish, Nova Scotia. The word was out on campus (and in my Cape Breton family and village) that MacSween was brilliant and that his classes were different. In 1974 MacSween was fifty-nine years old and he had recently begun to publish: *The Antigonish Review* had been founded by him in 1970 and he had also brought out two collections of his own poetry, *the forgotten world (1971)* and *double shadows (1973)*. As the years passed, those in, or interested in, the Canadian literary world acknowledged *The Antigonish Review (TAR)* as an important vehicle for literature and culture. Its founding editor, however, would not receive national recognition for his talents as a poet and critic until a few years before his death (and this recognition was critical rather than popular), when the late Louis Dudek praised MacSween as a major and neglected Canadian poet.

Because I came to know MacSween as mentor, colleague and close personal friend, this book was originally planned to be a memoir, but as time passed the project underwent a form of metamorphosis into what is now more or less a full-blown literary biography. When I look for someone to blame for the burden of this project I generally single out my brother first: Ken Donovan is a staff historian at Fortress Louisbourg, a professor of history at Cape Breton University and the author of numerous books and essays on the social and cultural history of Cape Breton Island. It was my brother who more than once reminded me that whatever MacSween's importance in the wider Canadian and English-speaking world might be or come to be, he was first and foremost a Cape Breton Scot. So, naturally enough, the early chapters of this biography trace MacSween's ancestry and family connections, mostly through oral sources.

The American writer and friend of Alistair MacLeod, Joyce Carol Oates, once remarked that there were no more biographies, just pathographies. Her word cuts, so I feel a need for some apologetics here, for justification. According to Oates, the writer, the biographer of the moment, now only looks for pathologies—sickness and flaws—something to bring the artist or gifted person down to our level, to say, "look, ah, I thought so!" And by so doing fulfill, among other things, those perennial stereotypes about dysfunction, sickness and madness in the lives of artists. It is my sincere hope that this exploration of the hardships in Rod MacSween's background and—more importantly perhaps, of the genuine suffering of his family—is seen for what it is, or what it was meant to be: an attempt to open doors, passageways to help the reader gain an entrance to and an understanding of the world that this relatively unknown, enigmatic and gifted man came from.

About three-quarters of the way through this biography readers will notice a slowing down in the pace of the narrative as I try to grapple with MacSween's poetry and criticism. This section was influenced, encouraged and guided by the late Louis Dudek. Finally, in the last sections of the biography, I have relied heavily on the personal correspondence and interviews of MacSween's niece, Dolores Crawford. Without Dolores' input it is doubtful that we would have got to see behind the curtain, got to view the genuine life and suffering that, partially at least, inspired the great poems so admired by Dudek and others.

The key sources for this biography are oral interviews, MacSween's correspondence and his published writing. The interviews with MacSween, his family, friends, colleagues and fellow religious were conducted over a fifteen-year period, beginning as far back 1986. If there appears to be an overreliance on these oral testimonies, it has to do with a legitimate necessity: they are a primary source because of the paucity of personal correspondence that has come down to us from MacSween and his circle, both private and public. Indeed, very few of MacSween's letters, either by or to him, have survived, and none of his sermons have come down to us in written form. Most of the correspondence quoted in the biography I obtained from relatives and friends, especially Mary MacKinnon and Dolores Crawford. The Archives at St. FX yielded few letters, but at least one of these was crucial to an understanding of the younger MacSween.

Fig. 1 Sketch of R. J. MacSween by Anna Syperek. Courtesy George and Gertrude Sanderson.

Introduction

*R*oderick Joseph MacSween, the figure who inspired this book, was born in 1915 into a rural, Gaelic-speaking community on Cape Breton Island. Shortly after his death in 1990, Louis Dudek, the renowned Canadian poet and critic, called MacSween our "great unknown poet."[1] There are many reasons that writers of merit, and poets in particular, go unnoticed or unrecognized in their lifetime. The history of literature has many examples: some are famous like the Jesuit priest, Gerard Manley Hopkins; some are writers passed over because of where they came from, a rural poet neglected by the urban centre; others, because of how or what they wrote, a style not in fashion with the prevailing taste or critics of the time, a content that appears archaic, arcane or simply outside the temper of the times; it could also be, of course, that the writer, like the once neglected Hopkins himself, simply chose to stay on the sidelines as a person not interested in attention or fame (if poets can still be said to participate in fame). It might be said of R. J. MacSween, as he came to sign himself, that he is unknown and unacknowledged as a poet for all of these reasons.

Like other Canadian writers—of the Maritimes in particular—MacSween grew up in conditions of extreme poverty and hardship; however, unlike fellow poets such as Milton Acorn and Alden Nowlan, MacSween's way out and up in the world would not be primarily through his writings, but rather through his religion. In 1941, when Rod MacSween turned twenty-six years old, he was ordained a Roman Catholic priest, a calling that would eventually lead him to a career as a professor of English at St. Francis Xavier University in Antigonish, Nova Scotia.

Father MacSween, as he was always known in Cape Breton and at St. FX, began his career in parish work: first, in the Village of Pomquet on the Nova Scotia mainland then, later, in the town of New Waterford, Cape Breton. After six years as a parish curate, he was recruited to teach at St. FX by Moses Coady and "Doc" Pat Nicholson, his uncle. MacSween had a distinguished career at the undergraduate school: during his tenure, he founded one of Canada's influential literary magazines, *The Antigonish Review*; he established the first creative writing course at a Canadian university; influenced the careers and work of writers such as Alistair MacLeod, Sheldon Currie, Lyndon MacIntyre and Leo Furey; and, last but not least, taught thousands of Canadian students from several generations. While doing all this, he also found time to publish a novel, a collection of short stories, dozens of essays, reviews and four major collections of poetry. It is all a very unlikely path for a priest who was also a poet or, depending on your point of view, a poet who also happened to be a priest. If you place the emphasis on the latter, the career becomes even more improbable, given that MacSween did not seriously devote himself to his poetry until well into his middle age.

Although he died in the last decade of the 20th century, there is much about Rod MacSween's life that harkens back to an earlier time. Like his parents and grandparents before him, he absorbed and experienced a pre-modern and now largely forgotten world. Today, in the popular imagination at least, Cape Breton Island has acquired something of a mythic status; it is seen, or at least often advertised, as a place apart, a land peopled by, among other things, Gaelic-speaking Scots fiddlers, step-dancing away in Highland kitchens. It is a recent construct, this land of the happy Gaels, and it is as prefabricated as a mobile home. It comes partly from development offices, recording studios and, most persistently perhaps, tourism brochures. It is partly a government response to high unemployment and outward migration, the end of a coal-mining heritage, the death of a steel plant and the legacy of the toxic tar ponds—industrial Canada's most notorious environmental legacy. But behind every rooted stereotype there is always a branch of truth, so we are not so surprised when we learn that Rod MacSween's parents did indeed speak Gaelic as their mother tongue, and that he was in fact born into the only surviving Gaeltacht (Gaelic-speaking area) in the New World and, finally, that his grandfather actually was a gifted Cape Breton fiddler.

In many respects, Rod MacSween, like Moses Coady and Jimmy Tompkins before him, was not typical of Cape Breton priests from his generation: though he spent seven years in parish work, he was born for the classroom, and his teaching—in all its ephemeral glory—is what he is now best remembered for. He was a humorous and extremely quick-witted man with an encyclopedic mind and almost instant recall. These gifts made him a formidable debater (and not just with undergraduates), but though he loved debate, it was never for its own sake—he always had a point to make. Like most gifted women and men of intellect, he did not suffer fools gladly, but his reputation among some students and faculty as an autocrat is silly—a product of the overly sensitive and often too easily bruised egos of the solipsistic young and the accredited academic. I do not want to leave the impression that this six-foot-four Cape Breton Scot was *The Friendly Giant* of a CBC children's show; he wasn't. Like most of us, especially those in the teaching or other public professions, MacSween wore masks, different ones for different occasions. And although he was never unapproachable, he was held in awe, fear and trembling by some academics and some students. The fear and trembling, at least where the academics are concerned, is a direct result of what Terry Eagleton once remarked as the difference between an academic and an intellectual (MacSween used the term scholar for intellectual). For Eagleton, "A snap definition of intellectuals might be that they are the opposite of academics."[2] Many academics tend to suffer from a form of myopia that prevents them from seeing beyond their narrow specialty. While it would be wrong to see MacSween as a public intellectual, given his role as a priest, he was nevertheless deeply engaged with fundamental social, political, religious and metaphysical questions that required him to be adept in more than one academic discipline. In Eagleton's words, he was an intellectual "concerned with the bearing of ideas on society and humanity as a whole."[3] Given MacSween's position, then, as this kind of intellectual among academics, he was bound to make enemies or, at the very least, generate hostility and fear when he expressed reservations about those who failed at what he saw was their professional and public duty. He did mellow, of course, as most us of us do with age, but when he died in 1990 at the age of seventy-five, there was no decline, no falling off of mental powers. He never became an old man.

This is one perspective and persona. There were many others: the champion of poor working-class children; the uncle who became a father to his nieces and nephews; the counsellor of confused and troubled young women; the priest who consoled the sick, the dying and the lonely; the scholar, polymath and artist whose mind seemed incapable of rest. Towards the end of his life, MacSween came to question the nature of his profession as a priest. He weighed the cost of his calling and the demands of its public world, a world that, as it aged, appeared to cast aside most of what he had believed in, fought and stood for. When the institutional church finally failed him, with its descent into sexual abuse scandals, he railed against it, both in his poems and in the presence of his bishops, colleagues, fellow priests and nuns. But despite the collapse and transformation of his traditional Catholic world MacSween never lost his faith, even though he sometimes gave the impression that he had. In his last years, he achieved and projected a serene equanimity in matters of the spirit, and while most of his poetry records a tragic vision, he himself was essentially an optimistic person.

As recently as the 1960s, the vocation of the priesthood was still regarded as one of the ways out of working-class Cape Breton. There is little doubt that Rod MacSween chose this route for himself, but there is nothing in the life or the work to suggest that he would have made another choice had the dice been rolled differently. His religion ran deep; it fuelled and drove his life and work. As a priest and a scholar MacSween knew that faith had historically united the common people and the intellectuals, the clergy and the everyday faithful in the strongest of bonds.[4] He knew as well that the narrative of religion was the grandest narrative of all because it could, in the words of Eagleton, "interweave art, ritual, politics, ethics, mythology, metaphysics, and everyday life, while lending this mighty edifice the sanction of a supreme authority."[5] If, during the latter part of his life, MacSween saw this authority crumble, both because of his Church's actions and its set of beliefs (dogma which seemed more and more improbable as time passed), he still firmly believed that the Church could be changed for the better, that it was not too late.

I have argued throughout this biography that for much of his life MacSween's Catholicism was akin to a form of nationalism, and that this nationalism was both a cultural and a political force in his life and work. Most intense in his early years, this cultural and political identification with his faith slowly waned as the old paradigm of Christian life and teaching, both Catholic and Protestant, gave way to the post-religious age. Unlike most of his calling, however, MacSween was able to make the transition to this secular world with relatively few scars. Though he was not a figure of the left, his powerful mind easily embraced society's movement towards more personal freedom in matters of faith and morals. More than most of his profession, MacSween knew that "religion could link questions of absolute value to men and women's everyday experience."[6] He also believed that religion was "by far the most resourceful symbolic form" the world had ever known and he believed that culture could not play surrogate to it for very long—Matthew Arnold's vision was not simply premature, but wrong. This is what many of his reviews and essays said, and it was how he spoke, taught and preached.

In his poetry a different story is recorded. His deeper self, as Marcel Proust would have it, seemed to acknowledge the other and darker side of the story. Environmental destruction, the commodification of culture, genetic engineering, the widening gap between the rich and the poor and many other such themes all surface. When he laments the death of the Church in his time, it is because he regarded the institution as a bulwark against the onslaughts of a consumer, materialist and imperial world devoid not only of the spiritual and the transcendent but, more presciently perhaps, of justice and compassion as well. Having grown up in a working-class Cape Breton coal-mining family, MacSween knew first hand the impact of uncontrolled industrial capital on the lives of ordinary people. Later, too, he came to see the vulnerability of men and women in a society that disregarded them. The death of ritual in their ordinary lives, the contempt of the consumer world for the human spirit, and the supremacy of power and politics would eventually lead MacSween to write a poetry that often renders the world as a place approaching apocalypse. This is not the welcomed or promised end so wished and willed for by many fundamentalists, but rather the inevitable and unavoidable tragedy of a world gone wrong. MacSween knew about the dangers of fundamentalism, but there is no sign in his verse that he saw how ugly and ferocious it would become in a post-cold war world. Still, the tragic dimension and sense of foreboding in much of his poetry has a symbolic resonance and relevance for all of us who now live on this side of the 9/11 world.

At the opening of the 20th century, when the Catholic Church began its battle with modernism in earnest, the French poet Charles Pèguy, off on his own and largely for his own purposes, articulated a formula which may help explain to a contemporary, secular observer how a poet and fervent Catholic could live within the orthodox and often reactionary confines of the Catholic Church. Pèguy wrote about the necessity of passing from *politique* to *mystique*.[7] Pèguy's case, of course, is politically and culturally of its own time and place, but his concern with mysticism connects him with both the present and the past. MacSween was not a mystic, but it was a condition he believed all true Christians—and of course Roman Catholics in particular—should aspire to; it was, furthermore, a state, a way of being in the world, that the poet in him could easily identify with and accept. In his later years, MacSween sometimes argued for his faith with artists and intellectuals from the wider and ever increasingly secular and skeptical world. In order to support his arguments, his faith, he invariably called upon the works of the great mystics that he had admired and taught over the years. MacSween's admiration for the tradition of mysticism in Catholicism increased and developed, not only with age but also with his own increasing awareness of the importance of art—and especially of poetry—in his life and work. As with his writing, MacSween's faith became more and more inclusive as he aged, and his omnivorous reading of the world's religions served the dual purpose of feeding both his faith and his insatiable hunger for knowledge.

The Irish poet Paul Durcan once remarked that the deeper he got into the life of an artist the more miserable, the more depressed he became, because of the suffering he encountered there.[8] He found it hard to finish reading a biography. The opposite, he said, was true of the work, which made him feel good, elevated his spirit, helped him to keep going. MacSween would give Durcan trouble, as neither the life nor the work is wholly celebratory or wholly tragic. Those of us who knew him might feel that the life was triumphant, a great achievement in the face of harsh odds. But there was much that was hidden. Even among his closest friends, MacSween was an intensely private person; there were always masks that never came off. His writing, too, perhaps somewhat predictably, is far from confessional in style or tone, but it is ultimately there—especially in the poetry—that the deeper self finally emerges and speaks.

As with his attitude toward religion and the church, MacSween's ideas on literature, art and culture altered over the years. He moves from a classic, if sometimes predictable, donnish conservatism, embracing primarily the high art sanctioned by a British imperial view of culture, to a wider and more inclusive view of the role art and culture in a postcolonial, postmodern and post-religious world. Somewhat ironically, perhaps, the Catholic writers he supported and championed throughout his life may have helped him on this particular journey. Predictably enough, Father MacSween wrote with a sympathy, openness and a generosity towards Catholic writers and artists that in today's secular world can really only be understood as a form of cultural nationalism—a partisan supporting and boosting of his own tribe precisely because they come from, record and are faithful to his world view, his sense of place both physically and spiritually. It is not surprising that MacSween would run into problems here, that his cultural loyalties, devotions and feelings would sometimes become conflicted. It is, as we shall see, both fascinating and at times painful to witness, as Canadian nationals, MacSween fighting these culture wars, especially during the nascent, fragile and not-so-long-ago beginnings of our own Canadian literary and cultural nationalism.

Any attempt, however, to label or place MacSween as a thinker or writer may prove futile. Though there were definite trends and leanings, as an intellectual he was both a polymath and, for the most part, an autodidact. His reading was voluminous and omnivorous: literature, philosophy, history, classics, economics, psychology and, of course, religion. What accompanied his extraordinary powers of concentration was a memory of equally extraordinary retention. It made him a formidable debater and a remarkable teacher. Because he never prepared lectures, his insights were new, not only for the students, but often for himself as well. This side of the man—the wit, humour and radical spontaneous insight—has been the hardest to reproduce on the page. The performer from the classroom remains, like the artist on the stage, elusive. While it is true that something of this natural and comic anarchy comes across in his letters, there are simply too few of these to give a complete or representative picture. Unlike one of his favorite writers, Evelyn Waugh, MacSween never successfully got the comic energy and wit of his conversation, lectures, sermons and everyday talk on to the page. Because of this, I have included some excerpts, both in the main text and in the endnotes, of conversations with MacSween taped during one of the many road trips he made throughout his life from Nova Scotia to Ontario.

Father MacSween would have deserved a biography had he not written a single poem: his life as a priest, teacher, critic and editor is remarkable and worthy of recognition; however, it is R. J. MacSween the neglected Canadian poet who inspired this book, and it is his poetry that most justifies and deserves our attention. Given this, I have tried in specific chapters—especially those concerned with poetry and prose—to give a critical overview of his work, to place it in the context of the Canadian, modern, Catholic, religious, cultural and literary tradition from which it came.

In an interview from the mid-1990s, the former American Poet Laureate Robert Hass looked back and reflected on the nature of modern poetry:

> Czeslaw Milosz, in his eighties, looks back across all the generations of experimental writing that he's lived through, from Valèry and symbolist writing and the early surrealist writing of his youth, through many of the forms of modernism, and as an old man, having seen an awful lot of the horror of the twentieth century, has an ideal of writing poems that are as plain and accessible as possible. So it's interesting to me to have been in Berkeley at a time when there was this terrifically interesting

postmodern poetics that was if anything even more difficult for ordinary readers than modernism, at the same time that I was translating this old poet who had tried on every avant-garde movement of his time and had come to the conclusion that they were mostly the vanity of wounded artists who hated the middle class that they grew up in. I think that an awful lot of American writing since the 1950s was in some ways anti-modernist.[9]

There is much in this quote that helps explain the nature of Rod MacSween's own poetry and poetics. Although Ezra Pound, the most difficult of the high modernist poets, was MacSween's professed favourite, his own verse, like that of Milosz, is plain and accessible. MacSween's poetry has been described by the late Louis Dudek as classical in style and content, a verse written in tempered, chaste rhythms with a pared down, minimalist diction. The underlying moral vision of a poet like MacSween further complements this chaste style in that it is informed by an awareness, if not a fondness, for the ascetic—a natural enough response, on reflection, for a priest in the age of rampant consumerism and unfettered technology.

One of Rod MacSween's curious strengths as a poet lies in what many have often considered to be a fatal weakness—his refusal to accept the consolation of being exclusive and apart. I refer of course to his unique upbringing—his Cape Breton Island heritage—that strong sense of cultural and political identity the island fostered and still proclaims. This is the world his former student, Alistair MacLeod, has so singularly and successfully made his own, especially in his award-winning novel, *No Great Mischief.* Why MacSween refused to write about his own past, both private and public, is complex, and I explore it at some length in the chapters that deal directly with his poetry and fiction. But whatever his reasons, MacSween spent half a lifetime developing a detached, historically-minded style without reference to his Cape Breton heritage. There is, of course, a great danger when writing poetry of this nature. Intellectual verse, the poetry of ideas, even when it is rife with irony, runs the risk of being cerebral, unemotional, passionless and detached. The scholarly and critical debate about this kind of verse goes back at least to the 18th century when, as many of us were told as undergraduates, Dr. Johnson accused John Donne and his fellow 17th-century metaphysicals of disassociating their sensibilities, of deliberately writing poetry without feeling. While we might acknowledge that taste does come into the matter, it is still true that when MacSween's poetry falters it often does so because it seems to lack feeling, that emotion we so often demand from our best poets. The risk, then, is great when writing a poetry that appeals specifically to the intellect, but, then so too are the rewards. When writing of this nature succeeds, it does so at the highest level of achievement; lyrics of no more than a few lines, and short narrative poems of a page or so, often carry as much freight and meaning as a novel or an epic poem. MacSween's verse at its most charged acts as a kind of moral barometer for the century in which he grew up. And more often than not it successfully and dramatic-ally gives utterance to those voices whose lives have been passed over, for those who, through suffering, oppression, or neglect, have been silenced and forgotten.

Given his calling as a priest and teacher, it is not surprising to find that many of his best poems are meditations on how we live; they are sermons that don't preach, lessons that shun the quick fix and the easy answer. Writing as late as he did, the poetry is naturally assured and confident, but it is never dogmatic. There is no closure, for instance, in a poem like "because," the last stanza of which ends with ellipses, ends by continuing:

> because there is no time
> because life is a rush
> and ends before we can speak
> because everything distracts us
> from the few important things
> we sense beyond the light
> because we should like to be free
> although we know that freedom is impossible
> except in limited and restrictive ways
> because...

In a late poem entitled "a door closes" MacSween talks about the dimin-ishment of life, "when all our dreams are denied," and he warns us that if we are not careful the door will close "upon the time of chances"; these chances are to be seized upon not only because they are redemptive and restorative, but because they are also deeply connected with our inner selves and our inner lives:

> within the soul
> the loom weaves
> a tapestry of many colors
> the embroidered fantasies
> willed into being
> by the secret self

There is, of course, as with all important artists and poets, a central idea, a fundamental theme that lies at the heart of the work. In Father MacSween's case, perhaps not surprisingly to most, it is his concern with the death of his Church in the postmodern world. This theme, which first appears in *the forgotten world* (1971) collection, manifests itself over time as one of the most complex, tragic and, eventually, enlightening spiritual journeys to be undertaken in our literature. Taken as a whole, R. J. MacSween's poetry, from his first collection to his last unpublished pieces, can be viewed as a spiritual autobiography, unique not only to our own literature, but, I would argue, to the literature of the English-speaking world, and not just the Catholic dimension of that world. With the end of theory as we have known it, writers like Terry Eagleton have highlighted the necessity, indeed the urgency, of returning to the questions and concerns that preoccupied the old grand narrative of eschatology. Religion, as we have known it, may be gone in the West, but death, evil and non-being, among other things, are still very much with us. And, as Eagleton says, "It is non-being which fundamentalists fear most. And what they plug it with is dogma."[10]

In the pages that follow I have tried to explore, with the biographer's often limited tools, both the public and the secret selves of this largely hidden poet; my goal, to use the poet's own words, has been to reveal something of the tapestry of many colours that this neglected artist so brilliantly willed into being. It is my further hope that this exploration, this mining of Rod MacSween's past, will flesh out the man behind the often iron masks of priest, professor and poet to show the reader something of the complex, compassionate, and compelling person who abided there. Finally, once readers have met this unknown figure, it is my fervent belief (to use the language of his paradigm) that they will seek out his poetry, a verse unique in our literature, a lyric and narrative voice that not only deserves our attention, but—as with all art— inevitably rewards it.

I   *I*ronville to the Bay: In Search of Family

*I*n the last week of April 1915 Mary Jessie MacSween boarded the Sydney and Louisbourg train at the small wooden station in Ironville along the shores of the Bras d'Or Lake on Cape Breton Island. She was nearing the full term of her pregnancy and was making the journey to North Sydney where her fifth child, Roderick Joseph, would be born on May 8th. During the past five years, she had made the same journey for three of her other children—Murdock, Michael and George—and she would make it again three more times, for Margaret, Catherine and Patrick, all before 1920, before the family left the small ancestral farm at Ironville forever. These trips to North Sydney were both a necessity and a homecoming for Mary Jessie, a necessity because the nearest hospital to Ironville was in the port town, and a homecoming because her parents, George and Catherine Nicholson, lived there.

In his later years, Rod MacSween recalled one of these birth journeys made by his mother:

> Pat and the two girls were younger than me. They had all the children when they were in Boisdale. I remember when Pat was born we were at table when the letter arrived (I don't know who presented the letter) which came from North Sydney where my mother had most of us. She'd go down to her home in North Sydney and then go to the hospital from there when her time was due. My father was reading the letter and we were all gathered around him and my brother, George looked over his shoulder and said we have a baby boy! It's a boy! My father wasn't saying anything, he was just reading the letter.[1]

Although Mary Jessie spent her years as a young adult in North Sydney, she was born and raised until the age of twelve on a farm in Beaver Cove, not many miles from where she now lived. Her father, George Nicholson, was a carpenter, a woodcarver and cabinetmaker, who had travelled much of Cape Breton Island building and finishing homes, churches and other public buildings. He had built the church in his own village, the Gaelic-speaking parish of Boisdale, the same parish where he met and fell in love with the local schoolteacher, Catherine Johnston:

> George went to work in the States when he was a young fellow. A few men from the parish of Boisdale had gone to Boston and they were working full time, so he mentioned to his betrothed that he'd like to go and she said yes. So he went, and of course he couldn't write; didn't know how to—and there were no telephones then. So there was no correspondence between them. But after a year, a friend of his came home from Boston for vacation and he attended a pie social at the Parish Hall in Boisdale—and Catherine Johnston was there having a great time! So when he went back to his work in Boston, he told George Nicholson that if he didn't get home soon Catherine Johnston would be picked up by somebody else because she was having such a good time the night of the pie social! So he didn't waste much time getting back. And they were married on St. Valentine's Day, 1876.[2]

George Nicholson and Catherine Johnston were in their mid-thirties when they finally married on that Valentine's Day in 1876. The career of schoolteacher, embodied by Catherine and passed on to the Johnston women, was also handed down to the Nicholson daughters[3]—so too, was the tradition of marrying late. Although well-educated for the time (she had her grade eleven), Mary Jessie did not end up teaching school like her mother and her sister; instead, she married Hugh Malcolm MacSween, at the relatively late age of twenty-nine, on June 30, 1908. Hugh MacSween, a large, handsome man of twenty-seven, came from the same Gaelic-speaking parish of Boisdale as his bride. An unskilled laborer with little or no education, Hugh was clearly seen as "marrying up" when he joined the Johnston/Nicholson clans.

Like many Scots Cape Bretoners, the Johnstons and the Nicholsons came originally from the Hebrides, those rugged, remote and sparsely populated islands off the coast of Scotland. In a similar fashion, the genealogy chart also locates the MacSween clan's origins on a Gaelic-speaking island off the Scottish coast. The first immigrant MacSween to arrive in Nova Scotia, Hugh (Rod MacSween's great-great-grandfather) landed with his wife and family in Sydney on the *William Tell* on July 25, 1817. Gaelic-speaking farmers and fishermen,[4] they settled in Beaver Cove and

Ironville near the shores of the Bras d'Or Lake. And it was on one of these homesteads that Rod MacSween's father, Hugh, great grandson of that original settler, tried to make a living from the land in the years before and during World War I.

Hugh MacSween did not return to the family farm in Ironville out of any particular love for the land—he had, after all, spent most of his young adult life as a coal miner. Beginning in 1909, however, the year his first son was born, Hugh had been involved as an active union member in what was to be one of the longer and more bitter strikes in Cape Breton coal-mining.[5] When the strike finally ended in 1910, after nine long months and a confrontation with the Canadian military, Hugh found himself, along with many other fellow miners, blacklisted. When he tried to get hired at different pits on the island, he was simply told there was no work for him. Unable to obtain employment in the mines—or anywhere else in industrial Cape Breton—Hugh was forced to sell the home he had built on Argyle Street in Glace Bay for a hundred dollars. Without a source of income or a place to stay, Hugh, his young wife and their infant son, had little choice but to return to the small and impoverished homestead in Ironville.

At this time, of course, it was not unusual for miners who were either blacklisted or injured to try and make a living from farming, but those who

Fig. 2 On the top of MacSween's Farm, *by Christine MacKinnon (courtesy Ron and Ruth MacKinnon).*

were forced to do so mostly lived on the fringe of the mining community. In so doing, they would often receive help from family, friends and others who were sympathetic to their plight, help they wouldn't otherwise obtain if they lived in rural isolation.[6] This isolation and poverty meant, among other things, that families like the MacSweens often had more in common with 19th-century pioneers than with 20th-century farmers. In his later years, Rod MacSween remembered scenes from his parents' constant struggle with the land, scenes that often seem to belong to another time and place:

> Out in the field one day my father kicked the horse to get him back in the traces, but he had the wrong harness on the horse. The big harness had broken but my father wanted to plough so he put the harness for a small horse on him, but the poor horse was always putting his feet outside the chains. My father would have to get him back before he could start plowing again so he would lift the horse's foot up and put it back. But my father got impatient and he kicked him on the side of the hoof, then the horse kicked him on the thigh. He barely managed to get home. He crawled into the house and I was there, and my mother greeted him and she was wondering what happened to him, and he told the story. Then I remember him lying on the couch with her putting hot compresses on him. It was probably the wrong thing to do but that was what she was doing—steeping flannel in hot water and putting it on his leg. Many years later, oh it must have been 30 years later, I asked him about it, and he had told me what had happened. No, they couldn't make a living at farming.

The young couple struggled for more than ten years to make a living from the small farm, but poor land (only 26 per cent of Cape Breton land is arable), great distances from markets where they might sell what they grew or raised, and, perhaps most importantly, an ever increasing family—all eight children were born by this time—made the battle with the land a fight they could not win. In the summer of 1920 Hugh and Mary Jessie packed their eight children and few belongings onto the train in Ironville and left the old homestead; they would never again return to live in the Gaelic-speaking parish of Boisdale.

Mary Jessie had no choice but to take her eight children to stay in North Sydney with her parents, the Nicholsons, while her husband returned once more to Glace Bay to try to find a job at the only work besides subsistence farming that he had ever known—coal mining. It had been ten years since the 1909 strike, and Hugh felt that with the passing of time he might no longer be blacklisted. Eventually, he did find work in the pits, but he was soon injured in a rockslide. Like all the MacSweens,

Hugh was a large man, over six-foot-two and two hundred and fifty pounds, and so mining for him, as for all big men, was done bent over, often on their knees. Hugh soon returned to work after the rockslide, but his injured leg continued to bother him, and the water (always present in the mines in those days) was a constant irritant that kept the leg from healing. Desperate to get better, the young miner asked the pit boss in his still heavily accented English (Gaelic being Hugh's mother tongue) if he could be transferred to a drier colliery. The company response was to send him to a pit where the salt water of the mine reached not to his knees, but to his waist.[7] Clearly, and perhaps not unpredictably, his days on the picket line as an active union member had not been forgotten.

In later life, Hugh spoke to his nephew—another Rod MacSween who had settled in Antigonish—about his early days, who relates: "When Hughie went to the mines to work as a young fellow, he didn't know any English. He could only write a little bit, and write in Gaelic. They'd make fun of him because of the brogue he had."[8] Unable to continue mining because of his injury, Hugh eventually landed a job on the railroad working for the Sydney and Louisbourg line where his brother, Jim, was track master; it was through his brother's influence that Hugh was able to hire on as part of the maintenance crew. Given his work ethic, it did not take Hugh long to become foreman of the maintenance crew, and in the years that followed he would help his sons get jobs working in the nearby shops and railyards. Although he now belonged to the railway workers' union, Hugh insisted—for the rest of his working life—on paying two sets of union dues, the second payment of dues was for the United Mine Workers of America.[9]

As was the custom in those days, children were often given the name of a close family relative: in Rod's case, it was Mary Jessie's eldest brother, Roderick Nicholson, who was so honoured and whose name would be carried on. Towards the end of his life, Rod MacSween tried to recall the man whose name he'd been given, an uncle whom he had met only when he was a boy: "He went early to the States to work. He married an Irish-American girl, Aunt May, with whom my mother corresponded all her life." His uncle Rod did leave one impression on the boy: "He seemed to me the reincarnation of his father. He had the same gentle, friendly manner and he resembled him physically as well."[10]

If Rod Nicholson never had the chance to be a model for his nephew or to make a lasting impression on him, his younger brother, Patrick Joseph

Nicholson, more than made up for this absence. This Nicholson was to have a very profound influence on MacSween. Doc Pat, as the elder man came to be known, would eventually lead his nephew to the priesthood and later to a career in university teaching. In the spring of 1915, however, Patrick Nicholson was far from his North Sydney home, having recently transferred from the Grand Seminary in Montreal to the newly opened St. Augustine's Seminary in Toronto. The institution had been recently founded by the newly appointed Archbishop of the city, Neil MacNeil, a Cape Bretoner and a former president of St. FX.

The autobiographical pieces written in the last five years of MacSween's life recall what life was like for a boy on a farm in rural Cape Breton at the beginning of the 20th century. While most of these stories and images are pastoral, if not idyllic, one of his first and earliest recollections was both industrial and political:

> A memory that has never left me for any length of time was the sight of the train going by decorated with flags and banners. It was mysterious and different but I had no idea what was the import of the decorations. I said nothing about it until I was about thirty years of age. At that time I asked my mother to give me the reason for the existence of such a train. "It must have been the end of the First World War," she said. The time must have been November 11, 1918, and I was in my third year.[11]

This intrusion of the outside world was rare in the rural life of the remote farmland, a place only slightly less isolated than the island of Barra, the home of those first emigrant MacSweens. In many respects, the customs, folkways and even the language of those early and distant 19th-century Scots, continued unabated in the lives of their great-great-grandchildren who could claim, however tentatively, to be citizens of the modern world. For MacSween, the most exotic and mysterious of these old-world trad-itions was the Gaelic language itself. Both his father and mother had grown up speaking Gaelic, and as the years passed this ancient tongue became a private language, something shared only between husband and wife, not unlike the language of love: "As long as my father and mother lived, they spoke Gaelic when together. We were accustomed to wait until they would turn to us in English. One reason we never heard anything gossipy or scandalous was that they had already exhausted those subjects between the two of them." Whether the Gaelic they spoke to each other was passionate or not, MacSween imagined it to be so, and he felt that "It made their English conversation rather bland, but their Gaelic was a matter of high mirth, of sudden outbursts, of roguish glances at each other and at us. The fun was buried deep in the language itself."[12]

The general culture of this rural area was still Gaelic, but none of the MacSween children learned to speak or understand the ancient tongue. And while the parents did not discourage their children from learning Gaelic, they made no special effort to teach them either, feeling, no doubt, as with most working-class people, that a minority or emigrant language would be a handicap, or at least a difficulty for them, in the wider English-speaking world—as it had so clearly been for the twelve-year-old Hugh when he first shouldered a pick and shovel to work in the mines of Cape Breton. MacSween recalled:

> My father showed no desire to teach us Gaelic. He himself had gone
> to school for only about three years. At that time the children all spoke
> Gaelic. The classes were in English and he learned very little. Then
> eventually he got work in a mine in Glace Bay. I've been told that he
> was only twelve years of age at the time. With his poor command of
> English and strong Scottish accent, he was often an object of mockery
> for the older men. Hence he regarded Gaelic as a drawback and a
> hindrance.

MacSween remembered though that his father regretted the loss of his language: "In his later years, there were times when he felt that what he had left behind was more precious and belonged to his very blood and bone, and also that no substitute, however worthy, would ever replace it."[13] An irony not lost on MacSween was the fact that his mentor, his mother's brother, "Doc" Pat Nicholson, became a leading scholar and promoter of the Gaelic language, not just at St. FX, but throughout Cape Breton and eastern Nova Scotia, wherever in fact there were native Gaelic speakers, and wherever the local Diocesan newspaper, *The Casket*,[14] was read.

In his memoirs, MacSween writes about the passing of this ancient culture, this forgotten world, and his tone is always tinged with regret and sadness as he records in elegy the time of his ancestors. There is a strong note of nostalgia, a feeling of loss; and so the recollections often read as a lament for a people, a place and a language that he could see and hear all about him as a child, but that he knew he could never belong to:

> It existed as naturally as the air and its outward manifestations were in
> music, song and folktale. The prayers of the older folk were in Gaelic.
> When we had finished our night prayers, said all together and led by my
> mother, we repaired to bed. But my parents remained on their knees to
> say their Gaelic prayers. It was as if English prayers did not count for
> those who had learned Gaelic prayers in their early youth. They were

good enough for the children—but not good enough for those initiated into the mysteries. My father entered into these prayers like a diver entering the water on a hot day. He let himself go with relief into the comfort of the old forms after he had moved to one side the inferior rituals that impeded his way.[15]

There were tragic stories associated with this Gaelic world, stories about people trapped, in the words of Brian Friel, in a paradigm of language that no longer matched the landscape of fact, of reality; one such story concerns an Aunt Mary:

If she were here now, I would be able to appreciate her properly—it takes that long to grow up to the stature of such people. When I was young, we used to laugh at her Boston accent, taking for granted that it was affected. But it wasn't. She went to Boston as a young girl and could speak only Gaelic. She landed at a police station, as she was unable to find her way. A policeman knew a family that needed a maid and there she went. She never reached the place she had been aiming for. It was in Boston that she learned English and, of course, the accent went with it. She must have known some English before this—but very little—not enough to become accent-proof. Peter Campbell's wife died, leaving about 6 children and the family decided that she was to marry him. She must have been at least 40. I'm not sure. She attended a family council—I think at Uncle Jim's. She said she would make up her mind after speaking with Peter Campbell. She did and refused to marry him. The family council persisted, saying that it was her duty—and she gave in.[16]

We could easily imagine the story and person of Aunt Mary amid the pages of Alistair MacLeod's short stories or his novel, *No Great Mischief*. MacSween knew many such stories, but as MacLeod himself has said, he chose not to record them in his fiction or his poetry.

MacSween was remembering and writing these stories from the vantage point of his old age, and so these recollections often read as the memoirs of a son inspired by his parents—and in particular by his father. It is very much a public record even when it is about private things:

I was too young to be present in the church at Boisdale and I never heard the hymns that were sung there. What I heard all the time was my mother singing. She sang day in and day out—as she worked. Most of her songs were in Gaelic. They had a fine impetus and a strong beat, good songs to work to. Later on I picked their melodies up here and there—I never learned the Gaelic words. I found out that most of them were love songs that she in turn had learned from her mother. To me, my mother was already old, but the incomprehensible lyrics spoke of youth, and love, and passion, and the fleetingness of summer.[17]

This, then, is part of the public picture that Father MacSween chose to present to the world; and what it records is by times courageous, compassionate, gentle and, almost always, nostalgic.

Though I eventually got to meet all of MacSween's living siblings, there was little to glean from them about the nature of their early life, especially their private life as a family. MacSween rarely spoke about his parents, brothers or sisters, and when he did it was always in general and public terms. Part of this was temperament, talk of his family would be small talk, and very personal small talk; it is not so much that MacSween would have regarded this as self-indulgent, but rather that he was always more interested and at home when discussing ideas about art, culture, et al. He never objected if students and friends wanted to pass the family album around, so to speak; he simply would not do so himself. This, of course, was, to a large extent, typical of his generation and his class; moreover, the Catholic religion in general, and the training of the priesthood in particular—the confidence of the confessional—always insisted on the subjugation of the self. MacSween, too, could call on at least one of his favorite writers for intellectual and artistic support in this area: the modern Anglo-American poet T. S. Eliot always insisted that the highest calling and the most sublime art were an escape from the ego, from personality. MacSween always took the time to emphasize this point in class whenever he taught the poetry of the author of "The Wasteland."

Like all of his friends, students and colleagues, then, we accepted without question what he told us about his family, and we believed that what he told us was all that there was worth telling. It was not until later, several years after his death in fact, that the stories, the details, about the nature of his early family life finally began to emerge. It is not a happy tale. The young MacSweens—especially the older boys—were raised in a crucible of violence. For those of us who knew MacSween, it landed like the shock of ice water on a summer day, especially as there had been no inkling that his childhood world had been anything but idyllic. It soon became clear, however, that the violence that surrounded him as a child was one of the reasons he left home as early as he did, and why he returned to his parents so rarely. It provided a clue as to why MacSween sought out so many other families throughout his lifetime; and why, perhaps, so much of his poetry was so often impersonal in nature and tragic in tone—especially the ones about family and childhood.

This discovery about MacSween's background, about the man and boy behind the masks, provides a certain level of insight into his poetry, but it is important to remember that this is only one road (and a back road at that) into the poet's world and art. In the age of the close-up and the biography channel, we have all been led to believe that the life is all. Yet we know that if poets, and artists in general, could be explained by environment alone, life would be simple indeed—so, too, would the art.

Fig. 3 Beaver Cove Cape Breton, 1919. From left to right Mary Jessie, unidentified woman, Margaret, George, Joe, Murdoch, Mike, Rod and Hugh MacSween with their maternal grandfather, George Nicholson. Courtesy Stewart Donovan.

In a family photo taken on the shore below the farm in Ironville, six of the eight MacSween children stare out at us from the summer of 1919. Rod MacSween, age four, peeps over his father's knee, while his four older brothers sit in a row beside him. Margaret, the only girl in the photo, sits on her mother's lap and smiles; Joe, the eldest, looks confident, his younger brothers shy. The father, Hugh, looks somewhat bemused, while his father-in-law, George Nicholson, stares sternly at the camera. The children are book-ended by the parents, but the men in the foreground dominate the photo—indeed, the explicit patriarchy of their presence almost overwhelms it. A half-century later, in the fall of 1974, MacSween, then fifty-nine years old, received a letter from Dolores Crawford, the only daughter of his eldest brother Joe. He knew *of* but did not *know*, his niece, having seen her only twice since she was a child: once at her graduation from high school in Glace Bay in 1957 (where he stood quietly at the back of the hall then left), and ten years later, at her father's funeral. Like many Cape Bretoners, Dolores lives in Alberta, where she moved in her early twenties. Her leave-taking, her "going down the road," like that of her only brother Michael, had something behind it, something driving it, besides the predictable economic necessity of earlier and subsequent generations; for this particular Cape Breton brother and sister, the journey out was also a necessary escape—a headlong flight in fact—from suffering and abuse. Their mother was mentally ill and their father, Dolores stoically recalled, "was very, very violent." She left home, "truly left home," before her seventeenth birthday.[18]

In 1974, with both of her parents now dead, Dolores MacSween Crawford wrote to R.J. MacSween—professor, priest, poet and uncle—in the hope that "Father Rod" might be able to tell her something about her family tree, about the history, public and private, of the world, the clan and the family she and her brother had come from.[19] In the months and years that followed, MacSween would tell his niece many things about his family, including his firm and stated belief that his parents should never have married. "The MacSween-Nicholson mix didn't work," Dolores recalled him saying, as he shook his head in sadness. Both niece and uncle confirmed that Hugh MacSween was an autocrat, a tyrant as father and husband who instilled fear in his wife and children. The record is grim, and it includes the severe beating of the two eldest sons, one of whom was the father of Dolores Crawford.

When I went to interview two of MacSween's living siblings, Michael and Murdock, I did not know then what Dolores later told me. Mike MacSween, much better known than his brother as a highly respected Cape Breton priest, began his recollections with his boyhood visits to his Gaelic-speaking paternal grandmother. Unlike his younger brother Rod, there is nothing nostalgic in these recollections, there is no sense of loss or longing; for Michael, his visits to the grandmother were painful experiences: "She lived with Mrs. MacIssac, one of her daughters, out in Paschendale and the greatest ordeal of my life was to go visit her. We couldn't talk to one another! This poor old lady was sitting there by the stove, and she couldn't speak a word of English!" Mike also recalled how "there was a feeling in the schools that if you spoke Gaelic you were considered a hick." His older brother, Murdock, had similar memories, not specifically about the grandmother, but rather about their own life on the small farm in Ironville:

> All I remember from when we lived in Ironville was poverty. All we
> ever farmed, for some reason, was potatoes and turnips. I remember

digging these in the fields. And you accepted these things when you were growing up. It was years after I began thinking about the hardships we had—they had—and the old house was that cold all we did was chop wood. You couldn't imagine how poor they were! Outhouses! No hot water! Today it's inconceivable, I guess, but I don't know.

Hugh MacSween and Mary Jessie Nicholson, had their financial circumstances been different, might have been better able to cope with the large family they now had in their care. Their story is a sad one. In Ironville, Mary Jessie and Hugh, who appear to have been poorly equipped as parents to begin with—especially Hugh—found themselves in desperate isolation. In his old age, Mike MacSween confessed to his niece, Dolores, that for all her love and effort, his mother couldn't cope:

> Father Mike actually said to me that he hated his mother—he hated his mother! And he hated her because she favoured the others over him, but he also said because she could never control the kids. She was always threatening them with, "Wait till your father gets home." And he was expected to go to work all day and then come home and discipline the children. And look at who the children were—these Godzillas on the hoof! It took me about two years to actually get through to him, "Look! This unwell mother had eight children." I cannot even imagine that myself.

When Hugh MacSween did get home from work the boys, especially the older ones, were punished—and punished severely. Murdock MacSween, by all accounts, was treated brutally as a child; he was a boy with a fierce will in an age when children were to be seen and not heard, as that fearsome Victorian cliché had it. Eventually—no doubt fearing for the child's safety—Mary Jessie contacted her parents in North Sydney, begging them to take the boy. They agreed, and so he was sent to live with his grandparents, as his brother Mike remembered: "Murdock was left with the grandparents for some years and when he was restored to the family—I think the reason they sent him back was because they couldn't control him—he was kind of the city boy against the country boy, and so he kind of looked down on us." Mike also remembered that "Rod hated Murdock when he was a boy," no doubt because Rod was younger at the time and would have been given more attention, attention that Mike also resented. Mary Jessie, it seems, made the fatal mistake of playing favorites among her children—and Rod was one of them; Mike and Murdock were not. In his old age, Mike recalled that "Rod created a lot of problems at home and he didn't take any punishment for it. He was resented." Mary Jessie's other favourites included the bright, articulate and affable George, and the eldest son, Joe. As the eldest, Joe naturally held a special place; a place, however, that eventually would cost him dearly, as his daughter, Dolores, discovered:

> Mary Jessie was very fond of my dad [Joe MacSween] because he was the oldest. And he was the one who would help her. When she was pregnant and she needed the floor washed, when she needed the bread kneaded, he was always willing to do that. Of course she had to close the door and make sure that nobody came in because this was not a masculine thing to do. But as long as she did that he would do anything for her. He was willing to scrub the floor, help make the bread, and help with the children.

Inevitably, when Joe became a teenager, he challenged his father:

> From what my mother told me Mary Jessie was very frightened of Hugh. My grandmother used to confide in my mother, they were kind of kindred souls, and that's how my mother found out about the beatings that Joe had taken. He always had back trouble, and my mother said it was because he had had a chair broken over his back by Hugh. I don't know what the circumstances were, but Joe himself was very violent with my brother—I witnessed that and my mother said that she had to stop Joe from wanting to beat the baby. She said that that broke her heart.

Fig. 4 Joe MacSween in the 1950s. Courtesy Dolores Crawford.

When Dolores first explained how hard life had been at home, with the violence of her father and the mental illness of her mother, her uncle Rod professed to be "shocked." But when she continued to talk about her grandfather, the son of Hugh Malcolm and Mary Jessie finally dropped his mask, and spoke from the heart about his father, mother and siblings. Dolores already knew much of the story: "I think he knew that we agreed about the family, I certainly never took any offence from it—none meant and none taken. I was in my late forties by this time and it was just like sitting here talking to you about it."

Dolores Crawford was not the only niece or nephew to acknowledge the disparate nature of the MacSween/Nicholson mix. Other nephews and nieces, like Jessie Sutherland and John MacEachern, were objective, articulate and compassionate about their parents, grandparents, uncles and aunts. If only Dolores ever received verbal confirmation from uncle Rod, it was probably because of her status as an exile. Her few and infrequent trips back East may have created a sense of ease, of freedom, between the uncle and the niece—a chance to say things long buried, but not forgotten. For Jessie Sutherland, Father Rod was also like a second father, though they never spoke about the dark side of their pasts—there was, it seemed, no need. They saw each other at least once or twice a year, and it was simply understood that things were the way they were.

From all appearances, Rod MacSween seems to have been spared the direct physical abuse visited upon his brothers, though he certainly would have heard or witnessed the beatings, seen the suffering; his age, and, no doubt, his temperament, seem to have shielded him. As he often told his niece, he kept a low profile and, as he grew to manhood, he had enough sense not to engage his father or, more importantly, to challenge his authority. He also had the luxury of his position in the pecking order: his older brothers had already laid down the challenge, taken the beatings. He became, as his niece relates, an outsider, able to stay on the fringe of the beatings and the violence by keeping himself legally busy playing sports and staying away from the house. Often he would come home late for supper. He said that he learned how to escape, and when the others were all getting into trouble, he wasn't; and most of the trouble he did get into came from his siblings because he didn't get the regular beatings they were getting.

Looking back, MacSween told his niece that he had found a "way of escaping it." He did not feel that "he had had a difficult time." He was at a loss as to why his brothers didn't see what they were up against, didn't see things for what they were; instead, "They would walk right into it. He would just sit back and say, 'Why are you opening your mouth?' They would just blunder right into it, create havoc and get half-killed." Dolores recalled that her uncle Rod "was pretty sensitive to the violence that went on around him, and he thought that anyone who had half a brain should have been able to avoid it. You know, he would say, that for very smart people—they probably had very good IQs—but, as far as inter-family and interpersonal relationships went, there was so much to be desired. They weren't clever in that way."

There were others outside the family circle who knew how fierce "Hughie" could be: another Rod MacSween, a first cousin and namesake, remembered his uncle: "Hughie was a hard man—a cross, hard man. They tell the story about his two oldest children, Joe and Murdock, when they got working they bought a car. But he wouldn't allow them to take it home. Had to park it somewhere else. They couldn't take it near the house. He figured they shouldn't have bought the car." There are other stories, too, that confirm Hugh's reputation as a grim man. His grandson, John MacEachern, who saw him almost daily in his childhood, recalled never having seen his grandfather smile.[20]

Fig. 5 Rod MacSween age 4, Beaver Cove, 1919. Courtesy Stewart Donovan.

Memory, of course, is selective, and so when MacSween chose to write about his own childhood he recalled (or perhaps in some cases created) only the beautiful things. He must have realized, too, that as a small boy, and the third youngest, he was somewhat protected—a boy who lived beyond the reach of the violence his older brothers endured. So with this relatively sheltered position, MacSween, in his old age, could recall his last summer on the family homestead as a time of joy, a time when he participated in a "Golden Age:" "When I think of my last year in Ironville, I can think of nothing but the sun shining on a fresh world. My Father was working in Winnipeg and my brothers ran wild. We lived on the beach at the front of our farm and the older boys swam like fish in the water of St. Andrew's Channel. To my memory we seemed to be nowhere else but on the beach all that summer." The summer "dragged slowly on, seeming to last forever." This time, then, without his father was "idyllic," the only summer he can recall as having been so, with a "lazy warm atmosphere and the bright water of the lake." He goes on to remark that he did not recall other summers because he was "too young." He does not say, naturally enough, that the freedom and nostalgia associated with that summer had to do with the absence of the father, but the sentence "My Father was working in Winnipeg and my brothers ran wild" speaks volumes about the absence of authority, control, fear and violence that Hugh so clearly represented. Later on in life, MacSween "judged other times and places" by his "experience of that early period," so that in the end, "Nothing else ever came near it."[21]

MacSween did not write many poems containing references to childhood, but there are a few scattered throughout his published work. One is entitled "turn back time," and it celebrates the house—but not the home—of his childhood in the rhymes and images of traditional children's verse:

> down the straight lane
> I saw my house
> in the deep trees
> crouched like a mouse
>
> fading from me
> shrinking inside
> the worn-out fence
> where I used to hide
>
> those trees were once
> up to my knees
> now they shiver
> close to the eaves
>
> trees thick with leaves
> you are not mine
> loved long ago
> in summertime
>
> these measure time
> express its will
> but I turn back time
> my heart stands still
>
> my heart stands still
> to catch in rhyme
> the early bliss
> of summertime

The charm and innocence of the verse are reminiscent of Walter de la Mare, Robert Louis Stevenson and of our own Bliss Carman, and there is no reason to read what we know of MacSween's past into what is, after all, a fairly conventional poem. Still, it is hard to resist seeing the second stanza as emblematic of his time in the home and not the house.

MacSween's most powerful, imaginative rendering of childhood is found in a late poem from his last published collection. An austere lyric, it reaches back past childhood, past infancy, to birth itself; entitled simply, "just born," the poem is about the pain, shock, mystery and loss associated with coming into the world:

> I think of myself just born
>   blood and filth on my mouth
>   air scorching my lungs
> and my cry quivering in the air
>   uttered not for nurses or doctors
> through the great spaces of the sky.
>
> and even up to God
>   my fierce cry
>   demanding an explanation
> why this rape from the infinite
>   into this question box of a world
> why this imprisonment in time and space
>   and in this animal body
>   made for limitation and suffering
>
> to be nothing and then suddenly something
> to hardly feel and then to be in pain
> to be in an envelope of flesh
>   and then to be open to sound light and air
>   to be pricked by numberless stimuli
> to be all alone and then to be the centre of touch
>   circled by voices and eyes
>
> much later in my crib
>   I reached out to catch the birds
>   that flew above the trees
> when I opened my hands
>   they were empty
> I saw only my empty hands
>   those symbols of captivity
> as I grow old shall I capture
>   and retain[22]

MacSween wrote this poem about birth and infancy in his late sixties and it reveals, through stark images and plain statement, much of the world view that his deeper self came to embrace. Though it is written about infancy, the point of view is clearly that of the aged man looking back to where and when it all began. As with most of his poems, it poses more questions than it provides answers: what, we might ask, is to be captured on the journey through life, and what retained? The empty hands as symbols of captivity: are these the penniless rich palms of a selfless Christianity? Or the forsaken hands of unfulfilled lovers? Perhaps they are the helpless hands of the child hiding forever behind the fence? No doubt the poem is about all these things and more.

When Hugh MacSween returned from working in Winnipeg at the end of the summer of 1920, he and Mary Jessie boarded up the old home-stead in Ironville, sold their few remaining animals to nearby neighbours, bundled up their eight children and boarded the train for North Sydney; they were going to stay with Mary Jessie's parents until Hugh could find work to support them somewhere in Cape Breton.[23]

MacSween was five years old when the family moved to North Sydney, so it is not surprising to learn that the impact of the large and elegant home on Archibald Avenue—and of the grandparents who lived there—was overwhelming. It is no wonder, too, that Murdock felt out of place when he returned home to the poverty and oppression of Ironville, having shared, if only for a few years, the comfort, privilege and affection that this house so clearly represented. Over the years, MacSween spoke and wrote at length about the presence and importance of this home and the maternal grandparents who lived there. One instance of the respect, love, and, indeed, awe in which he held his grandfather, is recorded in a reminiscence from his first years as a student at St. FX:

> When I was in college, I was asked to write an essay on the most
> wonderful man I had ever known. I did not hesitate. I grabbed pen and
> paper and poured out my admiration for my grandfather. Of course,
> he was unaware, or only partly aware of my feeling for him as I saw
> him but seldom, and even then I was completely tongue-tied by all the
> fears of early youth.

On reflection, it is a strange essay topic to assign to a first year university student—predictable, perhaps, only in its patriarchal subject matter. I can think of few male undergraduates who would write an essay praising their father like this; yet, it speaks volumes that MacSween singled out his grandfather for such praise, and not his father.

The Nicholsons were not middle class, but they were not of the labouring class either. Their relative prosperity came from the considerable building skills of the father, George, who, by all accounts, was a gifted carpenter, wood carver, and musician—he was also a man deeply loved and respected by all who knew him. For the children and grandchildren, he seems to have been the kind and gentle grandfather of legend to whom almost everyone could turn to in time of need, knowing they would receive the necessary comfort or help. The image of his playing the fiddle every evening, with the children gathered round to listen, is remembered and cherished by the

Fig. 6 Drawing of George Nicholson (1840-1932) by Christine MacKinnon, 1924. Courtesy Mary Gillis.

MacSween family. His wife, Catherine Johnston Nicholson, also had a reputation for generosity, especially when it came to befriending the local Mik'maq women who came to the fishing port from the nearby Reserves to sell their handmade baskets and other goods. As a boy, MacSween had witnessed this special relationship between his grandmother and the Mik'maq women: "Once, going in to dinner, I saw an Indian woman for the first time. She sat next to me while we ate and seemed completely at home. My grandmother treated her like one of the family." Over the course of the year that he stayed there, MacSween was "dimly aware of the coming and going of other Indian women," who "put their parcels in one of the sheds, ate with us, and also—I take for granted—slept somewhere in the house. When the selling stint was finished they went away with bags of various kinds on their backs." Years later, when MacSween was studying for the priesthood in Halifax, his grandmother died and he was unable to attend the funeral. One of his brothers recounted the event to him the following spring, noting with pride both the size of the funeral and the fact that it appeared as if all "the Indians of Cape Breton came and walked behind the hearse to the graveyard."[24]

In 1920, when George and Catherine Nicholson were still very much alive, they had once again become directly involved in their daughter's welfare. Before the year was out, however, the big home in North Sydney would be empty once again as Mary Jessie and her husband took their children and returned to where they had first begun their lives together a decade earlier—in the mining town of Glace Bay.

IN an essay on the life and work of the English novelist and poet, D. H. Lawrence, MacSween noted that:

> Others had written of the working classes and of their style of life, but none had realized them in literature with such startling truth. We can feel the life that Lawrence saw around him until the very spirit of the coal mine is ours, and the bewildering mental and physical life of his father—coarse, happy, intemperate, vigorous— is before us as though by touch. And then there are the beautiful natural scenes of field and wood and sky, as yet not destroyed by the savage machinery of men.[25]

MacSween was in a unique position to judge whether or not Lawrence was writing with "startling truth" about the working classes because he himself had come from a mining town that could easily have found a place in the pages of a novel like Lawrence's *Sons and Lovers*. Although Glace Bay, New Waterford, and Sydney are now relatively quiet communities and fledgling tourist destinations, these small cities and towns were once centres of working-class struggles; cauldrons of urban, industrial unrest that had few equals throughout the country. In the 1920s in particular, the fight for social justice in Cape Breton's industrial towns was similar to struggles in many of the world's larger cities. The battles between the left and the right, between labour and business, communism and capitalism, socialists and conservatives, took place at the pitheads and coke ovens, on the streets and in the courts, and at all levels of government. In the early 1920s, MacSween and his older siblings would have witnessed some of the dozens of parades and marches that took place on the main streets of his new hometown. Such parades boasted banners with "Workers of the World Unite" and were led by figures like the radical and fearless labour leader J. B. MacLachlan.[26] MacSween would have heard his parents talk about the battle of Waterford Lake, June 11, 1925, which culminated in the death of William Davis and the wounding of several other miners; his parents would have also witnessed the Canadian militia with its machine gun nests stationed throughout the town, and they would have known, too, about the desperate living conditions of the miners and their families—conditions that saw more than 12,000 people on relief from

Sydney Mines to Glace Bay. Like most urban Cape Bretoners, they were all-too-familiar with a setting created by a 19th-century form of predatory capitalism, a capitalism that was largely ignored by all levels of government; federal and provincial public policy consisted of *laissez faire* at best and, at worst, military intervention on behalf of the employer. Historians of the period acknowledge that only "the unprecedented relief effort by trade unions and service, church and welfare associations at the national level prevented wholesale starvation."[27]

Given these social conditions, it is not surprising that the religious, social and cultural life that MacSween lived and witnessed as a boy was often political in the extreme. Prior to the mid-1920s, the Catholic Church in Cape Breton was seen to be almost always on the side of the company and the establishment; content to maintain the status quo. When, for example, Hugh MacSween first stood on the picket line during the strike of 1909, armed men and machine guns faced him from their confident and secure post on Catholic Church property;[28] this was the same Church that sustained itself largely with miners' dues. Because of its importance and prominence in the dominant culture of the day, the Catholic Church was able to take notorious sides like this with both confidence and impunity—knowing it had the loyalty of its laymen and the backing of its hierarchy. An instance of this loyalty in the 1920s, was recorded when "Moscow Jack" MacDonald took the platform before a crowded hall of 700 miners in Glace Bay in 1925. One Stuart McCawley was not impressed:

> He started with a long quotation from an Italian poet, the audience didn't get it. He should have quoted Burns. He then scrapped the Bible, and the churches, told how the universe was made, took his hearers for a trip along the Milky Way, to Mars and the Moon ... flopped into the churches again. The audience sat dumb. The Highlanders can't stand knocking religion.[29]

In time, the emergence of the Antigonish Movement in the early 1920s would help change the Church's position, at least in Cape Breton and eastern Nova Scotia, by moving it from the company's camp and closer to that of the workers.[30] Although the Antigonish Movement was primarily a rural movement, born out of the need to help impoverished farmers and fisherman, it nevertheless also assisted and influenced the lives of Cape Breton miners and their families. It would be wrong, of course, to overstate this, given the traditional reactionary nature of the Catholic Church, and the presence of communism (the first "Red scare" took place in the 1920s in both the U.S. and Canada). It is not surprising to learn that the hierarchy and the clergy failed on a large scale to meet the miners' needs in areas of education and social justice—areas where it had much to offer.[31] Eventually, if reluctantly, the Church was able to introduce some progressive social policy within the diocese. That it did so was due almost exclusively to the vision and energy of two gifted Cape Breton priests, J. J. (Jimmy) Tompkins and his double first cousin, Moses M. Coady. These two Cape Breton priests of Irish heritage would help set the tone of the times that MacSween grew up in, and one of them, Moses Coady, would later have a profound influence on his career as a professor and writer.

Fig. 7 Moses Coady was born in Margaree, Cape Breton. Courtesy St. FX University Archives.

From the mid-1920s on, Reverend Moses Coady became the driving force behind the Antigonish Movement at St. FX. Chair of a then recently established Department of Education, Professor Coady founded and became head of the Department of Extension at the university in 1928, the same year in which he was appointed Chair of the Royal Commission on the Maritime Fisheries. In the twenty years that followed, Moses Coady would become one of Cape Breton's most famous sons, and his reputation as a teacher and social activist would gain international recognition for him, his university, his home province of Nova Scotia and the Maritimes in general.

It was during one of Coady's many trips to Glace Bay to promote extension work that MacSween first heard him speak at his local high school, where he was "spellbound by Coady's mixture of intensity and humour." In the years to come, Moses Coady would prove instrumental in getting MacSween a teaching position at St. FX, but in 1932 the young man was already under the powerful influence of a priest who was also a professor at the Catholic university and, more fatefully perhaps, this priest also happened to be his uncle—"Doc" Pat Nicholson.

*A*mong MacSween's papers at St. FX are a dozen or so pages of notes about his own life up until about the mid-1960s. Handwritten in point form, these notes begin with what seem to be his first readings. Interestingly, he began these notes, "this life," with literature, with his first encounters—or at least his first remembered encounters—with stories and books: "First story—'Bluejay' Second story—The Man with Glasses'." Notes two through five list some of his other reading material, books by and about pirates, Aztecs, Ted Strong: "His horse's hoofs were plopping the white dust," Nick Carter, Dick Merriwell, "Tales of a Grandfather," *Highways of History*, "Dickens for Christmas," history in "the funnies" which included stories such as "I ran money for Sparta" and "Lycurgus, Assyrian king shooting arrows." In number eight of these notes on ado-lescence he records "Fascination of history." All of this is very cerebral and bookish, but in case we think that MacSween was the stereotype of the pale intellectual and bespectacled boy, note six reads "My father chasing me to bed" and seven, "You're going to lose your soul over baseball."[32]

MacSween's older brother, Mike, confirms these notes and remembers when his younger sibling first began to read seriously:

> Well, I'll tell you what happened to Rod. He was lucky—see, when I was going to school there were no books. I remember the Sisters at St. Anne's letting me look at—when I was in grade ten—*The Last Days of Pompeii*. I took it home and I thought, what the hell am I reading this for? Most of the books I had were Frank Merriwell and Jessie James and Nick Carter. I read them every day, and *Western* magazine. But it was about this time that the St. FX Extension Dept. started a library in Glace Bay—and Rod haunted the place! He'd go down every day and take out a bunch of books, and then he would go up to his room and stay there until he read them. And he kept doing that. He was in grade ten at the time so he'd be about fifteen. Oh, I remember it distinctly; he just wouldn't come downstairs until he finished the books. He had an awful yen for reading.

*W*hat initially drew MacSween to the world of books, the world of ideas and imagination? Besides the obvious fact that he was gifted, there can be little doubt that he also sought refuge, escape perhaps from the oppression and violence that always threatened to break out in the home. There are many subtexts among MacSween's early readings, some of which are, no doubt Freudian and some of which, too, are formative. Joe and Murdock

MacSween would both eventually pass their grade eleven, leave school and go to work at the same job as their father. These two eldest sons were trying to move out and up in the world, trying to make the inevitable break with home; and so, like most young men, they went to dances, dated girls and longed for independence. The world of teenage girls and sex seems to have had little attraction for MacSween. In later life, MacSween would form many strong, emotional and lasting relationships with women, but sex never seems to have been a primal draw. Early photos show him to have been a very handsome—even striking—young man, and no doubt the young women must have cast looks in the schoolyard at the athletic teenager. The intense intellect, however, coupled with the fierce personality and the all-pervasive influence of his church, no doubt helped to keep the young 1930s women at bay.

There is, of course, the tragic example of his parents. In his public writing and conversations, MacSween often spoke of observing the love that existed between them, but we now know different; we know, for example, that Mary Jessie feared her husband, not only in his middle and old age, but from the very beginning of their lives together. One of the saddest confirmations of this fear occurred when she broke her hip—just before she died in 1950. Mary Jessie was outside walking in her backyard, hanging out some clothing on the line, when she slipped and fell, but instead of crying out to her husband for help she crawled next door to her daughter's home so as not to upset her husband.[33]

Inevitably, given the celibate nature of the priesthood, readers will no doubt wonder about MacSween's sexuality. But, as with women, there is no evidence of any inclination in this direction. He had, naturally enough, many strong male relationships—lifelong friends—but they were never more prominent than the women in his life, and at some stages they were less so. While he took the standard view of the time on homosexuality (he saw it as an aberration, a psychological illness socially acquired), and he held this view until fairly late,[34] he never regarded it as a sin—in his old age he acknowledged the folly of his Church's position.

If girls or boys did not preoccupy MacSween at this time, then books, baseball and hockey certainly did; the teenager would also be serving mass as an altar boy and like many other boys his age, he would be wondering about a call to the priesthood. We can imagine that the attraction of this calling would be all the more appealing given the conditions at home. There was also, on a more positive note, the shining example of his uncle, Doc Pat. Unfortunately, there is no one left to tell us what MacSween was actually like as a student in elementary or high school, but we can

Fig. 9 Grade Six, St. Anne's School, Glace Bay, Cape Breton, 1927. Rod MacSween is second from the right, four rows up; his best friend Dan is third from the left, second row. Courtesy Stewart Donovan.

These are pupils in Grade Six, Ste. Anne's School in 1927. In the front row, left to right, are Murdoch Steele, Francis Misener, Dannie MacDonald, Joe Bates, Bill O'Neill and F.B. MacDonald. Second row: Tom McEwan, Lloyd Livingstone, Dan Ed MacDonald (Kink) Elmer (Tug) MacCormick, John W. Devison and Joe MacDonald. Third row: Frank Novak, Dan Currie, Ronald MacLeod, John Gallagher, Joe MacDonald, Frank Anderson, and Leonard Nolan. Fourth row: Charlie Rooney, Alex Burton, John MacDonald, George Slamko, Bill McNeil, Rod MacSween, and Francis MacNamara Fifth row: Michael MacDonald, Henry Gates and Bill Burke. Sixth row: Gus Slade, Peter Stewart, Eddie Gaul, Duncan MacIsaac, and Malcie MacNeil. Seventh row: Steve Morrison, Jim AuCoin, Murdoch Dunn, Edgar Connor, F.J. McNeil, Don MacAdam Francis McNeil and Dave Flynn. Back row: Paddy Hayes, Charlie Gillis, Bob Desjardine George Petrie, Bernard McKay and John Mahe. (Courtesy of Elmer MacCormick)

guess that the bookish boy would answer when called upon by the nuns. His brothers, Mike and George, were also studious and had no trouble making the grade. And like their brother, too, the career and position of their uncle, Doc Pat, shone before them, and in a very short while the priest-professor would directly enter and change all of their young lives forever.

Patrick Joseph Nicholson graduated from Johns Hopkins University in Baltimore with a PhD in Physics in 1913—and he was among the first Nova Scotians to earn such a degree. The records show that he was certainly the first at his alma mater, the small Catholic college in Antigonish, where he returned to teach in the fall of 1916. The precocious Cape Bretoner had turned down many fine offers from both large universities and industry that final spring in Baltimore before his convocation.

Fig. 8 "Doc" Pat Nicholson. Courtesy St. FX University Archives.

Later, when he boarded the train to leave the southern American city, he would have known that another leg of his journey had been completed: from the outset, young Patrick Nicholson, like Tompkins and Coady before him, was headed for the priesthood and a career in teaching at his undergraduate alma mater, St. FX.

Wherever Patrick Nicholson's sense of "mission" came from, it wasn't, in the beginning at least, nurtured by his father, George Nicholson. Murdock MacSween, who lived with the Nicholsons for several years as a boy, recalled a story he had heard from his grandmother:

> My grandfather didn't want Father Pat to go to college—it was a waste of time. He wouldn't support him. So Father Pat took jobs down town, working until 2 or 3 o'clock in the morning. He used to scrub lawyers' offices and things like that. That's how he got the money to go. My grandmother was telling me this. Anyway, the first year he was at St. FX he took every prize but one, and everybody was making such a fuss about him that his father said, "Well, seeing as you're so stupid and can't be told anything, I guess I'll have to help you." So he helped him from then on. I remember my grandfather took me upstairs one day and showed me Fr. Pat's drawer full of medals. He was their pride and joy.

When Patrick Nicholson arrived on the campus of St. FX in September of 1916, the young scientist trained in the opulent laboratories of Johns Hopkins University would have seen little to encourage him. His long-time friend and fellow Gaelic-speaking Cape Bretoner, Fr. Malcolm MacDonnell (who would also become a president of St. FX) spoke of the world that greeted his mentor:

> He came up from Johns Hopkins, a layman with his doctorate in physics, and walked past some very attractive offers of employment, went into the seminary for three years, then came back here, where

he was going to take over physics. They took him over to the lab, and that was an empty room with nothing in it. He wasn't the type to back away from any challenge. He just rolled up his sleeves, picking up any bits of equipment he could find anywhere. We had just started to build a physics program. There's no question he is the founder of science here.[35]

To be regarded as the founder of science at your alma mater is no small achievement, but Nicholson also had other distinctions, including that of recruiter. Although the historian Raymond MacLean has shown that the tradition of recruiting young men for the priesthood—and having them educated in places as far away as Rome—began as early as the 1840s,[36] there is little doubt that Nicholson was one of the most zealous champions of vocations that the diocese had ever known. Like Tompkins and Coady, Nicholson wanted these young men to enter the priesthood so that one day they might return to help the communities that so desperately needed their skills in areas of education, social work and religion. Naturally enough, when he saw that two of his nephews might make good young men of the cloth, he lost no time in recruiting them.

The first of the MacSween family to be singled out by "Uncle Pat" for St. FX—and, eventually, the priesthood—was the third eldest boy, Michael. When in his late seventies, Mike recalled the day Doc Pat approached him about going to the college:

> Well, I was working for the Company at the time and I was shovelling—I was going to say shovelling shit all day. The first job I had was cleaning sewers out around the company houses in Caledonia. And I used to say to myself, "This is all there is to life?" Anyway, Doc Pat encouraged me to go to college. He asked if I wanted to go. "Well," I said, "I think I'd better. I'm not going to be cleaning sewers all my life, that's for damn sure."[37]

Sending young men to university, and eventually to the seminary, was no small financial matter. Murdock MacSween recalled the sacrifice made by his parents so that his brothers could go to St. FX: "You take putting those two priests through college—Father Pat helped them and they got help from different societies, but they had to scratch like hell themselves to get them through. My father had nothing to do with handling the money, it was my mother, and she scratched like hell to get whatever bills came in, tried to pay them." In later life, MacSween, too, recalled how poor his family was during these years, and he remembered going home once and finding his mother in a happy mood because she had finally paid off a debt:

We had this bill from the wholesalers. So every week when my father got his pay my mother drew two dollars out and sent it off to the wholesalers. And that went on for years and years—1920 to about 1938. My mother paid the bills, paid that wholesaler back. My father's pay was so low that all she could afford was two dollars a week. I came home from the seminary one time and my mother was telling me about it. She said, "I finished the last payment at Vooghts." The wholesalers name was Vooght. She said we got a letter back from them, and were they ever proud of it. They had said in their whole experience of wholesaling that they had never had such an experience as this one. They kept the money of course, but they praised my father and mother very much.

In later life, too, MacSween's older brother, Mike, once confessed to his uncle Doc Pat that, "I have grown up with a certain fear of debt."[38] It has been argued, that because of their long history of oppression and famine, the Catholic Scots, like their Irish cousins, have inherited a racial fear of the poorhouse; when this historical fact is combined with the poverty of Mike MacSween's parents, his fear of debt hardly seemed surprising.

Murdock MacSween, like the rest of the family, was naturally very proud of his two brothers going away to become priests, but he too, along with his older brother, Joe, had to make extraordinary sacrifices to make this possible. The fact that both young men were expected to stay home until the age of thirty was part of the extraordinary cost: "I felt obligated early on. I started to work when I was seventeen. Most of the money went home. I was getting $2.75 a day and that was the going rate. When I became eighteen I moved up to $3.25." Murdock, too, recalled, towards the end of his life, an incident from this time concerning his brother Joe:

Something terrible was done to Joe, I didn't realize it at the time, although I sympathized with him. He was working on the Sections and he'd be making $90 a month. My father was talking to the boss in the warehouse department, and they needed somebody. He asked the fellow would they give Joe the job and he said yes. He came home and told Joe he would have to go—I remember that night! Everything but the roof came off and my father wouldn't give in— "You've got to go! You've got to go!" They stood toe to toe that night in our living room—they almost squared off! My father couldn't go back to this fellow and tell him that he wouldn't come. So he stuck to his guns and finally Joe said, "To hell with you, I'll go then!" to the detriment of his whole life. Joe was reduced from $90 perhaps a $100 a month to $52! When the taxes were off he drew $42 a month, which he paid $40 home. He had nothing. When he tried to keep a little more than that, they'd have a fit. At the time we didn't realize what was happening to him, but—my God—that must have devastated him! Joe was reduced to poverty by the time he got married, and I didn't realize these things until later years. I think my father had the idea that working in an office was a big uplift, something better than the slaving down below that I was doing. But there was more money in it. So Joe was reduced to practically slavery for the rest of his life. Nobody realized it. Roddie never realized it. I never realized it—what an awful thing to happen.

In his old age, MacSween was asked by his niece Dolores why he had gone to the seminary? Why, in fact, had he become a priest? He replied, "Just to make it tough on everybody else." According to Dolores, her uncle was not joking at the time, but the statement, on reflection, seems to be more about escape than revenge.

IN an interview conducted shortly after MacSween died, Alistair MacLeod spoke about his former professor's poetry and the difficulty, the challenge, of really knowing the man behind the masks of priest and professor:

> When I read some of those poems, I think almost of what Matthew Arnold would call the buried life, or something like that. He obviously didn't want to write about his neighbors. But I think a lot of the poems are very deeply reflective and probably very, very honest. The critic Kenneth Burke has a phrase.... This is not quite accurate, but the gist of it is: In the depths of his imagery, no man lies, which means that when images are as refined as they should be in good poetry.... And as refined as they were in MacSween's poetry there's a kind of truth in them that shines. There is no subterfuge, no fooling around in art of that quality, and a lot of his poems have that quality. I think that some people may have said about him personally that you could never really find the man. You never knew when he was putting you on.... He was more like this with some people than with others.... But in the depths of his poetry no man lies, and in these poems there is a crystal-clear kind of intelligence that was always there, and a great sensitivity. There is great power there, and I think that in the better of these poems, he is really there himself. And his work will endure for a long, long time.[39]

The English poet, Philip Larkin, one of MacSween's favourite writers in his later years, had much to say about the tyranny of family life. Larkin's own parents, by all accounts, were toxic and thus became the inspiration, if not the subject, for one of his most famous poems, "This Be the Verse" the final stanza of which has a particularly patriarchal feel: "Man hands misery on to man./It deepens like a coastal shelf/Get out as early as you can./And don't have any kids yourself." MacSween may have felt that he too could have handed misery on, but he once remarked that he regretted not having had children, and his brother Michael, who was also a priest, expressed similar sentiments.

There is much in Larkin's lines that is emblematic of MacSween's life, the life of his parents, and that of his siblings. In his last years, when MacSween looked back and wrote about his childhood with nostalgia, the recollections are almost always poetic and idyllic and, one cannot help but feel, they are also mostly fictional as well. Auden, Freud, Dr. Seuss and many others have cautioned us about the world of children, about how easy it is to harm them, and how difficult it is to heal them. Much has been written about the influence of toxic parents, about the drama of the gifted child: MacSween survived his childhood, and his gifts, to all appearances, seem to have helped him make this passage—the inevitable journey out. Other children, equally but differently gifted, might not have fared so well. With few exceptions, the family, friends and admirers of MacSween regretted that his poetry was so often impersonal, so often lacking in the experiential, in human intimacy. On reflection, this wishful thinking seems mistaken, or at best misplaced: What if MacSween had been a poet of lyric sensibility, a love poet whose wellsprings celebrated the sensual, the erotic and the passionate? And what if his emotional life had outweighed his intellectual one? Knowing what we now know, it seems that what is most remarkable is not that he didn't write personal, experiential and intimate verse about human relations and love, but rather that he wrote poetry at all. The verse that he eventually came to publish is not a poetry based on the active view of life, but rather on the contemplative, meditative side, and its central concerns are ideas—at times bookish, intellectual and often detached; it is a poetry about religion, culture, society and death—being and non-being. It is also a tragic poetry and nonetheless powerful for these preoccupations and concerns. Finally, as his biographer and friend, I am conscious here, too, of the difficulties of distance and the dangers of wish fulfillment; of restraining the impulse to fictionalize a life into what it ought to, might have been.

ON the eighth of May 1933, MacSween turned eighteen years old. A month or so later he graduated from Glace Bay High School with honours at the top of his class; a few days after this he began looking for a summer job that would last him until the end of August. At the beginning of September, MacSween would leave Cape Breton Island for the first time in his life in order to begin his studies at St. Francis Xavier University in the small town of Antigonish on the mainland of Nova Scotia.

II   ⌠tudent and Seminarian

Fig. 11 Main Street, Antigonish in the 1930s. Courtesy, Pat Walsh, The History of Antigonish.

*I*n a memoir published in the late 1980s, Rod MacSween looked back over fifty years to his first arrival in the small but relatively prosperous town of Antigonish, located near the western shore of what all Cape Bretoners back then—and still—call the mainland of Nova Scotia:

I came by train and it was crowded with students on the way, like myself, to study at St. Francis Xavier. We arrived around midnight and we
scattered onto the platform like prisoners released into the light. We
were met there by a large man who drove a small bus for the Royal
George Hotel. However, such luxury was not for us. We headed up
Main Street for the university; everyone of us with some form of valise
in each hand. The way seemed very long that night before I finally found
myself in Broadway Dormitory and rested there, bathed in sweat and
with my arms weary.... Even in the darkness of the warm September
night, it was possible to feel the charm of the village. I had come from
a mining town where trees were spread sparsely over the landscape, and
here were mighty trees towering over Main Street and almost meeting
overhead.... I was surprised too by the pavement which was made of
concrete slabs.[1]

Coming from Glace Bay, MacSween naturally refers to the small town as
a village, but he is both delighted by and envious of its tree-lined streets
and slabs of expensive concrete pavement. The university's presence in
this rural area was due exclusively to the fact that Antigonish was the
diocesan seat for northern Nova Scotia and Cape Breton Island. For Cape
Bretoners, and for Catholics in particular, forming the majority population
of the diocese, the choice of the little "mainland" town as the site not only
of their Cathedral and their Bishop's Palace, but also of their university,
was a legitimate source of resentment and tension. MacSween would have
known about these regional and parochial battles; however, they were of
little concern to him as he settled in to the life of a freshman at "X."

The St. FX student life of 1933 had little that would be recognized
today by its student body, faculty, surrounding community or a *Maclean's*
magazine survey. Fresh "man," the term for first year students, was the *mot
juste* in 1933 when the small college had more in common with a British
public school for boys, or an Irish Jesuit school for young men, than it
did with the university as we know it today. In the 1930s, almost all of
the scholarship and bursary money the college possessed was earmarked
for those students intending to study for the priesthood.[2] The curriculum,
discipline and extracurricular activities also had much in common with
prep schools past and present, as James Cameron, the university's official
historian, records:

The daily lives of the students followed the long-established routine
from the wake-up bell at 6:45 in the morning to "lights out" in the
evening at 10 p.m. The regular activities included chapel, breakfast,
classes, dinner, recreation breaks, evening prayers, supper, and study hall.
Classes were scheduled for Saturday morning, and on Sunday there was

a class in religion, to be attended by Catholic students in addition to the normal religious services…. Priest-prefects, stationed in each dormitory wing, supervised the college routine, enforcing adherence to schedules and regulations.[3]

On reflection, the only modern-day equivalent for a routine like this might be a modified boot camp for military or police training. The courses offered under this regime included the standard fare of the time: philosophy, physics, chemistry, Latin, history, English, economics and French. Campus activities and clubs listed a student paper, the *Xaverian*, debating clubs, a choir, a drama society and the all-pervasive athletics. Rod MacSween was a lean six-foot-four in 1933, and he excelled at many sports, including hockey, rugby and baseball. Although he did not have a strong singing voice, Rod had a good ear for music and he could carry a tune. So it was also at this time that his interest in music began, especially after he became a regular member of the university's choral society. All of these activities, then, eventually helped make the young man into the proverbial well-rounded student, but this rather conventional side of university life absorbed a very small part Rod's time. What drew him to the university in the first place (besides, that is, the normal wish of most teenagers to leave home and get on with life) was his uncle, "Doc" Pat Nicholson.

It is difficult to overestimate the influence that Doc Pat must have had on the young man: though Rod showed no inclination toward the hard sciences (Nicholson's own field), he was a brilliant student with a reputation for voracious reading, and the uncle—who had a keen eye for spotting talent—must have been especially proud of his younger sister's boy. Rod, then, would spend much of his three years on the campus either in the presence of his uncle, or working for him in and around the university. Being so close to—and so enamoured of—his uncle was something the young man would come to both cherish and regret. All the evidence indicates that Professor Nicholson championed young MacSween and very quickly became like a second father to him, and the nephew was more than willing to be treated like a son. His roommate, John Hector MacGregor, recalled how "Rod spent most of his time in Doc Pat's room in the old arts building, reading, talking and doing things for him." Early photos show an uncanny resemblance between the uncle and his nephew, and these resemblances were much more than skin deep: both the professor and the student had a reputation for kindness, humour, quick wit and, when provoked, temper and sarcasm. Father MacGregor, who shared a dormitory with Rod and about thirty other young men, recalled some of these qualities and characteristics from their first year on campus:

He was a fairly good athlete, he could pitch, play football and was a good hockey player, but he wasn't fast enough.[4] I remember he sent for kneepads or elbow pads for hockey and his bed was next to mine in the dormitory. I went over and he wasn't in very good shape at all. They had gotten kneepads when they should have been elbow pads or something, and I said something, and he near ate me! You had to watch him because he had a bad temper as a young fellow. But I didn't mind him. I didn't mind the thing very much. He was very kind and, you see, I had great respect for him. People were in awe of him. There was just such an aura. He could talk about anything.[5]

John Ross, another classmate of Rod's, acknowledged that the boy from "the Bay" (as Glace Bay was always known) could show "flashes of anger," but Ross also remembered that "He kept binders on himself." A much more prominent—and attractive—side of the freshman was his ability to be funny and send himself up. Ross recalled a bare-chested MacSween clowning in the dormitory to the delight of the other residents: "He'd flex his muscles and MacGregor would do the same thing, but he was under the arms of Rod, and they would be parading with their chests stuck out wanting us to decide which one had the better physique." John Ross also recalled the young man's reputation as a student: "It's not that I observed him doing much reading, but rather that the thought processes that came out in his conversation would seem to indicate that he had. He was a deep thinker, even then." Finally, Ross acknowledged, with some healthy envy, the natural physical skill of his former classmate: "He had tremendous athletic ability too. Son of a gun, you know, if he were around today he could've played Canadian football. I'm sure he would be a place kicker."[6]

Fig. 12 MacSween as a sophmore, 1934. Courtesy St. FX University Archives.

If he wasn't attending class, playing sports, singing or socializing in the dormitory, Rod was usually in the company of his uncle. And while the virtuous Doc Pat rarely lost his temper, he could, at times, be very sarcastic—as his nephew Rod once experienced and remembered:

> We were doing an experiment on sound. We struck the tuning fork and made the whole column of air inside the tube vibrate. The tube had been cracked and repaired with sealing wax. The wax broke and the tube broke further. It was about four or five feet long. John MacClory from Ottawa was the fellow with me, and he said, "Let's run." I said we might as well tell him, he's going to find out. We might as well face it now and get it over with. So I went up and I decided to go easy. You see, when we broke the tube the thermometer fell down the middle and broke as well, so I started with the thermometer and I was going to say, "And we also broke the tube", but I didn't get a chance because he broke in on me and said, "You know what you should do? Go down and look around and find something else you can break—and smash that too!" I said, "Okay," and turned and walked away.

While the humor and defiance in the "okay" speaks volumes about the relationship, we might remember, too, by way of explanation about the uncle's outburst, how poor the college was, and how hard the physics professor had to work to save enough to equip the modest laboratory.

This uncle and nephew shared many things in common besides their blood ties, including a love of music—while a student, MacSween continually assisted Doc Pat with both his choir and his band. They also shared the cultural, spiritual, political and ethnic bond of their religion. They had more than passing interest in the history of their Church: its great writers, apologists and activists. And they did not have to look far for a tradition of activism to inspire or to promote: both Nicholson and his nephew would have been keen boosters of men like J. J. (Jimmy) Tompkins and Moses Coady—the two Cape Breton founders of The Antigonish Movement and the pioneers of adult education, both at the university and throughout the wider community in the People's School program. There is little doubt that Rod was heading for the vocation of the priesthood from very early on in his life, but these many connections and influences would have constantly strengthened and bolstered what appears to have been already a predestined world view.

There were, understandably, many differences between the uncle and the nephew. Like MacSween, Professor Nicholson was progressive in his views on education, and he believed a time would come when his university would hold a place as a worthy and acknowledged institution of higher learning—especially in his beloved sciences. Culturally speaking, however, things were different: Doc Pat, a Cape Breton Catholic Scot, was a man in love with the past—and a very specific past at that. Nothing illustrates this more clearly than his promotion, his championing, of the Gaelic language and culture of his parents. It is true, that toward the end of his life, MacSween came to value the importance of his uncle's work on behalf of this old world culture, but as a young man his interests lay elsewhere. He had a strong sense of and interest in history, but it was the world of avant-garde literature and art that most fascinated him and occupied the majority of his reading time. All his life MacSween felt a pressing need—if not a compulsion—to feel current, to be in the know, to be in touch with the contemporary world of art, letters and ideas.

Modern literature would eventually come to dominate most of his adult reading life, but during his undergraduate years at St. FX MacSween would receive little exposure to contemporary letters. Former president, Malcolm MacDonnell, a sophomore in 1935, shared the same dorm as MacSween and was eventually befriended by the senior student. MacDonnell recalled that the precocious undergraduate had little trouble with the formal course of study:

> I knew his attitude. He would seem very interested in the routine curriculum. But he would breeze through it. I don't think there was a blessed page in the library that he didn't read. Now, allow that our library wasn't very extensive in those days, but there was quite enough to keep us busy. Rod read. Read all the time. And he had such a marvelous memory. He not only understood what he read; he retained it. You'd ask him a question and he never looked through a book to answer it. It was really at his fingertips.[7]

IF MacSween didn't get the exposure he wanted to the avant-garde, to what was new in the world, at St. FX, he did get a grounding in literary history, especially from professors like Fr. R. V. Bannon. Shakespeare was Bannon's mainstay, though he was more than familiar with Chaucer, Swift, Dante, Homer, Virgil and all the other Western Europeans—the standard and classic "dead white males" who then made up the canon of college reading, and who now tend to be found ghettoized into Great Book and Great Ideas programs.[8] Rod also studied history and philosophy, where he would have read some of his favourite Catholic writers, both ancient and modern, including figures such as Alexander Pope, Gerard Manley Hopkins, Cardinal Newman, G. K. Chesterton and Hilaire Belloc.

Even while at home during his summer breaks, the young under-graduate continued to astonish his siblings and others with the sheer volume of his reading. As his brother Murdock recalled:

> He used to amaze me. He got a job on vacation out on the highway, a student's job. He would go down to McCall's Bookstore [in Glace Bay] and buy those paperbacks. He'd just take that many off the shelf—like that—yards of the stuff! I'd say did you pick out something important. "No, no, I'll read them all." I'll read them all!

Clearly, reading seemed to occupy most of his time at home during the summers, but Rod was also recognized for his ability to play baseball—and especially to pitch. His brother Murdock remembered this as well:

> He pitched for the collier leagues, the top leagues around here then. There was this big shot that came down here from Montreal to play the Glace Bay team, a home run hitter. Rod was on his team. He made a remark that if Rod wanted to go farther he could. Roddie did something that nobody else did, I'm told. He took every player in the league and wrote out his weaknesses, and said if he were bad or good so he could pitch to him.

OF the six boys in the MacSween family, three would eventually marry and have children. All of these marriages, in time, would prove problematic, many people—including MacSween himself—would later come to regard them as tragic affairs. It is difficult to speculate on the nature of human sexuality, and on the nature of love in particular, but we can pose safe and rhetorical questions about such matters in anticipation of perhaps vague and rhetorical answers. Questions such as: Did young MacSween possess the self-knowledge at nineteen or twenty that told him he would not make a suitable husband or father? Did he see his mother's unhappiness, the lack of love in her marriage, as proof of its failure? Or was he simply not interested in matters of love and sexuality, as he had always professed in his more senior years. The questions are not entirely moot, but they are, for the most part, unanswerable. Though historians have shown it to be a long tradition, the celibate is not—to put it mildly—popular; and it has become more difficult to defend the tradition in the wake of the crisis of sexual abuse of children which has recently been brought to light in the American Catholic Church.[9] To all appearances, MacSween accepted—and was content to live under—the conditions and restrictions that the priesthood imposed. Celibacy's place within the paradigm of Catholic patriarchy both protected and isolated this "way of life." The continued and, as many see it, reactionary refusal of the Vatican and the hierarchy to let go of this medieval construct has seriously challenged the credibility of the Church in the post-Freudian and post-feminist age, hindering its ability to engage in serious debate on all matters connected with human sexuality—from abortion to same-sex marriage, to women, gays and lesbians in the clergy. In his old age, when discussion of human sexuality arose, MacSween would always smile and quote the cliché, coined and refined no doubt by theologians and the hierarchy, that he was given "the gift of celibacy."[10] Most of us, like Dante Gabriel Rosetti's beautiful and famous Virgin, would curl up and back away at the prospect of such an offering, such a gift; the young MacSween, however, appears to have had no regrets, or at least he never expressed any. Perhaps, in his case, the "gift of celibacy" was simply low sex drive, a libido hard wired by accident (or providence, depending on your faith) to suit both the calling and the times. Ironically, when he was a young priest, the puritan code of behaviour and the Church's repression—and obsession—with all things sexual, might have made it somewhat easier for the young man to sublimate whatever degree of sexual drive he may have had.[11] In his last years, MacSween came to regard the celibate as, at the very least, institutionally anachronistic, a relic from a bygone era that his Church would do well to cast off.

OF the forty-five graduates from the St. FX class of 1936 four would eventually enter the religious life, one to become a nun and three to become priests—including Roderick Joseph MacSween. As we have seen, given his intellectual and religious bent, it is hardly surprising that young Rod would follow in the footsteps of his admired uncle, Doc Pat, or for that matter, of his influential brother, Michael. Furthermore, for MacSween, the transition to the world of the seminary would not be as difficult as it had been for so many others; it was, after all, just another step for him on the road to becoming a member of the clergy, a road so many of his family and close friends had already travelled.

Although Nicholson and Coady, and many less prominent young men, prepared for the priesthood in seminaries as far away as Quebec, Ontario and even Rome, for the vast majority there was but one choice—and that was the Holy Heart Seminary in downtown Halifax. If student life at St. FX under the diocesan priests resembled British or Irish public schools of the time, then life in the seminary under the Udist Order of French priests was just shy of monastic. Just. Arthur Doyle entered the seminary with MacSween in September of 1937, and graduated with him in June of 1941. Late in life, Father Doyle recalled the harsh, military regime of the Halifax seminary.

> We'd get up at five o'clock in the morning, and we were down to the Chapel at five-thirty for an hour. It would be very cold in the wintertime because the building didn't have much heat. It was very cold in our rooms—we had a pitcher of water there and sometimes we'd break the ice on the water. We had breakfast at seven, and then classes about eight o'clock, which went right through till noontime. We were not allowed to talk at all. After dinner we could talk during recreation. We had the cassock on from the moment we got up till we went to bed. We were never allowed to be without the cassock. Even when we played handball we had the cassock on. At that time all our subjects were taught in Latin except history, I believe. We were not allowed to go downtown alone; we went as a group on Thursday; most of the time we had our cassocks on. We went in pairs, so there'd be seven or eight going down the street two by two.[12]

This grim and austere routine made it difficult, if not impossible, for any meaningful human contact, which, of course, was its intention in the first place: "We didn't really get to know too much because we had private rooms and as part of the rules we were really not allowed to talk." Father Doyle remembered, too, that MacSween was good at "handball and softball," but most of all he was looked upon

> as quite the intellectual even in the seminary. Although we were pretty busy doing our own theology, he was doing a little reading on the side, too. He would bring in some books of his own (he wouldn't have too many because we weren't allowed), but he did a lot of theological reading as well. We didn't have a very elaborate library, but it was fairly good. He would be in there.

In an interview with a former student, MacSween recalled when he first began building his own personal library:

> I suppose the year I left college, I began to buy books, as many as I could. I got a job, labouring in Glace Bay. Hard work. I'd go down every payday and wander around the only bookstore, unable to make a choice. Finally, I would make a choice and buy a book. So, by the time I went to the Seminary, a year later, I had a nice collection—that is, nice for my age. When I was in the Seminary in Halifax, I discovered the Penguin editions downtown. Paperbacks were practically unknown at that time. When the Penguins appeared, I realized I could get a very good library by spending a few dollars every once in a while.[13]

MacSween's recollections are confirmed in his autobiographical notes, where number fifteen records with a comic touch: "Seminary. Penguins had just arrived. Poor as a church mouse? I *am* a church mouse."[14] The paperback Penguin book series gave him access, at a relatively cheap price, to many of his favourite writers. These paperbacks had other advantages too, not least among them for the young seminarian was their size and portability. Hugh MacDonald, another fellow Cape Bretoner and seminarian, recalled that the young man from "the Bay" had habits different from most in the classroom. One of MacSween's tricks involved piling four or five theological books on his desk to give the impression that he was being attentive to the subject if not the lecture, when, in fact, he was immersed in poems and novels. Hugh MacDonald noted that "Rod knew his theology well, but he didn't waste any time listening to discussion in class, he just read, his head bowed down almost in reverential prayer, his attention focusing completely on what was in the book, not on what was being said."[15]

In 1939, Moses Coady first published his story about The Antigonish Movement in a small book entitled, *Masters of Their Own Destiny*. The book was a short history of Coady's success with adult education through economic cooperation in the rural farming and fishing communities of North Eastern Nova Scotia and Cape Breton. At the time, the text became more or less standard reading for priests and seminarians, not only from the Diocese of Antigonish, but also throughout Atlantic Canada and beyond. At Holy Heart Seminary, Joe Marinelli was the senior member of his class, so he gathered a group of his fellow seminarians together to

> go through the book chapter by chapter. We were waiting to get the
> thing going, you know, name the fellow who was going to do the first
> chapter, and the second and so forth. Well, Rod took it over. He was
> right, I mean, because I didn't show leadership. So I said all right, go
> ahead.

The story is revealing in that it shows the respect and attention that Coady and his teachings received and was receiving from the younger seminarians. MacSween's taking over the session also highlights the young man's natural leadership abilities, at least in a classroom or group setting. It was an ability that would eventually capture the attention of teachers such as his uncle, "Doc" Pat Nicholson—and, more importantly perhaps, of Moses Coady himself.

Hugh also remembered that the young seminarian was a man of humour:

> At noontime, with the boys around when we were dressing up and
> going out, Rod would always have a smile on and he would make a
> nice little crack about everything. He was delightful—I liked him very,

very much. I remember one time we were in the Chapel for vespers. Rod would take advantage of the situation. His position was on the opposite side of the aisle; we were all standing up and Rod had his biretta on. Right opposite him at eye level was his great friend Danny MacDonald—who was also full of humour—and they both stared at each other for about three minutes, each one trying to stare the other down, and they had the most ugly faces that you could possibly wear—that they could wear—defiant. I was watching this whole thing from another angle. All of a sudden Rod lifts his biretta over his head to salute Danny who burst out laughing, as did Rod. And this was under high tension because we were all under high tension in the seminary—and especially in the Chapel! Another time we were both on for intoning the vespers and we had to move over to the centre of the altar and turn around and make the intonation. Well, you like to be over there in plenty of time, but Rod, no. I would whisper, "Rod, it's time to go." "No." "Let's go Rod, now!" "No."—and there we were. Rod would not move until the last split second. So, that was Rod's humour all the way through.

There were times of course when his humour was not appreciated, as his long time friend Joe Marinelli recalled: "Rod was sitting next to Father MacKenna from the Island [PEI]. You had to sit according to your name. On that day we had sausages. So MacKenna took up a plate and went over to Rod and Rod says, pointing at the sausage, 'Don't hand me that obscene thing!' But MacKenna got wild, he wouldn't talk to Rod for the rest of the year."[16] That MacSween felt comfortable enough to make a sexual joke may (or may not) say something about his own comfort level with the male celibate world he had just recently entered.[17]

Although MacSween was undoubtedly writing poetry from a young age, only one example of his early efforts survives and it is more a piece of comic relief, of parody, than serious verse or even juvenilia. "Ode to the Universality of the Toad"[18] has much of the in-house joke about it, a spoof no doubt on the constant diet of dogma, discipline, canon law and moral theology that was their daily bread in the seminary. The title and opening stanza of the poem give its flavour:

Ode to the Universality of the Toad
There is no transcendental as universal as a toad
Garrogous LaGrange
Being has many aspects: verity, goodness, toadiness.
Maritain
In the Middle Ages, the nearest universal solvent was toad juice.
Etienne Gilson

O Universal Toad
Buddha
The Toad Forever
Devison

To thee O Toad
I offer up this ode
The reverence of my heart
I lovingly impart.
Oh beauteous toad, who hops
My wonder never stops
In going over thee.

The Devison who is jokingly quoted at the beginning of the poem is Father John Devison, another friend of MacSween's from Glace Bay. Similarly, there is a mention later on in the verse of "the lamented Blue,/ who puffed." This refers to an unnamed seminarian who smoked, even though the penalty for being caught meant immediate expulsion. The poem highlights, once again, MacSween's comic side and his love and need for humour. These treasured moments of levity were rare in the dark, sombre and bloodless corridors of the seminary, where most of the professors and young men alike took themselves seriously, very seriously. Fr. B. M. Broderick of Chatham, New Brunswick, who knew MacSween both at St. FX and at Holy Heart recalled "that poetry for Rod was a distraction he cultivated while in the seminary, no doubt as an antidote to the inhuman side of seminary life."[19]

Two years after MacSween entered Holy Heart Seminary, Canada was at war and Halifax had become a boom town; its harbour jammed with ships for the North Atlantic convoys; the fast convoys left from the provincial capital while the slower ones departed from Sydney. The downtown streets were often overflowing and overrun with young men and women bound for overseas or looking for work in the military port. Not very long into the war, two of MacSween's brothers embarked from Halifax to join the fight in Europe. Pat, the youngest, a career soldier, was in the infantry and he eventually served in France, Belgium and, later, Germany; George, the third eldest, became a squadron leader, flying fighter planes for the RCAF as advance support for the allied drive through Italy to Germany.

News of the war, however—especially for the sheltered and sequestered seminarians—was very hard to come by; there was no radio in the

*Fig. 13 MacSween at Holy
Heart Seminary, 1940.
Courtesy George Sanderson.*

building and the only
newspapers permitted
were diocesan, religious
papers, *The Casket* from
Antigonish, and two or
three other papers from
Quebec and France.
Now and again, a vis-
iting chaplain would
give them news, or the
janitor might slip them
a copy of the *Halifax
Herald,* where hockey
scores were often more
sought after than U-
boat sightings, or the
progress Monty was or
was not making against
the Desert Fox in North Africa.

Still, many of these young men were very conscious of the war; men
like MacSween's life-long friend, Joe Marinelli, a Cape Bretoner of Italian
extraction. Marinelli recalled "feeling inferior" as an adolescent of Italian
heritage, but once he got to the seminary his life changed; there he met
three Udist priests who had all been trained in Rome and who "read and
talked about the Romans all the time." Years later, Marinelli remembered
his friend Rod's remark from their time together, "Joe, you were hard to get
along with in the seminary. What happened to you, Marinelli? You were
a nice fellow at St. FX, then, when you got in the seminary, you turned
into a miserable skunk." Marinelli admitted that he "became overbearing
to compensate for being Italian." MacSween of course knew what his
young friend was going through—the Canadian government had wrong-
fully imprisoned many Italian-Canadians during World War II. To this
day, many Cape Bretoners retain a deep sense of shame about this racial
profiling and imprisoning of their fellow islanders, many of whom came
from the coal-mining communities, like Joe Marinelli himself.

During the longed-for summer months, the seminarians returned home
to be with their families, to work, and, as was more often the case, to help
out at their home and other parishes. It was on his second summer vacation that MacSween first visited the small outport of White Point, Cape
Breton, a remote and beautiful place that would become very special in
his memory over the years. MacSween made the trip "Down North," as
the local expression has it, with Joe Marinelli. And over fifty years later,
Marinelli recalled—with vivid details—the visit he had made with his
friend those many decades ago:

> My first summer out of the seminary "Doc" Nicholson asked me
> directly to go down to Cape North, to White Point. There was no
> money involved. We had to take it out of our own pockets. I didn't
> have much, but I went there to White Point in the summer of 1938.
> What a great summer!

The two young seminarians taught catechism to the children in the morning and preached to the adults in the evening. Marinelli shook his head
in disbelief when he recalled how men who had been out swordfishing
all day would then come home "to listen to young guys like Rod and
me. To have *us* preach at them!" He remembered, too, how it "was the
best audience I had in my life—right there in White Point in the old
schoolhouse!" The following year Marinelli's friend, MacSween, arrived
and both young men slept in a fisherman's shack. For Marinelli, it was an
idyllic time: "Old nets hanging from the ceiling and walls. We had one
blanket underneath us and one above and we slept like logs. We went
swimming in the day and after catechism in the morning, and when we
came home often there'd be a nice hot bowl of soup cooked by the two
beautiful women who ran the store for their father. They were Lebanese."
According to Marinelli, MacSween returned again in 1940, but the Cape
Breton Italian stayed home because he wanted a summer off for himself
before heading into full time parish work. "Rod went alone that time. He
loved it there!"

In his autobiographical pieces written during the late 1980s MacSween
confirmed the words and memories of his old friend about this idyllic and
now forgotten world:

> After meeting a few people, I was astonished to learn that my own
> family had had an impact upon the place. A granduncle had managed
> the fish plant for years but was now dead. My grandfather had built
> the small church which was then used as a school. My grand-aunt
> had watched from an upstairs window while two young men had
> rowed a large dory across the bay. One of the men was her only child

and, while she watched, she saw the boat overturn in a squall and the rowers drown. She went to her bed and stayed there until she eventually died.... I went to sea for my first swordfish hunt. I found it a most thrilling experience.... The boat was steered by Francis [Dixon]'s son, Jellico, who was perched in a kind of crow's nest on the top of a mast. He suddenly shouted "swordfish!" and I leaped to my feet, dropping my book on the deck.... It was *Mein Kampf* by Adolf Hitler. World War II was on, and it was impossible to escape the hated name. I had read that the book would reveal all of Hitler's intentions for the conquest of Europe. I found the book very boring, perhaps because I was unable to give it my full attention.... At the time I did not know that memories from that period would crowd upon me year after year. There was a sense of isolation there that now could not be recreated. I could have been on some small island off the coast of Scotland—and the time could have been some early date, say before the time of Christ, when people often lived apart from others for long periods of time.[20]

The passage is a beautiful and fascinating evocation of time and place with its mixture of personal experience, coincidence and momentous historical references. The discovery that his beloved grandfather George Nicholson was associated with the outport must have rendered a strong, almost visceral, feeling of home to the place; and it was, no doubt, partly this feeling that inspired MacSween to write so eloquently and so elegiacally about White Point almost fifty years later. The section on the "grand-aunt" and the loss of her only child is especially moving and highlights, once again, the sensibility of MacSween both as a man and a writer. Similarly, the historical references tell us much about both the younger and older man: he is reading *Mein Kampf* to gain insight into the war, but quickly drops the text on the deck when the drama of the hunt—of sword-fishing— takes over. And if *Mein Kampf* evokes World War II, then Jellico Dixon's name recalls World War I and the Battle of Jutland, won by the British Commander, Admiral Jellico; no doubt the parish priest who baptized the boy must have had some connection either to the naval battle or the Great War itself. Finally, there is the older MacSween's observation about being on some small island off the coast of Scotland before the time of Christ. The landscapes and seascapes around White Point, as with most of Cape Breton, strongly resemble the Scottish islands and Highlands, so MacSween's geographical reference here is hardly surprising, especially given his Scots heritage. What is different though, is the time he evokes. Why does he choose a pre-Christian time, a pagan time, in fact? Surely, people lived alone and in isolation after Christianity. We might speculate here that during this time of war and destruction he imagined himself as some Celtic Druid priest celebrating what was good in the old pagan world, a person in touch with nature and the arcane, with the mysteries of an unspoiled and sacred place.

There is one final story connected with these White Point days, an anecdote that captures both the tongue-in-cheek humour shared by MacSween and Marinelli and—perhaps more tellingly—something of their own sense of themselves: who they were and who they were about to become, what their role would be as soon-to-be-ordained priests. The story concerns an inedible pie. According to Marinelli, young Leo Dixon had lunch with them every day, "He'd sit down for ten or fifteen minutes and talk about the weather and that. He was beautiful, about ten or eleven." One day the would-be curates are given a pie but there is a problem. "We were all for pies," Marinelli recalled, "but this one when you cut it, you couldn't cut it with an axe!" The seminarians could neither throw it out nor send it back, actions equivalent to shooting the fabled albatross of hospitality. But at this point, as with many stories about Scots Highland villages, fate conveniently intervenes. When the big Scot Cape Bretoner was holding the pie, Joe Marinelli asked:

> What are you gonna do, Rod? and Rod said "Well, I don't know. Can't throw it out because they'll see it." Sweet, innocent, Leo came in and I said "Wait, Leo." He looked around. "What is it, Joe?" "I got something for ya," I said. "What?" Leo said. I came around with the pie and said, "This." I knew he was going to kick about it. "Oh, no. I can't take that Joe. You and Rod eat that!" So I said, "Leo, you know Rod and I are going to be priests in a couple of years." "Yes," he said. I said, "You know what you're supposed to do when a priest tells you something?" Leo said, "Yeah, you're supposed to do it." I said, "Well, then, take the pie." He went out the door and turned around and said, "Joe, you're too good to me." Rod and I could hardly wait for him to get out of the door so we could just roar.

It is a charming story, but it is also a story that, in its innocence and naïveté, reminds us of the awe and respect that was regularly bestowed on these young men—not only by the children, but by their parents and the vast majority of their parishioners as well. In later years, both MacSween and his good friend, Marinelli, would reflect back in wonder—and in fear and trembling—at the paradigm of absolute trust in which they once had the privilege, terror and obligation of living.

The four years of seminary training ended for young Rod MacSween on Saturday June 7, 1941, when he was finally ordained as a priest by

Archbishop McNally in the Diocese of Halifax. The following Sunday, the young celebrant sang his first solemn high Mass at St. Anne's Church in his home parish in Glace Bay. "Doc" Pat Nicholson, his uncle, acted as deacon during the Mass, while Rod's brother, Michael, was one of the subdeacons. Later that night, following Benediction, the young hometown priest was presented with an address book and a purse from members of the congregation. A week later, it was MacSween's old Catholic High School that honoured him with a reception and two gifts: a gold engraved pyx and a sick-call case. Once again, the neophyte priest pronounced Benediction and local newspapers noted that, "Dan E. MacDonald, another member of the class and a student for the priesthood, was present during the afternoon and spoke briefly following the presentation to Rev. Fr. MacSween."[21] Returning home to such a reception, to family and friends, after four years in the cloistered world of Holy Heart Seminary, must have been a dream come true for the often homesick Cape Bretoner.[22] No doubt his head was a few hat sizes larger too—especially now that he was Reverend Roderick MacSween. It is difficult today to imagine what the role of the priest was like in Catholic communities—the influence they possessed and the respect they commanded. Their authority and status had few equivalents at the time: among the faithful, the lapsed, agnostic

Fig. 14 Holy Heart Seminary, Halifax, 1941. Rod MacSween is fourth from the left in the back row. His friend Joe Marinelli is second from the right, front row. Arthur Doyle, another friend and X man, is second from the left, back row. Courtesy Joe Marinelli.

and otherwise, they were seen as august doctors and, perhaps, like some (a very few) respected political leaders, lawyers and judges. MacSween's natural contempt for authority, fuelled no doubt by his artistic side, must have shielded him somewhat from the pitfalls that go with being one of the chosen. Still, there is little doubt that the young man could not but be aware of the prestige, power and aura that naturally went with the calling.

The young, would-be, curate spent the month of July basking in the praise of his hometown, adjusting to the outside world, and preparing for the intense religious and social work experience that awaited him. Whenever possible, new priests were permitted, if not encouraged, to cut their young teeth in the home parishes, so MacSween was to continue as an assistant to Fr. MacAdam at St. Anne's—his home parish in Glace Bay—until December 20, 1941, when his apprenticeship was suddenly interrupted by an urgent letter from his Bishop in Antigonish:

> *Dear Reverend Fr.,*
> *I have been endeavouring to have you remain as assistant priest at Glace Bay, but owing to a combination of diverse circumstances I find myself obliged to change that plan.*
>   *Rev. D. E. Chisholm, P. P. of Pomquet has been in the Hospital in Antigonish for some considerable time and there is every likelihood that he will remain there through an indefinite period. While his curate, Fr. Maillet, was still living, the work could go on, but when the latter died the place was entirely without a resident priest to go there for Sundays, but even this did not work, and besides there are the sick calls &c. to be attended to during the week days.*
>   *I must therefore appoint an assistant priest for Pomquet, and much as I regret it I have to call upon you to take over that duty, and so I hereby appoint you to be curate in that parish. The matter is urgent, as Christmas will be here on the 25th (Thursday) and there is no one else to be there for the services. So, dear Fr., I direct that you go to Pomquet by train on Wednesday the 24th instant so as to be on hand for the Christmas services. Pack up what is necessary from your belongings, and proceed to Pomquet as above directed. I am writing the housekeeper at Pomquet to have someone to meet you at the station to take you to the priest's house. I am sorry to have to take this step, but in the circumstances it is unavoidable.*
>   *With best wishes I remain*
>   *Yours sincerely in Christ*
>   *+ James Morrison*

MacSween's return to Glace Bay had been more than local-boy-makes-good. At twenty-six he was regarded as a priest with special gifts, a young man of promise; his undergraduate years at St. FX and his "post-graduate" years in the seminary in Halifax singled him out as an articulate scholar and priest with clear leadership potential. It is difficult to know for certain what the young curate's expectations and ambitions were at this time—there is no record of them. One can imagine, not unfairly, that MacSween saw himself as destined for one of the larger urban parishes on Cape Breton Island, a place where he would be kept busy and where, as he would later phrase it, all his talents and abilities could be put to use. This, as Bishop Morrison's letter highlights, was not to be his immediate future. MacSween's first independent parish assignment would be the most difficult, isolated and trying of his career. His apprenticeship in Pomquet, as he came to regard it, would teach him many things, but most of all it would provide a hard and up-against-it lesson about a side of the priesthood to which he probably had not given much thought during his busy and intense training as a seminarian—its intense and often desperate loneliness and isolation.

Clearly, Rod MacSween was intent on becoming a priest from very early on in his life. Like his brother, Michael, and his uncle, Doc Pat, he was participating in a family tradition that existed for at least two generations, if not longer. But if MacSween imagined that his role in the priesthood would be other than the implicit one of pastoral care, of serving his Church and community as a diocesan curate and priest, then he kept these thoughts to himself. And yet, even in these fledgling years of his vocation—a time of intense work and intense friendships—MacSween, the scholar-priest, (the contemplative if you will), continues to insist on his space and place amid the active (if not hyperactive) world of the diocesan curate and the committed social worker.

In his university and seminary days, MacSween, was regarded as a bookish intellectual, but he was also known as a talkative, affable, humorous and intensely social being. He made friends quickly, many friends—and enemies too—and he thrived on this human contact. Given the nature of his personality, the isolation and loneliness that the young man would experience in the parish of Pomquet was to be especially difficult. It is arguable, however, that these very years of isolation and apartness gave the scholar in him a chance to develop even more; he would read and think as he had never read and thought before; with a new intensity and a new hunger; with a passion, perhaps, beyond the accepted one that most polymaths and autodidacts naturally possess. If he could not have friends and family about him, he would fill the empty hours and lonely days with books, books and more books. In his youth, part of his motivation for reading was to escape the household world, the family battles; now that he was truly on his own—for the first time in his life—he would devour books and absorb knowledge, not to keep people at bay, but rather to atone for their all too remarkable absence.

III   *Y*ears in the Parish: Pomquet to New Waterford

*T*oday, the Acadian village of Pomquet is only a twenty-minute drive from the town of Antigonish, but on Christmas Eve 1941 it must have seemed a lonely spot indeed for the young priest who stepped from the train onto the snow-covered platform of the small station. Rod MacSween was just 26 years old in 1941, and although he had had four-and-a half months of experience in his home Parish of St. Anne's, it must have seemed little enough training to the young assistant curate, now left in charge of his first parish at the second busiest time of the Christian calendar.

The man MacSween had been sent to temporarily replace at Holy Cross Parish, Fr. Daniel Chisholm, had been pastor of Pomquet for 38 years; now in his seventies, he had been ill for many years. His reputation, as parishioner Leona MacDonald recalled, was not good: "Father Chisholm was a hard old knock. He was sick for many years. If he had anything against you, and you went to receive Holy Communion he'd skip you and go to the next one. When he had catechism for the children, the children were so scared of him!"[1] Joe Marinelli, Rod's close friend from seminary days, remembered a conversation he had not long after MacSween had been transferred from Pomquet:

> He had a tough time there. I was comparing notes with him because I had a tough pastor, too. I was in New Victoria for six years. I said to Rod, "I had a hard time." "Ah, Joe," he said, "you didn't have as hard a time as I did. That old Father Chisholm, he was kind of like a madman—you didn't know what he was going to do next."

A letter from E. A. Kelly also gives an insight into how the young curate was feeling at the time. Kelly had been in the seminary with Rod, but was

73

"prevented" from becoming a priest, from "going on" as he puts it:

> *The thought of loneliness was one thing I feared when I was a seminarian. If, I thought, the priesthood is as lonely as the seminary then it must be a bloodless, uneventful life, from a human point of view. And, as you paint it the ministry is far more lonely and humdrum. I think it is something that is far too little impressed in the seminary. Of course, in your case I would not be too affected by your pastor and what he said after recovering from his paralytic stroke. He would not be normal then. Anyhow, a sickness of thirty-five years is exceptional and would be more than enough to make anyone permanently depressed. All in all it may have been providential that I was prevented from going on. Loneliness goes hard with me.*[2]

In a photograph of MacSween taken in Pomquet in 1942, he is seen as a thin—almost emaciated—priest in his black robes, looking very much older than his 27 years. Indeed, the figure in the picture bears little resemblance to the smiling jovial face of the seminary graduate of only a year earlier. In many respects, of course, he was different and older. Later in life, MacSween acknowledged that little in the seminary prepared him for life in the parish, particularly in areas of social work and counselling—if anything it set him back a few years.

These young men, then, were poorly equipped to deal with the suffering they found around them, especially, as MacSween soon discovered, when the anguish concerned matters of human sexuality.

Although he rarely spoke out against the teachings of his Church, there was one area—and a central one at that—which he challenged all his life, first privately, then, with the appearance of *Humanae Vitae*, publicly. This was the Catholic Church's stand on human sexuality and, in particular, on birth control. In his old age, MacSween spoke of his years in Pomquet, when he had advised many of the women parishioners—primarily through the medium of the confessional—to

Fig. 15 MacSween in Pomquet, NS, 1942. Courtesy George Sanderson.

practice birth control through contraception. It is difficult today to appreciate how radical an act this was in rural, Catholic Nova Scotia in 1942: a young, newly minted, curate in his first parish, willfully subverting one of the central teachings of the Catholic Church. It is, of course, a genuine example of MacSween's accelerated maturity, and a marker of his independent spirit. But these distressed women, with their large and poor families, must also have reminded him, consciously or not, of his own childhood and of the often grim life his own mother had endured with her large family.

Eventually, MacSween did make some lifelong friends in Holy Cross parish—people like Leona MacDonald whose marriage he celebrated. On the whole, however, it was a difficult and lonely time. His tentative grasp of spoken French did not help matters. He could read the language and understand it fairly well, but he did not speak it with anything approaching fluency, despite his years in the seminary among the French order of Udists. This lack of fluency in French, his youth, his inexperience and his general shyness with strangers, all combined to keep his social circle painfully circumscribed. There was, however, one advantage to being stationed in Pomquet, one small compensation, as it were, for the isolation—the village was close to St. FX, and, more importantly, it was close to the university's library.

Betty MacDonald and her husband Jack, Rod's cousin, recalled him speaking about these years in the small French parish: "He told us that that was the greatest blessing in disguise. That's when he started reading seriously," Betty remembered. "He talked about coming in to the library here and taking away tons of books. He read volumes." Both Betty and Jack knew, too, about his isolation: "He was very lonely there, and I suppose he didn't speak French. I think that's why he did so much reading."[3] In an interview with a former student, MacSween recalled that at this time he began buying "many, many books. I mean, as many as I possibly could buy."[4] MacSween's own autobiographical notes confirmed these memories: note 18 read, "In parishes—137 books in one busy year. No waste!"[5] Although there is no way of knowing for sure, those 137 books could certainly have been read while MacSween was at Holy Cross Parish in Pomquet. Kevin MacNeil, long-time librarian at St. FX, recalls that in certain sections of the library—especially in the literature, history and philosophy stacks—"Father MacSween's name could be found signed in almost every book."[6]

It has been argued that fear is one of the central ingredients in the make-up of an autodidact, but wherever the impulse comes from, the need, or the desire, to know—to always have an answer—was an underlying part of MacSween's makeup. It was certainly as much a part of his personality as his love of verbal combat, his fierce determination and his self-discipline. The years in Pomquet tested and strengthened his resolve in these matters, but they also revealed a weakness, an anxiety that the young man had not yet experienced or, as far as we know, contemplated—the fear of loneliness and isolation. Luckily, MacSween's time in the parish was relatively short, and he would, in fact, never experience this particular type of prolonged solitude again. We might wonder here, though, what kind of lasting effect this unintended seclusion had on the young priest and how—or if—it affected his way of being in the world.

At the end of August, 1943, Rod MacSween packed many of his books and all of his belongings into the late Fr. Chisholm's old Chrysler and made his way to the ferry at Mulgrave. He was making the crossing to Cape Breton Island, and going home to Mount Carmel parish in New Waterford, one of the largest and busiest parishes in the Diocese, the main parish of a large and vital mining community. He was chosen to be one of several curates assigned to assist the pastor—the historian, Fr. A. A. Johntson, and Rod's cousin on his mother's side of the family. In later life, the five years that Rod MacSween spent at Mount Carmel parish came to hold a very special place in his memory; he came, in fact, to regard them as among the happiest times of his life.[7] This may seem strange to those of us who knew him as a teacher—as a person so obviously born for the classroom—but memory is selective and MacSween's nostalgia for those years is easy to understand when seen in the light of the loneliness he had experienced in Pomquet. In New Waterford, things would be different: this was a mining town like the one he'd grown up in, and he knew its streets, its people and the rhythm of their lives. Here he would make vital, lifelong and loving relationships with men and women of his own age and his own class; he would also make a contribution to the communal life of the mining community—especially in his work with youth—that was far and above the normal duties, expectations or achievements of a parish curate.

Like most coal-mining towns in Canada, New Waterford was experiencing a boom during the Second World War, not unlike the surge in its economy it had experienced twenty-five years earlier during the First World War. Toward the end of that conflict, on July 25, 1917, sixty-five miners were killed in an underground explosion, miners who had been meeting quotas for wartime coal production. While no such disaster took place during the 1940s, the men underground also continued to put in overtime, or as many shifts as they wanted, because of the constant demand for coal. One of the apocryphal stories about the town, and a staple myth about similar coastal towns of the Atlantic seaboard, tells of German U-boat sailors anchoring off shore and rowing into "Waterford" in "civvies" to go to the local cinema, no doubt to see the androgynously beautiful Marlene Dietrich in films like *The Blue Angel*.

There was of course real contact with the war: on October 20, 1942, former premier and Cape Bretoner Angus L. MacDonald, then federal naval minister, confirmed that the Newfoundland-Nova Scotia ferry SS *Caribou* had been torpedoed six days earlier in the Cabot Strait with the loss of 137 lives, including 22 women and 14 children. The U-Boats were in the Cabot Strait because the slow convoys with American Liberty ships left from the port of Sydney, a few miles from New Waterford, where hundreds of merchant marine vessels, escorted by corvettes, cruisers and minesweepers, jammed both arms of the deep and protected harbour.[8] Thousands of men and women from all divisions of the military crowded the streets, bars, dance halls and churches of Sydney and its surrounding towns.

Two of Rod MacSween's brothers were fighting overseas and they both frequently wrote letters home to family and friends. Regrettably, most of MacSween's correspondence during these years has not come down to us (there are no letters, for instance, about his years in Pomquet) and there is but one missive to him from overseas. His younger brother, George MacSween, was a Flight Lieutenant flying fighter planes on the Italian front in 1944, and his one letter home to his brother is both a document of the times and one of the few pieces of MacSween's correspondence to survive from the period. Written in October, 1944, the letter talks about the poor weather and the difficulty that the Canadian infantry is having because there is "very little open country and what there is, is dotted with streams and rivers and can be defended easily with a few machine guns plus the artillery."[9] George is proud of the air force, though, and sees it as their one great advantage: "We batter hell out of them continually and it is no more than they dare to try and stop us from the air." Still, he admits that it is tough going, and they "continue to advance slowly." Like most soldiers in the war, he is happy to make contact with men from home: "I found out that the Cape Breton Highlanders were in this part of the world, so I looked them up the other day." Elated, he discovers "four Glace Bay boys" and gives a description of them, telling in the process how, or if, the war is taking its toll on them: "Angus Norman is a major and looks very old now. The strain is telling on him. Allie Woods is the same old guy; a sergeant now and sporting a terrific moustache which makes him look about forty. Caut MacLean, you remember him. He played rugby for Caledonia. He is exactly the same and Angus Norman had great praise for him. Joe MacIntyre, you probably do not know. He played rugby for St. Anne's long after our time." George's next piece of news concerns a letter he received from their youngest brother, Pat, who is also fighting in Europe. Pat, we learn, was

> *concerned about having to drop one of his stripes in order to go overseas. He thought that they would think, at home, that he had been in trouble. Apparently, in order to go overseas he had to switch to another outfit and, in doing so, had to revert to his substantive rank. It was tough, after being a Sergeant so long, but I think he will be glad he made the step just the same. If he is in France, he should get an eye-opener.*

George then relates that he "spent a few days in Rome" and that the "feature of [his] visit was a private audience with the Pope." He is suitably impressed by the Pontiff, noting that: "He is quite a man. He is very athletic, oozes personality and speaks fluently in several languages."[10] George ends his letter with a reference to the Sistine Chapel and the Vatican art galleries that he will "never forget."

Like his brother George, Patrick also wrote letters home to his family. Rod's youngest brother, Pat spent a total of seven years in the reserve army before eventually going overseas. Father Mike MacSween recalled his brother's departure vividly because it was the first time he had ever seen his father take a drink: "Pat was in the reserve army and he came home and said 'I'm going overseas and everybody has got to have a drink with me.'"[11] A tragic figure, Pat appears by all accounts to have had a hard time during the war and, like many returned veterans, he suffered from mental illness. The war, however, was not the sole cause of the soldier's breakdown: Pat had been suffering from mental problems from as far back as his teen years when, apparently, he had run away from home and school in the ninth grade. The then-unknown term schizophrenia was eventually applied to his illness. The evidence does point to a bipolar condition, which the war would not have helped.

In October of 1944, however, Pat was very upbeat in a letter to his uncle and namesake, recently been appointed president of St. FX.

P. 22338 P. J. MacSween
110 11 cdn Base Rft Bn
25 Oct. 44

Dear Fr. Nicholson:

I intended to write to you before, but due to laziness etc I kept putting it off and I am just getting around to it now. From letters from home I learned that you have been promoted to President of St. FX and I am very pleased as in my humble opinion you deserve it. Since I left Canada I've traveled (at the taxpayers expense) through England, France and now Belgium. The people of France treated us very well and they seem to think that Canada is another part of France. They were quite surprised when they learned that many of the Canadians couldn't speak French. In Belgium many of the people can speak English and it is a little easier for us to get around here. Also, most of the films here are in English and although the films are twenty or thirty years old they help pass the time. There seems to be a shortage of food here at present, but as for clothing, hardware, electrical supplies the stores are very well stocked. I received a letter from George yesterday and he seems to be getting on quite well. He stated that his promotion to Sqn Leader was coming through and with that rank he is getting into the high priced help class. I am glad for his sake that he is doing so well. As he has completed his overseas tour of duty (3 yrs) he is expecting a trip to Canada. I have several more letters to write, so I'll end now and I hope to hear from you very soon.

Best regards,
Your loving nephew,
Pat

Doc Pat's promotion to president would eventually have a profound impact on Pat MacSween's older brother, Rod, but by the fall of 1944 the now seasoned curate was deeply involved in parish work in the town of New Waterford. It was a busy and intense life, but one that he gladly welcomed after the isolation and loneliness of Pomquet—he worked, read and constantly made new friends, and new families. Frank MacNeil, assistant curate with Rod for several years at Mount Carmel, remembered the always hectic days and nights of parish work. The biggest ministry of the time was to visit the individual homes of parishioners. According to MacNeil, he and Rod would "start out every morning after breakfast" with each of the young men taking a different street, an exercise they would do "day in and day out." Besides visiting these homes, MacNeil also recalled how, on a monthly basis, they "heard confessions from all the kids in the school." The toughest week of the month in the liturgical calendar—outside of Holy Week of course—was First Friday week: "We had to get the kids out of the way so the adults could come for First Friday confession." The long-retired priest shook his head in wonder when he recalled the gruelling pace, "So Tuesday afternoon you'll hear the grade three's and four's, or you'll hear the five's, six's or the seven's, eight's and nine's and so on. So you were either in the schools or visiting the homes—we had a hospital too—once a month you had sick calls, communion calls." The work was evenly spread between the curates, so that Rod would take one section of the parish and his colleague Frank, or whomever else might be curate, would take another. There were also, of course, regular Masses to be said and once again Father MacNeil recalled the frequency and the demand:

> There was a mission in the nearby town of Lingan, so one said the first Mass at Mount Carmel and then went to the mission in Lingan. The other two stayed home and looked after the Masses at Mount Carmel. So there must have been five masses in Mount Carmel, and one in Lingan. It was all Sunday morning. I imagine the first mass was at seven o'clock.

As any Catholic over the age of forty-five remembers, there were other rituals besides the obligatory Sunday Mass. These included: Vespers, one for The Blessed Virgin and one for The Holy Name; Benediction and the Rosary on Sunday afternoon, while Sunday evening was often devoted to the Way of the Cross. When the snows had gone, Corpus Christi would be held outside, as Father MacNeil nostalgically recalled: "We'd all walk over—must be a lot of pictures of the old Corpus Christi processions where they'd have the canopy out and the fellow with the white gloves carrying it!" During MacSween's time in the parish there were always three ordained priests on staff to minister to well over a thousand families, and these families would be large Catholic households, with anywhere from six to ten children—or more—per home. The majority of these families were mining households. While safety conditions had improved, there were still mine and industrial accidents on a regular basis; as Father MacNeil remembered, "some fellows got killed."[12]

Naturally enough, working at such a pace, and under such conditions, left little room for down time, and down time for MacSween's inevitably meant up time—occasions he used almost exclusively for reading or writing. In later life, when he reflected on this intense period of parish life and work, he remembered doing more—not less—reading, because his "free" time was all the more precious to him.[13] Once again, Rod's comrade in parish work, Frank MacNeil, confirmed his fellow curate's memory of this period:

Books! I'm talking about 45 years ago. There were books here, and
books there. You couldn't see the carpet in the room. He'd be reading three books at the same time. One was here and one was there,
one over there. He didn't believe in putting them on a bookshelf or
anything. There were books, books, books. You couldn't see the carpet!"

In addition to this intense reading regime, Rod also kept his hand in at
sports—on Sunday night when everything was done, the curates would
head down to the Strand. Father MacNeil could still see in his mind's eye
the old gymnasium and its young athletes: "There were some pretty good
basketball players, but Rod would hold his own—and he would get into
the game! He'd be soaking wet within five minutes. He was a big man and
he was very determined." MacNeil remembered that Rod was tough and
had attitude as well: "'Yeah, I can play with you fellows. I'm a little older,
but I got the strength and the energy and the determination to show
you.' I don't know how high Rod could jump, but look out when he said
he was coming down, you got to hell out of the way!" MacNeil recalled,
too, how "in those days Rod wasn't near as heavy—he was big but loose
as a goose. He used to go up to Raymond Campbell's parish at St. Agnes
where there was a tennis court. He used to go up there and challenge Fr.
Campbell. Rod was a good player without any coaching; he had natural
athletic ability."

Another free-time social activity was singing. Although he didn't
have a strong voice, MacSween had a good ear and enjoyed singing both
for its own sake and, no doubt, for the performance opportunity it also
provided. Frank MacNeil recalled how

> socially, they would get together—I couldn't sing—but Rod could
> sing. Johnston was a very good singer and he was very good at liturgy.
> He would get Fr. Devison from St. Agnes, or Fr. Marinelli, from New
> Victoria, and they would spend hours in the Glebe House singing
> parts of the Mass or anything.

Singing wasn't the only musical activity that caught Rod's attention. There
is an amusing and telling exchange of letters between "Doc" Pat Nicholson
and his nephew over some classical instruments. The affectionate and
humorous tone of the letters highlight how the relationship between the
uncle and the nephew had, if anything, deepened:

> *Dear and Reverend Fr.,*
> *Twice since Christmas we have had musical gatherings at convents in this*
> *area and have enjoyed ourselves immensely. If we had a cello and a viola*
> *we could begin to hope to build up a string quartet until the bishop shifts us*
> *into our various oblivions. So I have been put up to it by the Rev. Johnston*

to write to you for some antique tools of music that inhabit some sad attic in your building. He thinks that you have at least a cello. What sayest thou? I have so many irons in the fire myself that I hesitate to try such an endeavour even if I had the ability, but there is also the Revs. Devison and Marinelli, bursting with musical ability, and willing to try anything. If you are willing to give them tell how they may be taken down. My pastor is going up soon for a radio sermon.

Your loving nephew

The uncle responded, no doubt delighted and amazed at the prospect of having a string quartet in the mining town:

Dear Fr. Rod,
I have indeed both a cello and a viola. Neither one has been used for years. My claim to the viola is rather good, being an heirloom. Possession is my claim to the cello, except that I have spent $15.00 on repairs to it, and I dare say no one else—certainly no one living—has punished himself to that extent. My only misgiving in lending them is the possibility that they may get lost, and if you can contrive some way in which I can be assured on that point, the use certainly will be yours. There is no telling when we may be in a position to do something with them here. There should be no great difficulty in transporting both instruments in a car that has a good sized cavity behind. Even a rear seat would be satisfactory. The problem of packing them can be deferred until the road is clear. I have not looked at either to see whether they are strong. The cello ought to be because it is not long since a soldier borrowed it. I doubt that there is a bow for either. If you are set on getting these instruments, it might be well for you to get strings and possibly have bows ordered soon. With very best greetings for the New year to yourself and Fr. Johnston, I remain,
Yours ever faithfully[14]

These letters illustrate several things about their correspondents and about the nature of lives they were leading. Though the nephew-curate admits to having many irons in the fire, there is no suggestion that the work is drudgery—in fact the tone seems to imply the opposite.

For the vast majority of Cape Bretoners, their only exposure to "high culture" came from the church, whether it was in the form of a High Latin Mass or, as in this case, the chance visit to the Glebe House while the viola was being tuned for a private or convent performance. There was a vital traditional musical culture in Cape Breton, a culture that Doc Pat, as a Gaelic scholar and musician, was keenly aware of and determined to promote and support. But only in his later years, did Rod MacSween come to realize and recognize both the magnitude and the distinctiveness of this traditional culture, and, more personally, of his uncle's place in supporting and preserving it. It is not uncommon for young intellectuals from the working class to be at odds with their heritage, with what went on at home, seeing it—in those far away pre-cultural studies days—as quaint, unsophisticated and, in every sense, parochial. But there is more at work here for MacSween than the simple rejection of his class and clan: it is, for instance, ironic, comic and perhaps a little predictable, that the nephew would joke with his Gaelic-speaking uncle in the language of Shakespeare, in the tongue of the Sassenach, as it were. In later years, as we shall see, MacSween, the intellectual and artist, is forced to recognize—but not always accept—both the price that's paid for high culture and the legacy of cultural imperialism that *de rigueur* goes along with it.[15] His cultural studies education was always hard-earned in the hinterland, but at this point in his life it is enough to recognize that the nephew loved and respected his uncle, even though he would have considered his interests—and his heritage—very remote from the world of the avant-garde that he so admired and so wished to be part of.

Rod MacSween's brief letter to his uncle also raises questions about his own future, especially when he mentions being shifted into oblivion by his bishop. With all his reading, and with his reputation as an "intellectual" now spreading throughout the diocese, we might wonder if he had ambitions other than the normal one of wanting to have his own parish. There is no record of MacSween ever having said he wished to teach at St. FX, but there is no doubt that he was aware of the tradition of priests being moved from parishes so that they could help out at the Catholic college.[16] It is difficult to pin down MacSween's motivations and ambitions at this point—at least as regards teaching and writing—but it would, I think, be fair to argue that his faith, his ministry and the mission of his Church, were uppermost in his mind. This may seem obvious, but I state it here and in other places because MacSween—especially in later life—sometimes gave the appearance of someone who had lost his faith. In those later years, it is true, he abandoned the outer trappings of the ministry—the collar and the black robes—but like his much-admired, famous and often censored contemporaries, Ivan Ilich and Hans Küng, to mention two, he never gave up hope—let alone the faith—in his beloved, conservative and continuously frustrating church.

Naturally, there were ways of serving his church other than the traditional one of parish priest: he could always employ his skills as a teacher or a writer, if the opportunity so presented itself. At this point in his curate's life, however, the pedagogical or scholarly world would have to wait; he was too busy and too happy with the active and hectic life of parish work, work that kept him going from dawn until he collapsed on his bed, dog-tired every night.

"*Doc*" Pat Nicholson was also corresponding with his other MacSween nephews during these first busy days and months of his tenure as president. Mike MacSween, the second eldest and Doc Pat's first MacSween recruit, was now stationed as a curate in Sydney Mines; George and Pat were both still overseas. In anticipation of returning veterans coming to St. FX, Nicholson wrote to Pat, in January of 1945 to encourage the veteran to attend the college, "We are crowded and are expecting a lot of ex-service men back with us when this miserable war is over. I do not know of any good reason why you yourself should not be included."[17] Pat's reply to his uncle concerning his education is both moving and revealing:

> *With regard to my entering college after the war is ended, I'm afraid that it would be a bit out of my class. Besides not having the necessary ability, I've drifted behind so far I would have difficulty in passing a Grade V examination. I have given this matter serious thought before receiving your letter and I am certainly regretful that I didn't take my education more seriously. There seems to be a penalty for everything, and I've lost out on some wonderful opportunities due to not having completed high school.*[18]

Like all the MacSweens whose correspondence has survived, Pat demonstrated a gift for language—the letter itself might be enough to gain him admission as a mature student today. His lack of self-esteem, no doubt had something to do with his class, with where he came from, but mostly, perhaps, it was an indicator of his mental health—Pat was fragile, and would become more so with the passing of time.

By all accounts, Rod, like his uncle Doc Pat, was a faithful correspondent with his friends and family. One letter he received about this time comes from his longtime friend, Dan E. MacDonald. Dan E. was assistant curate at the Cathedral in Antigonish from 1943 to 1950. In his handwritten letter, MacDonald has drawn a little house in the top left corner with the heading, "The Palace Grill!" It refers to the bishop's residence, always known and recognized by Catholics as the Bishop's Palace. The letter highlights the spirit of this young man and hints, too, perhaps, at why Rod was always so attracted to him—and why they remained best friends from childhood:

> *Amigo meo I am in a quandary! Que faire! Tonight I have a wake; tomorrow a funeral—a trip to the country and so I write to you! I meant to write long ago. I held back—see what iron will I have! Anyway your book—a jewel! Your letter a tonic! Yourself—a treasure! and I bankrupt!*

I haven't read the book as yet, took a peek or two but now have to lay it aside for the duration! Why??? My pastor has evanuit I am alone cum episcopo! Tre solus sanctus! He solus dominus! Ego solus serious—woe is ego! Fr. Gallivan went driving for funds St. FXers in the Ontario region! He'll be gone for over a month—I'll be gone for the duration by that time. A Holy Hour coram episcopo this Friday—Subject: Blessed are they who hunger and thirst after justice ... and I've been famished all my life. Will he take the hint if I should ask for a sandwich and glass of water during the sermon! Your Book Reviews are splendid! Honestly, the last one I fear you tried to out do the poet. My dear Shakespoke such choice of language ... and I knowing what other choice language you could use***###!!! Friend—fly thee hence and go up higher. How goes life at H20 ford? Is the noble Jones still plying his way with his ignoble steed! I owe you an admission, a confession no less. I had to tear up the page I had written—the written word once writ stays writ and what I had writ (though funny!) had to be censored ... do we go prosaic again!

With its wit, Latin quotes and puns, this letter would not look out of place among the pages of James Joyce, though the anti-clerical Irishman would cringe no doubt at the thought, despite his admiration for the Jesuits. The letter also highlights, sadly, the predictable self-censorship of this world, the repression of the comic and satiric flow of language and ideas that these men were clearly capable of writing. What would MacSween, the non-priest, have written at this time in poetry, fiction and essays had he not been so circumscribed by the world he lived in and the church he served? We will never know, but we can imagine that these born-in-the-closet-iconoclasts would have given us a madcap world to read and laugh about; a counterculture to the fiercely conservative postures they were forced to live and maintain.

Dan MacDonald's letter also contains the first reference to the only kind of writing that his friend was publishing at the time: book reviews for the diocesan newspaper, *The Casket*. It was during these years in New Waterford that MacSween first began publishing reviews in the Antigonish paper. These review articles were important for several reasons: they gave MacSween an outlet and an audience to share his vast reading with and, perhaps most importantly, they got the attention of the university community, not least of all Moses Coady and the new president of St. FX, "Doc" Nicholson. Both of these men were interested in scholar-priests who could teach and—especially for Coady—write. We might wonder what was going through the young curate's mind when he submitted his short articles to the newspaper: he was clearly ambitious to write, to share his growing knowledge with a wider audience than those in his immediate circle, but was he also looking for a way out of the parish? MacSween was also practising the art of poetry at this time, and though he did show it to friends and colleagues he did not, as far as we know, attempt to publish any of it at the time.

MacSween was kept extremely busy as the senior curate of Mount Carmel and, on at least one occasion, he had the opportunity to help out at New Waterford's other large parish, St. Agnes. It was an opportunity, though, that he could have done without. The Halifax riots on VE Day 1945 are now common knowledge to most Canadians, as is their cause: the simple-minded authorities who chose to close the liquor stores on that most longed-for day—the arrival of peace after six long years of war. In New Waterford, there was a large Italian community made up mostly of miners, but also of some shopkeepers. Many Cape Breton Italians—as Father Joe Marinelli knew too well—had been imprisoned (euphemistically called internment) during the war; and so, on VE day it was predictable that Italian Canadians—and storekeepers in particular—became the target of a post-war euphoria that was sweeping the nation. On that day in New Waterford, MacSween was called to a mob scene and stood in front of Favretto's store with his fellow curate, Raymond Campbell. A crowd had already gathered and they were shouting epithets such as salami and Mussolini; eventually a few stones were thrown. In his old age, MacSween recalled being "scared to death" at the time, but he stood his ground and eventually the mob dispersed. More than thirty years later he published a novel, *Furiously Wrinkled*, in which he used something of this post-war New Waterford experience:

> ...his nerves began to shake as memory awakened his emotions. He could still hear the stones whizzing through the air above his head and the crash as they landed against the walls or the windows. He cringed as he felt again the fearful anticipation of being struck on the head with a stone—or worse, of being torn to pieces by the enraged crowd.[19]

Like many other towns in Canada, New Waterford experienced a post-war baby boom with the return of its veterans. Although in his later years MacSween expressed little interest in the company of children, he took a very different view during his time at Mount Carmel. Fellow curate Frank MacNeil remembers that "he did so much for the people and their children. "At that time, we didn't have the welfare system, so Rod had control of the Strand bingo money and he was very, very generous to the people. He was like a one-man welfare system." MacSween remembered being surprised at how the poor gave in comparison to the prosperous:

I didn't realize that at first, but I was in a parish in New Waterford, and every Monday we had to count the collection and I did it for a year alone. And the next year we got another curate, and he was counting the money with me and he said, "Look at this doctor, he gives $150." and I said, "That's pretty good, eh?" "Like hell it's good," he said, "He should be putting in at least $500, possibly a thousand or two!" And I said, "But look, that's quite high." And he said, "No, it isn't. Look at this fellow, a miner, and he gave fifty dollars. What proportion of his salary is he giving and what's that doctor giving? He's giving almost nothing." And every parish I've ever been in, whenever we discussed this matter, it was the same. The rich don't give as much as the poor.

Another of MacSween's special projects—and one he was extremely proud of—concerned the building of a summer camp in Hay Cove for the children of the parish. Again, Frank MacNeil recalled that after getting help from an important Liberal party member of the time, they were able to buy one of the buildings from the army base in Victoria Park, Sydney: "We picked the officers mess—the best building that was there. We cut the buildings up in sections, took them up by truck, and then the carpenters from New Waterford came up and put them together. [Michael] Mick MacKinnon was transporting and Howard Conway was the carpenter in charge of the building—taking it apart and putting it together again. From then on Rod was able to have his camp for the girls and boys of the town, the Guides, Scouts, Cubs and Brownies."

Constructing a summer camp in the woods beside the beautiful Bras d'Or Lake, for poor mining-town children, was no small achievement for the young curate. And an added satisfaction must have been the location: Hay Cove was not far up the Lake from where MacSween had spent his own idyllic childhood summers. Through the building of this camp, Rod came to meet two of his early and closest friends, Mary and Mick MacKinnon. Mary MacKinnon was a beautiful and vibrant young woman with a strong personality, a vivacious wit, and a love of conversation and argument. She recalled that long after her husband and the children had gone to bed, she and the young curate would be talking and debating late into the night. Mary was involved with the Girl Guides and, like the other women from the parish, she helped with the cooking at the summer camp. Through Mary, MacSween came to know her husband, Michael, or Mick as his family and friends knew him. He, too, had a strong and expansive personality, and like his wife he also was extremely good-looking, charismatic and talkative. A resourceful handyman, Mick made his living primarily through trucking, construction and odd jobs—both he and Mary were also active in the local Liberal Party.[20] MacSween came

Fig. 16 Hay Cove, Cape Breton. Building a parish summer camp for Girl Guides and Boy Scouts. Courtesy George Sanderson.

Fig. 17 MacSween setting up camp in Hay Cove. Courtesy George Sanderson.

Fig. 18 MacSween, standing far right with men and women from New Waterford. Hay Cove, 1945. Courtesy Mary MacKinnon.

to know and regard this family as his own; in many ways at the expense of his own family. Mary MacKinnon recalled, for example, that when her only daughter was born, it was Father MacSween who drove her to the hospital. Similarly, and perhaps not surprisingly, her youngest son, Roddie, was named after the priest.

Despite the close friendship that evolved with Mick MacKinnon, it was clearly, his wife who attracted the young curate. This intelligent and attractive young woman from New Waterford was to be the first of several women who came to play a prominent role in MacSween's life. Over the years, these women provided a desperately needed contact that celibacy and the patriarchal life of the priesthood denied the young MacSween. Although he accepted "the gift of celibacy," he still clearly longed for the feminine world. In his later years, MacSween wrote an essay about the women, the "ladies," as he phrased it, who peopled the world of one of his favourite writers, Evelyn Waugh. In this essay, MacSween spoke about

Waugh's need to have intelligent and beautiful women as friends and confidants; people with whom he could share his world view, his art and ideas. MacSween shared the same need, but his women friends—their husbands and children—also became substitute, if not surrogate, families. He seems to have desperately needed to be adopted and loved by these families and friends; and these families were more than happy to have an articulate, witty, intellectual and compassionate priest enter their lives. Though he had little time to visit his own family, just a few miles down the road in Glace Bay, he also had little inclination—it was not his home anymore, and had not been so for some time. In a few short years, MacSween had, whether consciously or not, set relationships in place to ensure that his parents' home would never be his home again.

Although Mick and Mary MacKinnon were to become Rod's closest friends for many years, there were others who also entered his life, or rather whose lives he entered. Effie Duggan, a friend of MacSween's recalled a woman named Anna MacPhee, who died young of cancer, as a person who was drawn to the curate: "Anna and Fr. Rod were great friends. Anna wasn't married. They were very good friends through parish work." Anna MacPhee, it turns out, was a handsome woman: attractive, vivacious and broadminded, with jet black hair and an "infectious smile." Effie Duggan remembered how "Fr. Rod and Anna and the Guides made a trip to Kentville for the Children of Mary or CYO or Knights of Mount Carmel—some group. She was a phone operator years ago in New Waterford."[21] Mary MacKinnon remembered that Anna MacPhee lived with her mother and two sisters; she recalled that she and MacSween visited Anna for her famous cooking, most of it sweet. Like the curate, Anna could be sarcastic and comic at the same time.

There were other women whom he knew from the camp and with whom he kept in contact on and off over the years, including Helen and Merle MacLeod. These sisters often teased both Mick MacKinnon and MacSween about their politics: committed Cape Breton socialists, they were forever urging the men to vote NDP instead of their traditional Liberal. There was also a young girl who entered MacSween's life at this time and who would eventually become like a daughter to him. Margaret Beaton was a Brownie at the Mount Carmel summer camp who accidentally got hit with a stone and lost a tooth. MacSween witnessed the accident and took the child home to her parents and, after a short while, he became a close friend of the family. As the years went by, he continued to visit Marg, eventually becoming like a second father to her.[22]

Fig. 19 (Right) Catholic Girl Guides, 1945; Mary MacKinnon is on the far left, back row. Courtesy Mary MacKinnon.

Fig. 20 (Left) New Waterford women and girls at Hay Cove. Anna McPhee is fourth from the left, back row. Courtesy Mary MacKinnon.

Fig. 22 (Above) Winter outing for wartime women and children of Mount Carmel Parish, New Waterford. Courtesy Mary MacKinnon.

Fig. 21 (Left) Anna McPhee, New Waterford, 1944. Courtesy Mary MacKinnon.

The busy curate was also something of a second father to his adopted sister, Theresa. This orphaned girl from Pomquet had been adopted by his aunt in 1939 (it was Rod, in fact, who had brought the child home to Glace Bay from Antigonish). In a short while Theresa found herself living at Hugh and Jessie's, and from there she often went to visit New Waterford where she would stay with the MacKinnons or other friends of her adopted brother. Theresa remembered going to the summer camp in Hay Cove, and she also recalled crying to her older brother because she didn't have a bicycle like all the other kids her age. This, she remembered, was soon remedied.[23]

Besides looking out for his stepsister, MacSween would also visit his mother and father, his sister Margaret, and brothers Joe and Murdock, all of whom were still living in Glace Bay. The visits were always short and, as his siblings and their children recalled, never private because MacSween was sure to bring someone with him. He would visit his family in the company of other priests or with friends like Mick MacKinnon. As a priest, Rod was already treated with considerable deference in the family, so bringing other priests or guests was a further way of distancing himself from any possible intimacy; it also provided a ready excuse for an early retreat. If this seems harsh or ungrateful, it must be stated that he did not enjoy visiting his immediate family for any sustained period; it was not that he disliked them—far from it—but he found them hard to relax around. Part of this had to do with their personalities, they could be difficult, combative—especially the sons—and they were easy to anger and quick to argue. Hugh, himself, of course, as we have seen, was a patriarch who brooked no contradiction.

Pat and George MacSween, the two most easy-going of the brothers after Rod, both returned from overseas and went back to school. George would eventually become an engineer after a short stint in a seminary and some time at Dalhousie University and the Nova Scotia Technical School in Halifax. Pat would not be so fortunate. Already unstable, the war had taken its toll on him and, after a short time spent trying to study at university, his illness soon became worse and he was forced to quit. He then spent time in and out of mental hospitals, where he was often visited by his brother, Mike. In a letter to Doc Pat, Mike noted that his brother told him he was "going to Dalhousie and I suppose that is to be near George and to be by himself, I guess. He is still a problem and he will have to work it out by himself now for he resents direction as most of us do."[24] Nicholson was compassionate and concerned. There is a sense that he felt he should have done more for his nephew at the university:

I dare say nothing can be gained through standing in Pat's way. Several times during the past year some of us spoke of trying to get him some psychiatric treatment but it was not easy to discuss the topic with him. We have hopes of having better facilities during the coming year. Our plans include having a physician on the campus full-time and perhaps we can have a psychiatrist visit us occasionally. A small percentage of our students have something to gain from such treatment. I understand that George wields more influence over Pat than anyone else and he might persuade him to go to Camp Hill during the Christmas vacation or at the end of the year.

Fig. 23 Pat MacSween ca.1946. Courtesy Theresa Gallant.

MacSween also visited his brother and he, too, soon came to regard him as a tragic figure, gifted but unstable, and now incapable of making it in the world on his own. At first MacSween, like his parents and his uncle Doc Pat, blamed the war, but eventually he too came to acknowledge and accept the fact that his youngest brother's illness was congenital and long-standing. Between his visits to the mental hospital, Pat spent a short time in Hay Cove living in the camp his brother, Rod, had built for the children of New Waterford; while there, he carried a large army issue knife and expressed openly the fear that "his enemies were out to get him."[25]

There were other sufferers, other people in pain that MacSween was concerned with and whom he visited on a regular basis. In his old age, MacSween recalled panicking one night when he was called out to give the last rites (extreme unction): "I thought I was going in the right direction, then I realized I was on the wrong street. I started to panic and ran trying to find the house." He did eventually get there "covered in sweat" and out of breath. He remembered, too, visiting a woman with a huge cancerous growth on the side of her neck. He was there to give comfort. "She had been told by another priest that things would be okay. And she believed him, took him at his word." When Rod saw her again, the cancer had spread. "This poor woman looking up at me. Suffering and betrayal in her eyes. I'll never forget it."

In the midst of this demanding life, MacSween continued to develop as a scholar and still pursued his great love—and at times, no doubt, his great escape—reading. He was also now and again writing reviews for *The Casket* newspaper and poetry for himself and his immediate circle. Frank MacNeil remembered that although MacSween had little money he continued to buy books, to build his library, "Personally, himself, he was always broke, and he would be looking for money, a Mass stipend, for instance, he had saved up to pay a bill that arrived for books that he bought." His reading, as always, was omnivorous: history, philosophy, theology and, of course, literature. There were favourite areas and favourite writers: the great Russians—Tolstoy, Gogol, Dostoevski and Turgenev, with their deep spiritual roots, appealed to him early on. In later life, MacSween acknowledged that he was often first drawn to writers because of their strong spiritual sense.[26] There were also, inevitably and naturally, the Catholic writers that he followed and admired. His love for these writers or writers he perceived to be sympathetic to Catholicism was never parochial, nor was it by any means strictly religious. But it is perhaps best understood as a form of Catholic cultural nationalism with religion rather than ethnicity as its central tenet.[27] If, in his old age, MacSween's love and defence of these Catholic writers sometimes seemed strident, it had more to do with cultural nostalgia and Catholic cultural nationalism than with literary criticism. It was, partly at least, the underdog cultural and "national" identification of converts like Graham Greene, Evelyn Waugh and later, Robert Lowell and Marshall McLuhan that helped draw MacSween to these writers in the first place. At the very least, artists and thinkers of this stature converting to Catholicism gave him comfort in a society that seemed rapidly heading toward the secular.

Similarly, MacSween's lifelong love of T. S. Eliot's poetry stemmed largely from the Anglo-American's spiritual sense, his knowledge of Augustine, the early church and, most importantly, the mystic tradition. The mystic tradition preoccupied and fascinated MacSween all his life: the combination of artist and religious in writers such as the Spanish mystic and lyric poet, St. John of the Cross, the English writer, Dame Julian of Norwich and the anonymous author of *The Cloud of Unknowing*, became, as the years went by, increasingly important writers and texts for him. At the end of his life, when secularism became triumphant in the West, MacSween was able to make the transition, in Charles Pèguy's phrase, from *politique* to *mystique* in a relatively painless way. He had, as we shall see, much less "political" and "national" baggage to hang on to than most. In the end, he never loses his faith, but I would argue that it did undergo a metamorphosis: all religions, all faiths eventually come to exist for him on a single, open plane of understanding. Admittedly, in the 1940s, the young curate was still somewhat partisan and very much committed to the cultural and political side of his Cape Breton, Scots Catholicism—as he was to the world view of his Roman Catholic Church.

MacSween was drawn to writers like T. S. Eliot for reasons besides religion. Eliot's verse, as many undergraduates remember, was bookish—very bookish—crammed with allusions, myth, history and foreign languages. If this high priest of the Modern movement was a student's nightmare, he was a polymath's dream-come-true; witness MacSween's 1943 edition of Eliot's *Four Quartets*, dated and signed January 17, 1945—the book is crammed with notes.[28] This (1945) was also the year that another American poet first came to the scholar-priest's attention; Ezra Pound would be arrested for treason in Italy. In New Waterford, MacSween, his ear to the short-wave radio, would listen to the poet's broadcasts all the way from the Rome of Pius XII. Pound's preoccupation with history, myth, art and religion made T. S. Eliot's work look (almost) like a grade school primer. It was shortly after this introduction to the soon-to-be-labelled "Fascist poet" that MacSween began a half lifetime of studying, teaching and reviewing dedicated to the work of this complex, thorny and soon-to-be-imprisoned American genius.[29]

IN his later years, a folklore developed about how MacSween came to be teaching at St. FX; his eventual arrival on the campus had more to do with simple economics than his acknowledged reputation as a reader, preacher, conversationalist or writer. By Christmas, 1946, his uncle "Doc" Pat Nicholson, president of St. FX, was feeling the pressure of postwar expansion at his university; a burgeoning enrollment of veterans meant new buildings had to be built including residences, classrooms and a chapel. Always short of money, the university could ill afford to pay scholars to come to Antigonish, so the president relied on the long-standing tradition of recruiting young priests from within the diocese.[30]

In the spring of 1947, MacSween was visiting his alma mater as part of the yearly retreat of priests that was organized for the diocese. Unknown to himself, he was being groomed for one of the positions at the college and his uncle, the president, would soon be lobbying the bishop to assign Rod to the university. It would not be a transition as dear to MacSween's heart as we might imagine. Some of his letters that survive from this time show how deeply involved and personally attached he had become with certain parishioners. Not least among these, were his friends Mary and Mick MacKinnon:

> *(This time Mary, I have put him first in order to pretend that he is the more important. Of course, Mary, we both understand that he isn't—we know that he's below zero in almost everything, especially in the thing he calls a "nose." But it's good policy to humour him once in a while. Don't tell him what I'm saying here.) As you see, (if I have included the money) I am still trying to pay my debts to the camp fund. Already I am becoming rather confused as to the number of weeks that have passed. Strangely, for some reason that I cannot fathom, I always make the number smaller than it should be, never larger. I hope that you enjoyed your trip down here as much as I did everything. Sr. Gilbert was pleased with everyone too—I wonder why? Are you all "special," as Fr. Finochietto says about everything? Anne sent me pictures—all horrible. Everything was blurred and my nose didn't look as long as it should—thereby I was deprived of half my distinction. Mick, you looked as though your nose were cut off. Is it? Or is it naturally stubby. So long—I shall be seeing you soon, I hope, I hope, I hope.[31]*

The letter highlights how he missed his friends and that his heart was truly back in the parish, but the coming fall was to be the beginning of his last year in New Waterford—and his last year in parish work. Although colleagues and friends insisted that he did not want to leave New Waterford, to leave the parish, he must have felt the attraction of the classroom; he was, after all, a natural teacher and performer who thrived on the give-and-take of debate. And those who heard his sermons knew that he was a man of wit and humour who appreciated an audience. It would also, of course, be a chance for him to share his great knowledge, his love of history, philosophy and literature. The choice seems obvious—no choice at all really—and yet his loyalties were clearly conflicted; the decision as to whether he should stay in the parish or go to the college was by no means a simple one. His aspirations, hopes and fears are found in a crucial letter to his uncle, Doc Pat.[32]

This letter is, among other things, an autobiographical essay, an *apologia pro vita sua*, as Cardinal Newman might have put it—a justification of his life as it has been lived thus far. The initial reason for the letter has to do with a "conversation" that has passed between the nephew and his uncle. The New Waterford curate, it transpires, had apparently offended one of his fellow clergymen with a sermon he had given. Doc Pat seems to have been caught in the crossfire by defending his nephew's accuser; but the nephew, it seems, was not in a mood to back down:

First of all, I am very sorry for having been so queer and proud—and I will add undeveloped and afraid of everything strange. But I suppose that you know more about me than I do. Secondly—the sermon. That famous sermon. I am sorry here too for having offended so nice a fellow as Fr. Kane, but quite often even nice fellows deserve a rap on the knuckles to shatter their complacency. The more I thought about it on the way home the guiltier I felt—and although I cannot now remember exactly what the mistakes were and their correction, still I felt that even when an improvement had been done upon my work it was uncalled for, because I was giving the sermon and not Fr. Kane. In other words, I, with my peculiar knowledge, idiosyncrasies, passions etc was better able to determine what my sermon should be than even a Fulton Sheen or Bossuet. Sheen can prepare for Sheen's sermons but not for mine—only I can do that. And so my peculiarities should be respected. It was for this very reason that I was asked to preach—that I should instill into that course of sermon something entirely of my own flavour. If anything else were desired the whole course should have been a series of readings by Fr. Kane himself, because in this he is superlative. So corrections should have been confined to a minimum concerned with bad grammar (not peculiar grammar) and heresy. And if I remember rightly in a few cases I was grateful for that very service. But when I looked over my paper, overwrought and afraid as I was (feeling the push of the powers that be a little too near for my feeling of inferiority) I was outraged at what I considered an insult to my individuality. This feeling was heightened by my belief that such treatment would not have been meted out to a pastor who presented a sermon of equal value to mine. Anyway, now I do not care two hoots about it—and the explanation I have given sounds too grandiose for such a small affair. I cannot find the corrected sermon. It may turn up some day, but I have found the rough draft which I retained for myself. I did not intend to send this, but having read it over again I have decided to do so. Pardon me for saying so, but where the writing is my own and not the product of some sermonizing hack I am satisfied with it, and to a select audience would not be afraid to preach it again. It is not good—that is, not excellent if compared with great sermons; it has queer expressions—but why not? Every sermon is an attempt to break "the cake of custom," or should be. Within certain limits this must be done.

The Fr. Kane referred to is George Kane who taught grammar in the English Department at St. FX. Many years later, MacSween said of Kane, "In his own field of grammar he was supreme. We'll never have another grammarian to equal him."[33] This may have been so, but at the time of the letter the curate clearly had a low opinion of this grammarian. At any rate, after having dismissed Father Kane and rebuked his uncle, the nephew-curate then proceeds to tell the president of St. FX where he may obtain samples of his "famous style." It is at this point in the letter that we make the rather comic discovery that this is, in fact, a job application and, furthermore, that it is an application that has already been through the initial stages or hoops. Part of the reason for such arrogance on the curate's part comes, no doubt, because of the people he has in his corner. It is revealed, for instance, that no less a figure than Moses Coady is one of his champions: "They [the reviews] made a very favourable impression on Dr. Coady and he has done a certain amount of planning my future himself. His idea was that I should go away to some university and come back prepared not to teach but to write. Is it possible that you and he might conflict over this?"

At this point in the epistle MacSween delivers an impassioned and partial explanation of his own life: why he has chosen the path he has and why, too, he might make a good professor. It highlights many things, including his "philosophy" of art, and what place this art has in own life and world; it also draws attention to his extraordinary ego—his sense of himself, his confidence in his own talents and abilities:

> *Personally I have no opinions. Everything I have learned, everything by which I have enriched myself serves me some useful purpose in parish work. Not a thing is wasted. I deplore only the lack of those qualities that would make me more learned and more gracious in style of living and expressing myself. I find that knowledge and art are useless unless they do work—they must be useful. So I find that my literary labour has helped me in speaking and sermonizing and countless other ways. When I had to direct the choir at Pomquet and when I try to teach some singing knowledge to Scouts and Girl Guides, my experience told me that musical knowledge was a necessity so I learned to know and love music to a certain degree. When I began to hear confessions and try to straighten out lives I saw the fearful complexity of minds and began to study psychology in order not to stumble and cause ruins. I had tried to draw pictures in an indifferent way when young and now seeing its necessity for handicrafts (by which personalities are allowed to grow and flourish) I have taken to it as seriously as time will permit. And so with history—and so with everything else that a person can acquire—it is in the process of being useful that culture actively grows upon one. I know that there is much more that can be said contra on this point but I am emphasizing one phase. I also write poetry of some sort and once upon a time thought very highly of it. Now, although I can write much finer stuff I think much less of it. Because it is performing nothing useful for me. If by it I could make money or move people to good I would write much more—I know that I would, but can I? It would, if any*

good, cause only wonder and notoriety. (Pride is mixed up in all things but because all pervasive I ignore its existence—a constant) I'm rather confused but this is what I'm driving at—if I have any ability due to native endowment of body and mind and general education of character then this ability should be put to use by being given some occupation that will bring out all my latent powers. If I'm going to be chosen to become a professor because of style in prose and poetry I must be given the task of composing in prose and poetry and not some other occupation that will make a drain upon other powers and cause a consequent atrophy of the stylistic. Right now I am so engaged in so many different things that I seldom have time to think. But I would be perfectly happy to continue this way if I can continue to be useful.

Toward the end of this letter, MacSween admits that "there is much more to be said contra on this;" his theory of art, his aesthetics, seem utilitarian in the extreme and would not look out of place in the writings of Bentham or Mill, or for that matter, in the pages of Dickens's *Hard Times*. It is as if he took W. H. Auden's dictum that "poetry makes nothing happen" literally. It is reminiscent, too, of Chekhov, the medical doctor, wishing to justify his writing with a pilgrimage of duty to the penal colony on Sakhalin Island, or Seamus Heaney questioning his role as lyric poet in a country at war. Finally, the would-be-professor's statement that "it is in the process of being useful that culture actively grows upon one" brings to mind MacSween's soon-to-be favourite poet, Ezra Pound, and his now famous dictum, that ideas are good only insofar as they are put in to action.

The upstart curate closes this encyclical, this unique job application, by asking his uncle to "forget all this blather. The sermon is yours—you can read it with the same mind as did Fr. Kane on that fateful day. You know where to get some prose pieces. I enclose one poem which you shall hate with all your heart but which is me just as much as the prose is." This final emphasis, once again, on his writing and the references to Coady, certainly qualifies—if it doesn't contradict—the story of how MacSween came to be a professor at St. FX. In interviews and conversations throughout his life he always gave the impression that it was his uncle—and him alone—who was responsible for getting him to the university; moreover, he confirmed this version of the story in an interview with his former student, Pat Walsh, in the summer of 1980:

> I think Dr. Nicholson picked me because of my library. He'd come down to where I was staying and look at my books, at a time when I was only a young priest. There was a look of envy in his eye. I'm serious. I think he believed that my books should be up at St. FX, not

down in New Waterford, where they were. So, he just figured out some way of getting them up here. He concluded that I had to go along. He used to come into my room, again and again, and walk around looking at my books. Then he told a friend of mine that a man with such a library should be up at St. FX.[34]

That Doc Pat was instrumental in getting his nephew to teach at St. FX is undeniable and understandable, especially given the close relationship between the two men. What is new and revealing, however, in MacSween's letter, is the fact that Moses Coady was also championing his cause. On reflection, this too is hardly surprising, especially given Coady's interest in education and his ability to spot and promote talented people, young and gifted individuals he could use in furthering the cause of adult education. Coady no doubt would have known about the curate's extraordinary personal library; he would also have heard about MacSween's strong personality and his reputation for argument (the parish world of priests was large but not that large, and the Sunday sermon was always a showcase of sorts). Finally, Coady was no doubt reading MacSween's articles in *The Casket* and would clearly have been impressed by the writing, by the "famous style."

There is a reply from "Doc" Nicholson to the extraordinary job application he received from his nephew and it is, perhaps not surprisingly, short, tactful and to the point:

Dear Father Rod,

This is merely a belated acknowledgement of your letter and enclosure which reached me ten days ago. I think it does not call for protracted discussion at this time. At any rate I am very pleased to have the manuscript you sent me, but it is difficult to say now whether I shall make use of it later. Now that Father Marinelli is with you your household should certainly be a cheerful one.

The manuscript, which must be the "famous sermon," is, sadly, gone; there is no record of it among the President's papers—none, in fact, of MacSween's sermons have survived; the poem, too, is missing, lost. But we have the letter, and it says much, more than enough, about the 32-year-old MacSween. If nothing else, it must be one of the most hostile job applications ever penned: the arrogant tone and self-confidence are clearly those of the artist as young man, even if the artist is writing to his uncle. We might wonder, as a concluding observation on this letter, what kind of an artist MacSween would have become had he had the chance to pursue the career of writing which Moses Coady had initially envisioned for him, rather than the career he ended up with—that of teacher, counsellor, chaplain and administrator.

Whoever was finally responsible for getting MacSween to St. FX, in the summer of 1948 the New Waterford curate got the latest and last letter of posting from his bishop; this dispatch would not send him into oblivion, but rather requested that he leave the parish of Mount Carmel and take up teaching duties at his alma mater in Antigonish. His close friend of the time, Mary MacKinnon, recalled packing his books with him; the final count, she tallied, was three thousand volumes. The beloved curate's departure was twice recorded by the press under the headings, "Named to St. F X teaching staff" and "Farewell made to parishioners." The former noted that the curate's "departure was received with regret by the parishioners of Mount Carmel especially the youth for whom he worked unceasingly." "Father" Rod was described as being of "kindly, genial nature," and was "responsible for the flourishing of the Boy Scout and Girl Guide movements in the parish during the past few years."[35] The second notice informs the reader that the popular curate returned to New Waterford to say a formal goodbye to his parishioners and friends. He spoke to them directly and personally in two sermons: "It is only natural to expect as time goes on and new faces and new duties occupy my mind, many of your names will gradually fade from my memory, but I shall always remember you in my prayers and I ask that I be remembered in yours." MacSween went on to say that his stay at Mount Carmel was "the five happiest years of his life."[36] It is not often that publicly uttered platitudes correspond with personal and heartfelt truths, but in this case it does seem to have been so.

MacSween was 33 years old (an auspicious time for a Catholic priest) when he received his last posting letter from his bishop: he was leaving for good the town of New Waterford, the Parish of Mount Carmel, and the world of the curate as he had known it. The time he had spent in parish work would return to him again and again in his teaching, his writing, his conversations and his memory. MacSween's exposure to this wider world, to this vast range of human contact with its suffering and joy, would help form the poet, professor and writer in ways that he probably never envisioned or imagined.

IV   *R*eturn to Campus

*I*n the fall of 1948 MacSween packed up his books and belongings, said goodbye to his family, friends and parishioners, and left Cape Breton Island for the mainland of Nova Scotia. His was heading to Antigonish, to St. FX, where he was to take up a post as an assistant professor of English. When he left New Waterford, his pastor, the historian A. A. Johnston, lamented his going, and spoke about the close friendship he had developed with his curate and cousin. Fr. Johnston was a saintly and scholarly man with but one minor failing: he was, in the words of another of his curates, "whacked out on time."[1] Apparently, if you were one minute late for anything—Mass, Benediction, bingo or lunch—you would get a blast from the time-keeping historian. On reflection, this minor quirk in his former boss must have seemed small potatoes to young professor MacSween, especially in comparison with the demands made by his new boss. It is an old adage that family and relatives demand more from one another and, moreover, that they often expect that what is given is to be given freely. Doc Pat never expected things to be free, but as his nephew Mike recalled, he did make demands on those he had helped: "If Doc Pat did you a favour he expected you to repay him. And he didn't want money—he wanted work!"[2]

None of the clichés about work—workaholic, driven—seem sufficient to cover this man. Two former presidents of the university, both close friends of Doc Pat's, simply acknowledged that he was the hardest working man on the campus, probably the hardest-working person the university had ever known.[3] MacSween, in his old age, remembered the work ethic, drive, demands and expectations of his uncle:

101

Dr. Nicholson was a fine upstanding man, honest, holy, very devout, but one thing you could hold against him was that he made slaves out of his young friends. They had to work for him. He couldn't drive so they were driving him everywhere, and in some ways there was justice in it—in that he was so much more important than the rest of us were. And I think that an important fellow has to be served in some way. He was the president and he had his finger in many pies, he was important and he had to be present at many things. But, well, at times he went too far with his demands.

One of the demands that nephew Rod had to contend with was the caretaking of—of all things—a mink farm. In a desperate attempt to raise money for the university, Doc Pat had started a mink ranch. The image of this university president raising minks to help his students is both endearing and quixotic. The experiment failed to generate money partly because of falling pelt prices and poor management, but Pat Walsh, one of MacSween's proteges, and long-time friends, remarked that the real reason the venture failed was that "all the minks were male!"[4]

Fig. 24 A. A. Johnston circa 1948. Courtesy St. FX University Archives.

Mike MacSween recalled, with more than a little indignation, his younger brother's plight as a fledgling professor during these years at St. FX:

> As soon as Rod got there Doc Pat demanded that he come up with him and work with the minks. And here he was—he had to get up at six o'clock for Mass and he was responsible for discipline—so he didn't even have time to study for his classes! And here was this brute of a man forcing him to clean out mink pens and put in new bedding and all that kind of thing.

In a published interview in 1980, Rod MacSween spoke about the nature of his early years at St. FX, and although he doesn't mention the hated mink farm, he does record how demanding his work schedule was, and the fact that he wasn't prepared at all for teaching:

The administration thought I was prepared because I had read a great deal. But I hadn't read many of the things that came into the curriculum. A great deal of the work was new to me. First of all the teaching of grammar was new. Also, that first year I taught what is now English 350. Many of the things I had to teach, I hadn't seen before. I had read many important works that were not in the textbooks. So, I had to work very hard the first years I was here; the first two or three years, I guess. Once I learned grammar the rest was easy.[5]

Fig. 25 MacSween crossing on the ferry at Mulgrave 1948. Courtesy George Sanderson.

The transition from parish curate to university professor was not, intellectually at least, a challenge for the scholar-priest, but the workloads—especially in these early years—were not dissimilar. Besides trying to keep up with grammar and feral minks, there was the discipline of prefecting residences. An onerous task at the best of times, it was especially difficult during the postwar years, even though MacSween's first freshman class, the class of '48, had few war veterans. Jack MacDonald, MacSween's second cousin, and a war veteran himself, recalled what postwar student days were like on the campus of the Catholic college. Initiation week, Jack recalled, had a different meaning when the students were "a bunch of guys" who had been in a war: "These guys just looked at these upper-class men and said 'come on, get real'. They stopped a lot of the nonsensical things that used to go on at initiation when the veterans were here."[6]

These students were adults, many of them as old as or older than the faculty. "Imagine," Jack commented, "trying to tell a guy to turn his light out at ten o'clock who'd just come through a war!" Most of the priests and professors understood that they were dealing with men who had been "through some pretty terrible experiences," but some of the faculty were, predictably enough, rigid, "and stupidly so." In most cases, however, compassion and leniency were exercised. Jack MacDonald recalled an example of this from his first year in Tompkins residence:

> I was 26 then, most of the veterans were that age or a couple of years older. Anyway, this guy who was a POW [prisoner of war] and who was not in good shape, got drunk one night, very drunk. Fr. Malcolm MacEachern was the prefect in this particular building. The guy got up to his room, but he couldn't make the upper berth of his double bunk bed. He fell down on the floor. Long Mal picked him up, put him in his bed, covered him up and closed the door. He went back to his room and never said a word. The priests knew that these guys were veterans and they just couldn't treat them the same way as the young students. Those vets used to go out and get wild once in a while, but they were a pretty damn good bunch of students. They're all over the world now as doctors, engineers and lawyers.

Prefecting, up at six to say Mass, teaching four courses, attending extra-curricular events—plays, hockey games, movies, etc.—not to mention looking after minks and boning up on grammar, kept the professor-priest busy enough during his first year at the university: "We priests all got up at six o'clock and said Mass at seven and then we didn't get to bed until twelve or so, so I was always tired, terribly tired."[7] Indeed, at times, this ostensibly "academic" life must have seemed much busier than the active parish work he had just left behind in the town of New Waterford.

With this much work to preoccupy him, we might imagine that there was little time for Fr. MacSween to be lonely: he had close friends among the faculty, young priest-professors who like himself had just been appointed, including Malcolm MacDonell, who taught history, and Charlie R. MacDonald who was in the philosophy department. Charlie R. had helped MacSween out at the summer camp for guides and scouts in Hay Cove, and Mary MacKinnon remembered him well: "We would be playing cards for matches in the little shack at the camp—Fr. Charlie and the other women, and myself. We'd see Fr. MacSween coming over from the tent and we'd hide the cards. We were frightened for him to see us playing cards or anything like that." But despite these close friends and this hectic schedule, life was still lonely for MacSween—mostly, he missed New Waterford and his friends. Part of this loneliness, no doubt, had to do with the nature of his work; teaching veterans and high school graduates was very different from helping scouts and guides—there was no contact with the parents, with the families; there was also much more formality and, above all, there was almost no communication with women.

In New Waterford, MacSween had established strong friendships with several women, either through their children or husbands, and these friendships became very important to him. The relatively large working-class town of New Waterford, where he was known, loved and respected, gave him a kind of freedom within the priesthood—within the code of celibacy—that he could not possibly have had in a small, conservative and largely middle-class town like Antigonish. Moreover, the conditions at St. FX in these early years were nothing if not monastic. It does not take a Freudian to point out that Doc Pat's all-male mink ranch, while a financial failure, was symbolically appropriate for its place and time.

How little free time MacSween spent in his new home in these early years is confirmed by his close friend Mary MacKinnon, and by his own letters: "Every chance he got he ran away and Fr. Pat wouldn't know." There were people that he did visit in the town from time to time: his first cousin Rod MacSween and his wife, Geraldine, fondly remembered when he dropped in: "He used to like to visit here, he liked the little ones. He was in good shape then, he hadn't put on the weight."[8] He visited people he knew from New Waterford or Glace Bay, working class-people like Effie and Jim Duggan. Effie's sister Mary had been a Girl Guide; now she was working in Antigonish: "She was only seventeen, and she worked as a telephone operator." He would go to their house quite often and "the kids loved to see him coming. They would hang on every word that he'd say." The young professor told stories and drew pictures of the children: "He got Peggy and Sheila and Mickey to sit, and he'd sketch them and sign the drawings. It's up there in the cedar chest."[9] The Duggans remembered, too, that he always wore his clerical clothes and that he never took his collar off. The house they lived in was part of a co-op housing project begun by MacSween's school and seminary friend, Dan E. MacDonald, during his tenure at the Cathedral. To the Duggan's, Dan E. "was a saint, a beautiful man," a common sense man of action who dedicated his life to the ideals of Moses Coady. But Jim Duggan also remembered the young priest's fear of small town talk: "There was no way you were going to get into a car with Dan E. if you were a woman, and he was alone. There wasn't going to be any talk about him!" Dan E.'s fear of talk highlights, once again, how different the attitudes were in the small town, especially when it came to the company of women.

At the end of his first year at St. FX, MacSween was assigned to teach summer school at Xavier College in Sydney; he stayed with his brother Mike, who was stationed in the parish of Johnstown. Mike recalled Rod's struggle with the teaching of grammar: "Every morning he would have to get up at seven o'clock and drive to Sydney. He would leave the papers for me to go over. I'd have to find the answers because he didn't know a damn thing about grammar." Mike didn't have a great grasp of grammar either, so he relied on "books by Churchill or somebody." He would read these authors to find out how they used grammar and then corrected the papers and explained the terms—when MacSween came home at night Mike would have them ready for him.

MacSween also taught a religion class, and years later his brother was not impressed by his younger sibling's grasp of theology: "I found that the students knew just as much as he did because different times he was wrong—that's in religion. See, it's easy to be wrong in religion." Of all his brothers, Mike was the closest to Rod, and all his life Rod believed that his brother, like himself and his uncle, should have been at the college. He had the energy and temperament of a Moses Coady, and he was a superb communicator too, as evidenced by his popular radio show that ran for years in Cape Breton. Whenever "Father" MacSween was mentioned to someone on the Island it was always assumed to be Mike and not his younger sibling, Rod. Whether or not Mike would have been happy at the college—or as effective as a social worker and community leader—is something his younger brother Rod must have pondered over the years.

Despite MacSween's troubles with grammar and religion, his reputation as a teacher grew quickly and his classes soon developed a characteristic style. The young professor could easily have swamped his students in a morass of facts and details, but he shared with his brother Mike the natural gifts of a communicator, if not a performer—humour, too, was prized by both men. Mike had an enormous repertoire of jokes because of the endless public talks and performances he gave, but like Rod—who rarely told jokes—his humour was spontaneous, anarchic and always bursting out in conversation. There was also a strong sense of the absurd in both men—and they enjoyed the shock value of their humour. Oscar Wilde's dictum, that people without a sense of humour are not serious, was one that both men would have subscribed to.

MacSween's professed style in the classroom—especially in his later years—was always to cultivate a sense of fun, and he learned early on "to develop an atmosphere of humour in the classes."[10] The religion class he taught in the old assembly room in Xavier Hall soon became legendary, a course hard to get into because of sheer numbers, and there are many anecdotes. A favourite comic technique he employed concerned names: unlike his uncle Doc Pat, who, it is said, could name every student on campus, MacSween had trouble remembering names. If a student did something out of the ordinary, however, he would recall it and use it. Freeman Whitty, a former student and friend of MacSween's, recalled putting on a passion play "and one Sister, when the Crucifixion was happening, had to say the line 'It can't be true', and she could never quite get the line right. Whenever MacSween saw her he would always say, "Hello, It Can't Be True."[11]

MacSween's other great love, in addition to the classroom, was the library. From the moment he arrived on the campus, he more or less took possession of the small building known as the old library. Its holdings, when he first visited, were meager enough, but there was one great advantage for a bibliophile—he could do almost all of the ordering himself—and order he did. He once calculated that he ordered 90 per cent of all the books that came into the library each year, and he did this for many years: "I used to order everything," he confessed to Pat Walsh, "even economics sometimes, if the book was a classic. I did the same for music, art, history, psychology, and philosophy."[12] MacSween would spend whole weekends marking catalogues, sometimes as many as fifty catalogues at a time.

Sr. Madeline Connolly, long-time librarian at St. FX, recalled his arriving "faithfully at mail time." "No child, excited about his Christmas gifts, was so eager as he to see and feel the contents. He would sit in the midst of the clutter, inspecting, examining and perusing each book, giving us as well a brief review of each."[13] Katherine Chisholm, who also worked with Madeline Connolly, remembered the new professor-librarian: "He came in before supper at about three o'clock every day. If he didn't come, we wondered if he was sick. Did he have the flu? Actually, in later years, when he got a car, he would tell us when he was going away. I think he knew that we expected him. He was a collections librarian. An unpaid collections librarian."[14]

Fig. 26 *Madeline Connolly in 1965. Courtesy Pat Walsh.*

There are many anecdotes about MacSween at the library, a place, as Chisholm recalled, that became like a second home for him:

He lived in Mockler Hall directly adjacent to the old library, so he was going home to Mockler before supper, probably to have a little appetizer. Anyway, Madeline and I were looking out and it was a snowy day and I said to her, "Look, I'd like to make a bet with you. See, he's heading for Mockler, but watch. Watch those feet!" The head was pointing toward Mockler, and when he got to the walkway to the library, sure enough the feet turned in. And he arrived in and he looked at us with a sheepish grin on his face. He was sheepish, and we told him. We told him we had a bet. He thought that was great.

MacSween, of course, also had his own extraordinary collection of books in his rooms, as former students like C. J. Fox, the writer, critic and London journalist, remembered "Word simply got 'round' that Father MacSween's room in Mockler House was crammed with books—modern novels and verse of all things—and that anyone dropping in could browse among banks of brightly coloured volumes, representing the output of such far-off figures as Waugh, Greene and Eliot, and even take some away."[15] MacSween was also considered a good prefect, good in the sense that he didn't hassle the students about curfew if they were quiet. In his interview with Pat Walsh, he spoke of trying to get the university to ease up on discipline; however, a letter dated January 1950, from his uncle, reminded MacSween and his fellow priests about their duties, and about how difficult it would be to change the status quo. Nicholson is explicit about two points: "1. It is highly important that every student in every section be accounted for at 10:45 p.m. every day [and] 2. When a Prefect finds it necessary to be away from the premises overnight, he should have an understanding with the Head Prefect regarding the necessary temporary arrangement."[16]

Although he was still in good physical condition, MacSween did not keep to any regular exercise routine. With so many jobs and with so much work, it was difficult to find the time. Moreover, the sports he played in New Waterford—tennis, basketball and hockey—were not always available to him as a young professor, and when they were he felt uncomfortable about performing them with the students. Walking, although practised by some, was not the pastime or fitness routine it is today, and it only interested MacSween much later—when he had a golf club in his hand. His perennial and persistent efforts to keep in shape are in evidence in a letter he wrote to Mary and Mike MacKinnon on Nov. 16, 1949:

How are Adam and Eve today? Has Adam washed the dishes and swept the floor—at a single glance from Eve? I hope so—because I want him to be in good physical trim for the Christmas holidays. I am in very good trim

*myself. [Here, MacSween has drawn a picture of a torso and arm with
muscle written on the arm and dishwasher on the torso.] The stretchers
have me tied up in knots. The day after using them found me very tired.
Now my left shoulder is sore. Nothing, nothing comes without pain in this
valley of tears. Fr. Rankin saw them. [Here, he has drawn a picture of the
spring loaded, muscle stretchers.] Need I say more? He wants a set. The
money is enclosed. Send them to me and I shall give them to him. I believe
that in his heart of hearts he thinks he will be able to beat me. What a hope!
Before he moves I shall crush him flat as a pancake in a pan. He also wants
a few shirts like mine, nylon socks, a sun-lamp. But he's going to get only
the stretchers now. He looks at my nose and envy makes him green. I can
hear him thinking: "What a noble prow. With that a man could be king of
the United Nations. I shall get…. No, those can't be bought. They come in
such perfection only once in a thousand years. I must live all my life with
this ugly, insignificant schnozzle. I wonder if there are any more in the
world as foolish looking as this." Yes, I say to myself. I know of one.*[17]

The letter ends here but there is another that survives from that academic
year, dated April 26, 1950. In this letter MacSween has inserted a drawing of a car, a roadster of the time, with three men flying from being
struck, their hats in the air. The drawing is his way of announcing that he
has been travelling: "I went to Halifax and saw George and Betty." He
then goes on, rather ominously, to describe how he can now drive "fast"
because he can stay awake, "I don't feel sleepy at the wheel now as I used
to. I guess that shows how tired I was all the time last year. I can't begin
to tell you how tired I used to be—with a dead, ugly tiredness that gives
no comfort at all." Though he might have been a candidate for chronic
fatigue syndrome, it is more likely that his exhaustion came both from the
nature of his new job and from the fact that he no longer had the opportunity to exercise as he once did. With classes now over, he was travelling
around the Diocese to say Mass: "Last Sunday I went to Guysborough,
Queensport, and Dover. I said Mass in the last two places." Although the
roads are bad, he clearly enjoys the travelling, and looks forward to the
trip back to New Waterford: "This Sunday coming—my sermon. Dear
folks, have mercy on me. (Don't think I haven't shivered as you took apart
Fr. Marinelli and Fr. Morley!)." He ends the letter with an invocation to
spring and once again inserts a small drawing, this time of a flower bent
over to a caterpillar: "Spring is coming at last. What does it hold in store?
Let us not guess. Let us only hope with a great hope. Of all the nice things
that summer brings, surely there are a few for us alone. So long."

As with most faithful correspondents, when MacSween wrote his
letters he often completed several in one sitting. The following is the only

letter to his parents that appears to have survived. It was written on the same day as the one to Mick and Mary MacKinnon:

Dear Mom'n Pop,

It's a long time since I wrote—so here I am again. I do not think that I shall be home again until the end of May. It is not too easy to get down anyway—especially since Fr. Mike moved—and then I'm very much broke, as usual, and have to save something for the summer. I was in Halifax two Sundays ago and saw the Royal Embassy there. Both of them looked very well—and in spite of the fact that George had exams next day. I had a very fine time with them. They are in very good cheer and hopeful for the future. I believe that I shall see them again in a few days—but I am not sure yet. I am to preach on the Radio next Sunday—so listen carefully. Then I'll feel right at Home. Also, I'll know that someone is listening—really listening. (Of course, I'm only fooling. I would prefer that no one would listen—personally. But—?) I may get a contract too for the Fun at Five Program. That would recoup my fortunes and give me a chance to throw a lot of sly digs at my enemies, whoever they might be. I hope that you two wonderful MacSweens are in good shape. Also that amazing collection of bone and muscle in which Pat, Catherine, Margaret, etc. have their share.

So long.

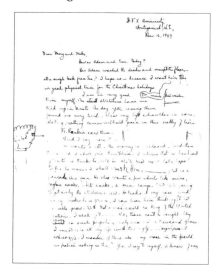 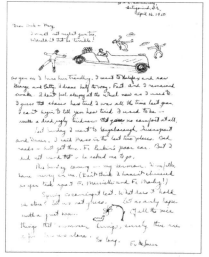

Fig. 27 MacSween letters to MacKinnons. Courtesy Stewart Donovan.

It is both a curious and revealing letter. There is a photograph from the same time of MacSween standing behind his father who is seated in the living room of his home; the son's fist is clenched and his head is raised in pride. The father, too, seems to share the same pride—"This is my son, the priest," might be the caption for the photo. The summer of 1950 would be a fateful one for MacSween, beginning with his leaving for Washington, DC, to do postgraduate work at the Catholic University of America and ending, sadly, with the death of his mother, Jessie.

IN the years immediately following World War II, St. FX, like many other universities throughout the country, experienced its first great expansion and transition. Hand-in-hand with this new growth, with increased enrolments and new buildings, was a heightened concern with standards and image. Almost since his first arrival on the campus, Dr. Nicholson had been a strong advocate of higher standards at St. FX; thus, he was naturally troubled at what he saw as the decline of staff qualifications, a decline which he truly believed was undermining the university's prestige in the Maritimes and throughout the country—especially in the English speaking Catholic constituencies. He lamented that St. FX was "getting loaded up with untrained personnel." Dr. Roy J. Deferrari, who returned from the Catholic University of America that year to inspect St. FX (as he had done back in 1938) confirmed Nicholson's troubled conclusion. Of twenty-seven faculty members in 1946, twenty were clerics, six had bachelors degrees, eight had masters, and thirteen had doctorates; by 1951 only fourteen out of forty-nine had doctorates, twenty-nine of these were clerics, sixteen had masters and sixteen had bachelors.[18]

Fig. 29 Rod MacSween with his father, Hugh, ca. 1955. Courtesy Stewart Donovan.

Given these conditions, it comes as little surprise perhaps that Doc Pat would insist that his nephew go to graduate school to get his MA and, eventually, his doctorate. Even MacSween himself sometimes complained about the low intellectual level of the priests at the college. This was a legitimate concern, but not unpredictable in many respects—or, in some respects, fair—after all, these men were trained as diocesan clerics and most of them expected to begin and end their days in parishes, far away from intellectual pursuits. They were not—nor should they have been expected to be—the intellectual equivalents of the Jesuits, the priest-scholars we associate with the world and writings of figures like James Joyce.

MacSween had little patience with trained academics—especially in the arts—but he did expect his colleagues, his fellow clerics in particular, to be dedicated, enthusiastic scholars and enlightened teachers. For the most part, the expectations of men like Jimmy Tompkins, Moses Coady and Patrick Nicholson were unrealistic for the majority of these diocesan priests; the small, but indelible renaissance of thought and action that these men had initiated at their college—and in the surrounding com-

munities—would not last another generation. Its demise had as much to do with the evolving secular nature of the world as it did with any internal factors. In many respects, MacSween was the last of a generation of remarkable and influential Cape Breton priests and, as such, his future position at the university would, ironically, be made problematic.

Fig. 30 MacSween in Mockler Hall Residence at St. FX, 1955. Courtesy George Sanderson.

MacSween's chosen discipline, his terrain, so to speak, was culture. But the influential men who had established the university's reputation—especially Coady and Tompkins—were men of action, men who participated in politics and economics, and who took pride in the contact they established with the wider community, both at home and abroad. Furthermore, these men, along with "Doc" Nicholson himself, lived in a time when the church and the university mutually supported one another. Unlike his predecessors, Father MacSween would be forced to fight his own battles in a very lonely—and often secular—field and, what is more, his antagonists—more often than not—would be his own fellow priests.

Although it is not in their correspondence, it is reasonable to assume that Doc Pat made MacSween's pursuit of graduate studies one of the conditions of his coming to the university in the first place. The nephew, not surprisingly, resisted at first, but to little avail: at the beginning of the summer of 1950, MacSween found himself headed south, with another colleague, Fr. Merchant Bauer, to the fierce heat of America's capital city, where he would begin studies toward a masters degree in English literature. Forty years or so later, his travelling companion, Fr. Bauer, recalled their journey: "We drove down together in my car. We went late in June the year his mother died. I know that because before the end of the school he got the phone call saying that his mother had died. He flew home, and I remember I drove home alone. So he took those courses anyhow, he took English. I took courses in Theatre."[19]

Several of MacSween's letters from this time have survived, and in them he talks about his studies, the city of Washington, and always—and often—the heat. The letter that follows (only part of which survives) was written to the MacKinnons shortly after his arrival in Washington:

Today I went to Chesapeake Bay which is about 40 miles away. (Find it on the map and educate yourselves.) It's a lovely spot—but it was just as warm as the city and no privacy. I was never so hot before in my life. It was terrible. The Americans were all hot too. Then we returned home—without supper and burnt, although we had taken care not to be exposed too long. On the way home I saw a hardware store and stopped. There I found a lovely electric fan ($11.95). I bought it. I'm broke now and I've been here only two days—but I'm desperate too, and which is the state that all good men and true prefer? It's blowing on me now! Great! If I survive Sunday I shall go to class Monday. That will be a new experience. How hot will the classrooms be? How tough or how dry the professors? How much homework for each class? Flash! When at Boston I weighed myself—230lbs! The scale? A good one. Others tried it and found it accurate. Think of that! And for 3 years I have been undergoing insults because of a faulty scale at the glebe house. I must admit though that the soft life is taking away my sylphlike figure (!) —but those days are ended, I think. I shall return a mere dry skeleton. A man offered to give me voice lessons. I refused. How else are you going to know me when I return? In no other way. Pardon me for speaking so much about myself. I know myself best—and it's such a pleasure to speak of what I know without constant interruptions from the peanut gallery of MacKinnonville. I'm going to end here. I could write on and on for ages, but every letter must be given its quota of news. I'm writing to you, Anna, Fr. Mike, Dr. Pat in a row—I've already written home—and I assure you that this takes more ingenuity than a mere story. This is two days later. I have just been reading a book in *which the writer declares that a succession of 6 or 7 short noses in a family is enough to doom that family to obscurity people will think so little of them. Long noses—prominence in public affairs. Proof comes slow—but comes.*

The letter contains his now characteristic wit and, as with his other letters to the MacKinnons, there are drawings: there is a sketch of a car and traffic lights with "honk honk" scattered all over the page, and a caption which reads, Me driving through Boston. Other things of interest in the letter include his physical description, and the fact that he is battling weight but really not that badly out of shape, given his six-foot-four height and bone mass. The fact that he is writing to Anna McPhee affirms, once again, the presence and importance of women friends in his life.

In his first letter, June 25, 1950, to the man who sent him to Washington, MacSween addresses his uncle as Dear Dr. P. J.—the comic informality shows once again how close the nephew and uncle were—and also how much confidence the nephew had gained:

Dear Dr. P. J.

A few words from the innocents abroad. This is our third day at Washington and both of us are beginning to feel at home, at least to a certain extent. My one big difficulty is the heat and the humidity, especially the latter. Whenever I move, I perspire like a fountain, become embarrassed, and look for a convenient exit. Yesterday the temperature was up to 95. It was a terrible day. Today is not so hot yet, but the humidity is up very high. I registered and received my course—the English Novel, Introduction to Literary Theory, and Pro-Seminar in Philology (or something or other). I intend to drop the last one, which was pushed down my throat by Dr. Cain, as it is unnecessary at this stage of the game. I do this realizing that my primary purpose here is to divest myself of complexes. This is being accomplished rapidly. Complexes are flying around everywhere without an owner. If this continues and the sun refuses to retire, I shall be a new man, mentally and physically, when I return. As a new man, of course, I shall have to be reintroduced to everybody at the college. (Facetiousness) We had an interesting journey on the way down. We ran along turnpikes until they sickened us, we became lost in Boston at night, we saw queer things on television, we lived 21 stories up in an hotel near Broadway, we walked around Rockefeller Centre, we visited an exotic bookshop from which I have been buying books for ten years (but was prevented from introducing myself by a complex), then on to Jersey, Baltimore and Washington, arriving late at our goal but managing a berth for the night. The heat was always with us in the cities—and for me this is the bane of existence—and this factor takes away true enjoyment from this venture. Nevertheless, it is only six weeks—so short a time!—and then we shall again be on our way to the island of fruits and flowers. There are few seculars here, mostly Benedictines. Everyone is friendly, but not too friendly. The lay-people we met everywhere astonished us by their friendliness. Ordinary people are very nice people, generally. They have not walked into that stage of introspection that doth make cowards of us all. So long. Pray for me.

On the back of the letter there is an account, more or less, of his first Monday at summer school:

Monday I went and asked Dr. Cain to be allowed to give up the Pro-Seminar, about which I have heard dreadful reports, for a course in Modern American Poetry (which I can use immediately in my work). He demurred. I insisted. He redemurred. I outlasted him. He gave in on the course, but whipped back with a refusal to give me graduate credit for it—and for the other graduate course that I have. I let it go. I shall get the knowledge if not the credit. I had a class to day—Introduction to Literary Theory. I believe it's going to be good. Then The English Novel—Dr. Litz. I don't believe that he's half as good as Fr. Bannon was in practically the same work. But that's the way the world goes. Dr. Cain is now concerned that I'm stubborn. What a strange and what a novel accusation to level against me, of all people![20]

This trip across the American border contained many firsts for MacSween: it was his first time outside Nova Scotia, his first encounter with graduate school and his first experience of a large urban society. Despite all his bookish sophistication, we can imagine the impact that modern urban America must have had upon him: the turnpikes "sicken them" as they head south, but they would not have sickened his brother Mike who had recently reported to his uncle Doc Pat that the "Louisbourg-Sydney road is being paved much to the rejoicing of all."[21] Washington was a beautiful and imposing classical city in these years. It was also relatively crime-free and safe to be about in at night. The reference to television in the letter is also interesting, as it would be several years yet before they could watch it in their own hometowns on "the island of fruits and flowers." The comic lines in the letter about complexes are part of the continuing battle he had with his uncle about being in Washington in the first place.

Obviously, MacSween did not think graduate studies would make him "a new man." His reference to the exotic bookstore in New York is the famous Gotham Book Mart, a haunt for modern avant-garde writers and a store MacSween had been buying books from as far back as his seminary days. His refusal to take the seminar in philology shows that Catholic U was still instructing on the old European model, a model still used today in Catholic universities such as Louvain, in Belgium. Finally, there is the heat and more heat, always the heat. Those who knew MacSween in later years can sympathize with this giant Cape Breton Scot—six-foot-four and two hundred and thirty-four pounds at this time—from the temperate coastal island, sweating in the subtropical sun of a high Maryland summer. Washington was built upon swampland, and when it came to the heat, he got little sympathy from his uncle, who, after all, had been a student in that same southern heat forty years earlier—if Doc Pat could bear it, so could his nephew. He put it somewhat more gently in a letter of July 3, 1950: "There is nothing much that can be done about the heat but to grin and bear it. It is just one of the experiences of life that one needs to go through in order to talk about it later!"[22]

Doc Pat, by all accounts, was not a puritan, but he was an ascetic with a fair sprinkling of Jansenism in his spirit—that French-Catholic inheritance from Port Royal bestowed on the Catholic Scots and Irish whether they wanted it or not—but which they certainly embraced. Doc Pat never drank and was fairly strict with his family and friends on matters related to alcohol. A former president of St. FX and Nicholson's long-time friend, assistant and fellow Gaelic speaker, Malcolm MacDonell recalled his mentor's attitude toward alcohol on a tour of Scotland the two made together in 1948:

> He was a pretty tight teetotaller, but I was just beginning to succumb
> to temptation in those days, and of course how does one resist the
> offerings in the Highlands and the Isles? But he didn't hesitate to
> censure me quite publicly every time I had a little sip. He'd look at
> me and say, "There's the fellow we have in charge of discipline, and he
> throws people out of the institution for drinking!"

MacSween, too, like most religious of his generation, was infected with a mild case of this French-Dutch affliction, the puritan spirit of Pascal, but much of MacSween's own temperament—especially in relation to the physical world around him—was open and uninhibited. If, in later life, and especially in his last ten years or so, MacSween was conscious of his body, it had more to do with his physical size than with his religion or the culture of shame that his and previous generations shared and lived in. Big men—as any former football player knows—are more subject to obesity than most, especially when they become inactive and have the added burden, as MacSween clearly did, of low metabolism. Because of this obesity, then, he suffered more than he should have in his final years; he came, in fact, to fear hospitals, not because of medical treatment but rather because of a phobia about physical exposure, a feeling of vulnerability around doctors and nurses.

Mike MacSween, like his uncle Doc Pat, also received letters and progress reports from his brother from Washington. Although these letters have not survived, there is a reference to MacSween at Catholic U in several letters that Mike sent to his uncle. Not surprisingly, the subject of weather comes up often: "I had a letter from Fr. Rod this week and he really seems satisfied although the heat bothers him." A few days later Mike reports on something literary and notes that Rod, "nearly caused one of his instructors to die of heartache when he spent an hour in class tearing Thackery to pieces. When the poor instructor questioned him after class and found out that he was Scottish, he was delighted, for he said that a Scotchman could never appreciate Thackeray because Scottish people all want things said as quickly as possible…. Fr. Rod replied that whether a thing was said quickly or not it would not help Thackeray."[23]

Although the heat continued to plague MacSween, it does not seem to have affected his studies. That the work was not a challenge for the mature student was made abundantly clear in a letter to his uncle, Doc Pat, on July 20, 1950:

> One more missive before the semester is over, all over. Don't bother to answer, as answering letters is very hard work. One look at the date above will show that we are almost home again. I shall be very glad to escape the heat. We have been rather lucky though. This has been a very cool summer, the Washingtonians say. Rain almost every day. This means high humidity—but not high temperature. As I write a thunderstorm is going on. It was unbearably hot around suppertime—when suddenly this rain came along, and now everything is wet and cool. Tomorrow it will be hot again—and so on. My studies are progressing very well. The heat in the library is simply frightening at times, and I often stay away when I should go there. But I get over enough to get along. I'm going to return with a long list of books and periodicals in English. I looked at the reserved books in History and Philosophy and could see nothing unusual. There are many deplorable gaps in their own library. The Lib. of Congress is near but that is only a last ditch—too much trouble involved in getting a book. In our quizzes I cleaned up—this is strange at my young age and with my past life secluded from books—making an "A" a 95, and in the other class where no exams were taken, my paper was read out all by itself. But it seemed so easy that I am rather suspicious of their marking—or something. Everything seems too easy. Fr. Bauer is very healthy and happy, and up to his ears in play production. (I heard that you have been seeing Ghosts yourself lately—and have not been the same since.) The CU play was very enjoyable, The College Widow. I liked it very much. Fr. Bauer with characteristic humility was prop man and had to run all over town gathering props. Fr. Peter [Nearing] is taking many classes and is interviewing

more people than a reporter. Sometimes I blink my eyes to see whether or not he is the rector of CU. If there are complexes there, they are very scared complexes, and have long given up the struggle for a place in the sun. I shall see you soon—unless I go through town so fast that I shall be invisible to the naked eye. Pray for me.

This letter, along with his brother Mike's, explains one of the stories surrounding MacSween's refusal to return to Catholic U to finish his degree: the fact that he knew (or felt he knew) more than the professors. The other part of the story—that they said they had nothing that they could teach him—has not come down to us in written form.

One of the ironies surrounding MacSween's time in Washington was the presence in that town of the American poet he would spend a quarter of his lifetime teaching and promoting—Ezra Pound. Pound was a prisoner of the United States government at St. Elizabeth's mental hospital for the criminally insane. The American poet had made broadcasts during the war over Rome radio and was indicted for treason. The punishment for treason was death by hanging, but Pound was found mentally unfit to stand trial. Although the "mad" poet eventually recovered his sanity, he continued to be kept locked up because he remained an embarrassment to the government, especially since the Library of Congress had awarded him the first Bollingen Prize for poetry in 1949 for the Pisan Cantos. By 1950, when MacSween was in town, Pound had already spent five years locked up in the asylum, and he would spend eight more before his release in 1958.

Two years before MacSween's visit to Washington, two other Canadian scholar-professors came to the city: Marshall McLuhan and Hugh Kenner arrived to visit with Ezra Pound, the "founder" of modern poetry; a third Canadian, poet and critic Louis Dudek, who was studying in New York at Columbia University, also visited and corresponded with Pound.[24] Curiously and coincidentally, MacSween, as we shall see in later chapters, would eventually end up promoting and teaching all three of these Canadians, while one them, Louis Dudek, would end up—forty odd years later—championing R. J. MacSween as Canada's "great unknown poet."

As graduate school slowly wound its way down during those last hot, dog days of a Washington summer, MacSween received a telephone call from home. He must have known it was something serious—if not tragic. Despite Alexander Graham Bell's celebrated connection with the island, phones were still a luxury in many Cape Breton homes, and this was probably MacSween's first long distance call. Predictably, the news he got was not good: his mother, who had been hospitalized with a broken hip for almost two months, and who had undergone surgery, had died. It was August 6, 1950, and Mary Jessie MacSween was seventy-one years old.

In a letter to Dr. Nicholson a week before his mother's death, Fr. Mike had written to say, "I saw my mother in the hospital last weekend, she was resting comfortably and she seemed happy but the most serious part of the operation is yet to come. My father is lost at home alone and these two certainly have given us an example of pure devotion in spite of much hardship."[25] In his old age, his brother Rod remembered wandering about the streets of Glace Bay and New Waterford in a daze, as former parishioners approached him offering sympathy. He recalled the words of an older coal miner:

> He knew my mother when she was young, and when he saw me he asked, "And how is your good mother, how's your mother?" He would do it with such feeling, you know. And then my mother died, I felt terrible myself, I was home for two or three days then I was back walking down main street, Plummer Avenue, in New Waterford and he met me, he came over and shook hands, "Sorry for your trouble, Father, I was going to go to the funeral then, I said, no, I'd better not go. You know, Father, these things come in life." Then he ran because he would have been crying in a minute.

Like many sons from big working-class families, MacSween felt guilty about his mother's difficult life:

> My mother was terribly overworked and we were too dumb to help her enough, and she was overweight which made her work even harder. She was very sweet-tempered. I only appreciated her when I grew up. What a lovely person she was. Everybody in the world I think catches on too late, how nice their parents are. I always appreciated my father, but I didn't always appreciate my mother.

MacSween's poetry is not a personal poetry. Even when he wrote about death, a subject he engaged often, it is almost always in general terms. There are elegies, but only twice does he directly name a family member. Although he may have written a poem for his mother—for therapeutic reasons if nothing else—the only reference to her is in a poem entitled "within the shell" which he published in his first collection, the forgotten world (1971). The date which the poem was written is uncertain, but it was most likely in the early 1960s. It is a complex and deeply personal poem that appears, on the surface at least, to be about birth and faith. The lyric opens with the poet (no doubt as an infant) encircled in a golden seashell by strangers, and as he whispers his "dreams" to himself, the strangers speak an exotic tongue (possibly the Gaelic of his youth) that to him is unintelligible, a fable. Eventually "pale hands move before" him and "call for a song," but the poet is mute: "I am a violin held in the air/but never breathed upon." In the next stanza Christ comes at night with a comforting smile, but when "he opens his lips to speak" the poet's own language, he does not hear a word. The silence continues in the final stanza:

> then my mother comes
> her face is brown wrinkled in a smile
> she doesn't speak
> she only looks at me

The poem seems to be about the poet's birth and journey towards faith, and it is interesting that MacSween ends this affirmation of his faith with an image of his mother. But in the end, the poem focuses rather strangely and—some readers might feel—coldly and dispassionately on the priest and his faith, and not on the spirit or memory of his mother.

A poem like "the focus," also published in his first collection, is one of the few lyrics MacSween ever published about the nature of love, and it is a work that could easily have been written with his mother in mind:

> some people are a focus of love
> they concentrate life
> within a compass so fine
> that flame leaps into being

The poem moves from this opening stanza with its personal evocation to a more public stance, "travelers come from foreign lands/to warm themselves at their fire/they hitch into town/from odd corners of the globe," The lyric returns in the third stanza to a couple—not, interestingly, an individual—who are the source of the focus:

> the lovers they have come to see
> burn before them
> like campfire flames
> on their faces an inscrutability
> like the Buddha's
> or Christ's bearded countenance

The poem does not portray the lovers as individuals, and the love that is finally celebrated is not romantic, personal or even familial—it is, in the end, a somewhat formulaic religious poem about transcendence, devotion and altruism.

When MacSween returned to the St. FX campus in the fall of 1950, he knew that he would not be returning to Washington the following summer to pursue his graduate studies. He had made up his mind that when the time came to go, he would simply refuse, and his uncle, the President, could do what he liked. If the Washington heat and the relatively unchallenging workload did not fully convince him of the futility of his being there, then the death of his mother certainly did. In his later years, MacSween always insisted that it was his age—even more than his knowledge—that justified his not returning to complete his graduate studies. In the spring of 1951, he would be thirty-six years old and only part way through his MA, an MA that he knew would never be enough. "Doc" Nicholson wanted his nephew to be "Doc" MacSween—he must "get the paper," as the saying went.

It is impossible for MacSween to have foreseen the eventual political importance of "getting the paper," of accreditation, but it is doubtful, given the way higher education—especially in relation to religion, culture and politics—eventually changed, that it would have made much difference in his professional life. By the end of his career, St. FX, like many other institutions of its kind, had moved not only in the direction of secularization, but, more critically perhaps, towards the larger "multiversity" model with its strong emphasis on science, social science, engineering and business. The liberal arts, which "Doc" Nicholson—as a man of science—regarded as fundamental, would no longer hold the high ground in the eyes of those who set policy and did hiring. Hand in hand with this shift away from the liberal arts was of course the rapid and inevitable secularization of the school. The role of religion—the direct influence of the Catholic Church and of the diocese, in particular—would soon be greatly diminished; greater dependence on non-religious and government bodies, especially in terms of funding, meant that St. FX would soon go the way of all former religious institutions of higher learning—it would be religious in name and tradition only.

*A*mong the St. FX Archives' papers of Fr. Moses Coady is a letter to Edward Skillen, editor of *The Commonweal* magazine out of New York. The date is January 23, 1953:

Dear Mr. Skillen:

I am sending you an article which Father Roderick Joseph MacSween, a member of our English staff, has written more or less in defense of Cardinal Stepinac in answer to the attack of Sherwood Eddy in the Christian Century. It may be too late because you may have already attended to this matter. It was my doing that Father MacSween is giving permission to submit this piece to you for publication in The Commonweal. *Father MacSween is a gifted young man and has, for a beginner, a great knowledge of history and literature. He might easily prove to be our greatest Christian apologist in this part of the world. He has not written much yet but I predict a great future for him. He is the nearest thing to a walking encyclopedia that we ever produced in this part of the country. I asked him to do this only a few days ago and in the meantime he read a couple of books and looked up all his old authorities.*[26]

Moses Coady's high opinion of MacSween must have helped his case for not returning to graduate school, but the kind of writer that Coady expected the junior professor to become—a Christian apologist—was a pipe dream. Even with his great love of history, MacSween was first and foremost a literary man and, as we have seen, a reticent but persistent poet. As the years went by, he continued to promote Catholic writers, to be a "Christian apologist" of sorts, but his vast and omnivorous reading prevented him from being parochial, if not partisan. There is no doubt about his allegiance to Catholicism, with what I have termed a strong "nationalist" quality, but as the years passed and as the Church declined in power and influence—especially in the West—MacSween moved slowly away from this public, political view towards a more private and argueably complex, meditative, if not mystical, stance in matters of religion. It could be claimed that he had been heading in this direction all along, but the nature of his study—and his life—certainly helped, rather than hindered, his progress.

MacSween's early admiration of controversial literary figures such as D. H. Lawrence and James Joyce—controversial, at least, in the eyes of the Church—highlighted the fact that when it came to art, dogma (politics) would have to take a back seat. When he first arrived on the campus in the fall of 1948, he recalled Doc Pat wandering about his room looking at his collection of books. When the Jansenist Scot came across a copy of James Joyce's Ulysses, a sour look came on his face:

Dr. Nicholson thought it was so bad, but he hadn't read it of course. He told me to hide it, but I didn't bother. And then a fellow from England came in and grabbed it, a Professor Healy, who was a fallen-

away Catholic. "I can't get this in England he said, it's been banned."
He asked me for a lend of it and he read it in about a week I guess, and
returned it right away saying, "I tried my best to read this book but I
could never get a copy."

MacSween's own well-marked edition had been bought in 1942, his first
year out of the seminary. What Dr. Nicholson would have objected to, of
course, was not so much Joyce's anti-clericalism, but rather the author's
reputation for portraying explicit and erotic human sexuality—the reason
it was banned and censored in the first place.

Similarly, D. H. Lawrence, because of *Lady Chatterley's Lover*, was an
even more controversial writer; he was also much more accessible than the
Joyce of *Ulysses*, and much more explicit, or at least candid, when it came
to sex. We remember, too, that Lawrence was often and popularly referred
to as the "Priest" of sex. Ten years or so after his uncle had first scanned
the shelves of his library, MacSween wrote an essay on Lawrence in which
he discussed why his most notorious novel had been written:

> It seems that Lawrence had reached the stage when he felt that he had
> to be even more direct in order to make men listen. It was as though he
> were saying: "Look! this thing you call unclean is indeed clean. Look
> with open eyes! I will not use symbolism or vague words anymore."
> What many called obscenity was truly an attempt at health.[27]

Interestingly, as we shall see, Fr. MacSween will himself come to a similar
crossroads in his own life, where he believed he had to be more direct
both in his writing and speech. To give "Doc" Nicholson credit, there is
no record of his ever having intervened with his nephew's right to teach
or read whatever he wanted—whether it was on the Index or not.[28] Of
course, given what we now know of the nephew's personality, it would
have been futile to try to do so in any case.

In October of 1953, the same year as Fr. Coady's letter to the editor of
The Commonweal, the South African poet, Roy Campbell, visited the St.
FX campus. The Canadian critic and poet John Sutherland, editor of the
Northern Review, had organized Campbell's tour. MacSween, who went
to the poet's reading and had lunch with him, remembered Campbell's
thick Natal accent and his imposing presence. There were other things
about Campbell that drew MacSween to him. The South African of Scots
heritage was, after all, a fervent Catholic and defender of the Church. He
had also produced some of the finest translations of one of MacSween's
favourite poets, the Spanish mystic, St. John of the Cross. Much later in
life, MacSween published a moving tribute to Campbell entitled "Talking
Bronco":

A spirit within him seemed always in struggle to break out from the bonds of restraint. At the same time, this spirit is wonderful in its very existence and is Campbell's distinctive mark. He seemed endowed beyond most mortals in his ability to love food and drink, the beauty of women and of animals, the stormy sea and physical endeavour. His enemies, who gathered in crowds behind him as he stormed through life, are an anemic group by comparison. They felt the whip of his scorn repeatedly and resented him as a barbarian unfit for the company of civilized men.[29]

The year of Campbell's visit, 1953, was also the centenary of St. FX's founding, and the month before the poet arrived on campus the frontispiece of the celebrations took place. A fall convocation ceremony in September was attended by the Prime Minister, the Governor General, premiers of Nova Scotia, Newfoundland and Prince Edward Island, twelve bishops and archbishops and 114 representatives from universities in Canada, the United States, Scotland, England, Ireland and many other countries.[30] MacSween's contribution to these august—if not overwhelming—celebrations was an article commissioned by his uncle entitled "Little University of the World." In later life, MacSween recalled the article and felt that "it wasn't too bad." The passages on Hugh MacPherson and on Coady are noteworthy:

> Dr. Hugh MacPherson was probably first in introducing the spirit that has made St. Francis Xavier the university of the people. He spent much of his life in an effort to improve the lot of the farmers as he traveled from place to place, inculcating the scientific spirit into minds proverbially conservative; and not least of his tasks was that of inspiring his fellow faculty members.... Dr. Moses Coady was born to teach. No man has ever had a greater desire to communicate to his fellows what he knows and what he wanted done. This was a necessity of his nature. He combined great intelligence with a complete lack of inhibitions.... He was a farmer's son who had engaged in manual labour during his youth. When someone was needed to focus the social spirit of the University in himself and to breathe that same spirit abroad among the people a better man could not be found.[31]

Besides this article for his uncle and alma mater, MacSween also took pride in being recognized that year as a great reader by what he regarded as an outside authority. Because of the number of dignitaries and academics in attendance for the centenary, certain priests in residence gave up their rooms for the university's guests. MacSween's room in Mockler Hall was occupied by Sir Alexander Grey from Edinburgh University. After spending a night in the room, Professor Grey told Dr. Nicholson that any university that has a professor with these books—and he gave a list—in his toilet, need not worry about its academic standards. Despite the comic ring, it must have made a strong impression on Nicholson, because he apparently repeated it frequently and with some pride. It certainly made an impression on Professor MacSween, so much so that he recorded it in his autobiographical notes: note 20 begins with "collection of books—watching for bargains eschewing book clubs." Above this note is written "no academic degree." Then note 21 states: "A mingling of the new and the old. 22: A fighting off of the fad of the moment until it proves itself. 23: A dipping into other literatures in the original or in translation—Europe, Asia, Psychology. Then, finally, 24: approval from Sir Alexander Grey."[32] In his introduction to "Talking Bronco," written twenty-nine years later, MacSween said of Roy Campbell that he "suffered the penalty of being brought up outside a great centre of Anglo-Saxon culture. When we read that Robert Service was one inspiration of his youth, we know all about the handicaps that the ordinary 'colonial' endures." Handicaps indeed.

Although he continued to buy as many books as he could, he announced in a letter to Mick and Mary MacKinnon that:

> *I have given up buying books for 5 years. And why? To buy a car! I'm serious. I think it's time. I want to be independent and free. I want to be able to run to Halifax, Port Hood or downtown if I feel like it. ("That's pride, Father!") I'm getting older and when old, it is not nice to be too dependent. Don't you agree? The question is this: how can I pay for it? Sounds foolish, doesn't it? Sounds like you two buying something with nothing in sight but Duggie's brains and Bobo Petrie's muscles. "What kind of car?" A Volkswagen (?) is too undignified for a big shot like me. What do you think? A big car. Any kind. A new one. In good shape. Not a lemon. I lean towards a Ford. But anything will do. The Credit Union will lend me about $1600 if I raise about $800. Perhaps I could get an advance on my pay. Or borrow from friends— if I have any. I think it possible for me to borrow a few hundreds here and there if I crawl low enough and speak softly enough. If you have any brilliant ideas that won't put me in the same mess that you're in, let me know. I really think that the time has come when a gypsy like me must have a bicycle of sorts of his own. Perhaps you could sell Bernie and Mick to the salt mines for a few years.*
>
> *See you some time, dear friends.*

He eventually did scrape the money together with the help of his old friend, Joe Marinelli.[33]

MacSween continued to be away from campus as much as possible, noting in the same letter that "I'll be away so many week-ends that I'll be

afraid to go away any more." On one of these weekends MacSween went
home to Glace Bay to officiate at the wedding of his brother Murdock.
This was Murdock's second marriage; his first wife, Julia, had been killed
in a car accident two years earlier. Murdock spoke of the tragedy in his old
age: "I was walking on the path on the outside like the gentleman usually
takes and she was complaining about the stuff that was getting in her
shoes—so, you walk here; I'll walk there. Ten seconds after, she was killed.
This car climbed the curb, picked her up. I was trying to run and my feet
were just like lead. She never regained consciousness." Julia MacSween was
thirty-eight years old, and she left behind five young children, the oldest
a boy of ten. Desperate, Murdock asked his father and sister, Catherine,
to move in with him: "I asked—they never said anything, but they came
right away. They stayed about two, two-and-a-half years" until he married
his second wife, Catherine Ann MacDonald.

There would be other tragic accidents in the MacSween family
over the years, including the death of two children of George and Betty
MacSween. Murdock recalled the deaths of these children and the impact
it had upon the family: "George was taking his engineer's course and got
a job up at the gypsum plant at the Little Narrows. They had a bunga-
low right on the water and he bought his little fellow a boat, a birthday
present, I think. From what they could find out, the boat got away on
the rope. The little fellow followed the boat out—the Little Narrows, the
water after two or three feet goes straight down—and he was gone."[34] The
second child died after receiving a bicycle for grading. They were living
in Moncton at the time and the highways were under construction. On
the way to the store the boy was hit by a truck and killed. As a priest,
MacSween had to confront death and dying all of his adult life: that there
was more tragedy in his own family circle than most, may partly—but
only partly—explain his life-long preoccupation and meditation on the
subject of death in his fiction and poetry.

A poem like "pain shall be no more" has the gentleness and deft-
ness of touch we associate with Emily Dickinson; it is not a comfortable
poem—none of MacSween's poems are—but many of the images in the
first three stanzas do suggest healing if not hope:

> pain shall be no more
> when that day shall be
> I shall be no more
>
> the bird beside the spring
> drinks the clear water

some of it falls like blood
upon the green stones

then the bird sings
the flowers awake like stars
the gentle cress
bends in the quiet water[35]

ON February 15, 1954, MacSween's uncle received a letter from his Bishop:

Dear Monsignor Nicholson:

It is with mixed feelings that I write this letter. Your regular term as President of St. Francis Xavier University ended in 1950. At my request, you remained in that position until the Centenary Year of the University was completed. It is now my duty to relieve you of the obligations of that office and assign you to other duties.

The letter was not unexpected by President Nicholson, but the other duties were: "Effective Wednesday, March 31, 1954 you are hereby appointed Pastor of St. Joseph's Parish, Sydney." Nicholson was sixty-seven years old—he had never been in a parish in his life—indeed, he had never been away from the university—now he was to be pastor of one of Cape Breton's largest and busiest parishes. There is little comfort in the fact that Nicholson was joining the company of other distinguished exiles such as Fr. Jimmy Tompkins, who had been sent away from the college in the 1920s and, for that matter, the old Bishop himself who had also been banished for supporting Tompkins. Publicly, Nicholson had said he was pleased to go;[36] privately, he felt a great injustice had been done. John Young, an alumnus and close friend of Doc Pat's, visited his old professor and mentor shortly after his exile. The recently retired president, and new pastor of St. Joseph's, confessed to his young friend that he felt that what had happened was "an injustice that only God in his good time will understand."[37]

Nicholson was not alone in feeling that an injustice had been done. The impact of his exile on his nephews—Fr. Mike and Fr. Rod especially—would be long lasting indeed. Although Bishop MacDonald had the final say, it is generally agreed that the driving force behind Nicholson's removal, his exile as it were, was his long-time colleague and nemesis, Fr. Hugh Somers. In his old age, MacSween recalled Moses Coady's private remarks to him about his uncle and what had happened to him:

Coady knew I was his nephew. And I had heard that Coady wanted to get rid of Dr. Nicholson. So one day Coady said to me, "They can say what they like about Dr. Nicholson, but he's worth ten of that man over there," and he pointed to Dr. Somers. Nicholson was criticizing the Extension Department but Coady still voted for him, he told Fr. Hogan this, too.

Mike MacSween also felt that Somers was plotting against his uncle. "He was catering to the faculty and of course he was a good businessman." Of all the letters President Nicholson received on his retirement, one of the most moving to be found among his papers is from Fr. W. X. Edwards, a professor in the English Department who was confined to a wheelchair and who died young from multiple sclerosis:

Dear Dr. Nicholson,

I would like to tell you something that, for various reasons, I don't think I could say to you personally. It would not, as a matter of fact, need saying at all except in view of the strained relationship that existed between us at one time in the past. I appreciate beyond all measure that at no time have you made any reference whatsoever to one or two very unpleasant conversations we had at that time and that you have shown towards me since then nothing but the friendliest feelings. The result is that tonight I can honestly say that like all the rest of your faculty I feel nothing but the most profound regret that you are leaving us. Some of my years as a priest have been most difficult ones but the consideration I received from you helped me (more than you will ever know) to turn a losing battle against multiple sclerosis into what seems, please God, to be a winning one. For this I can only say a simple "Thank you." Be assured that the best wishes and the prayers of all of us go with you to St. Joseph's.

Dr. Hugh Somers would be president of the university for ten years. Politically, these would be very difficult times for MacSween—twice within his mandate, Dr. Somers would try to get rid of him, to force him to leave the university and return to a parish. With only his BA, and his uncle now in exile, MacSween was vulnerable and had to rely more than ever on his reputation as a great teacher and intellectual as his main defence.

In some respects, MacSween's path to campus was conventional enough, a commonplace story over the years. Like many another priest, he was recruited from a parish to teach at the Catholic college of his diocese. There is much, however, that is unorthodox about MacSween and his journey from the parish to the campus. Unlike his contemporaries, MacSween had never expressed an interest in becoming a professor. His letter to his uncle—that remarkable job application—highlights a strong, passionate

Fig. 31 A newspaper clipping from MacSween's private papers: The farewell dinner for his uncle "Doc" Pat Nicholson. From left to right: Cyrial Tobin, Moses Coady, Nicholson and Bishop J. R. MacDonald. Courtesy Stewart Donovan.

belief in himself, in the active life and in participating in the wider world. Given how bookish a person he was, this seems, on the surface at least, paradoxical. There are, of course, many examples of poets who sought the active life, but we would have to dig deep indeed to find scholar-poets, bookish men, who preferred the street to the library. MacSween's return to campus would allow him to have his cake and eat it too; he had led a full, even tumultuous, life in two parishes where he played many valuable and important roles, accomplished things anyone—religious or secular—would have been be proud of. Now, with these active years and deeds behind him, he must have looked forward to the more contemplative life of the scholar-writer, which men like Coady had originally envisioned for him. That Coady had direct contact with—and approved of—MacSween's career change in such a fulsome manner would come as a surprise to many who knew MacSween well. On the other hand, Doc Pat's use of, and plans for, his nephew—mink ranch and all—came as a surprise to no one; no one, that is, except for the young MacSween himself.

MacSween's early years back at his alma mater were far from contemplative, but as time passed, the veteran professor got to spend more and more hours and days in his beloved library, a place he could later claim—given his reading, cataloguing and collections—as a personal domain. Although his teaching still required some background preparation—especially where grammar was concerned—in general it was not a challenge for him. He soon acquired a reputation for wit, humour and sheer brilliance that would eventually inspire, alarm and amaze St. FX students, faculty, clergy and administrators for almost forty years.

When the academic year began in the fall of 1954, MacSween was thirty-nine years old and his career at St. FX was now firmly established, so much so that he soon attracted special students, undergraduates in English, philosophy and Romance languages who would become his proteges. Before Dr. Somers's term as president ended, several of these students returned from graduate school to teach at St. FX where, eventually, they provided intellectual and emotional support for their mentor in what would come to be the most productive period of his life as an artist, scholar and professor.

V

*M*ockler to the Mount: Professor and Chaplain

*I*n 1952 MacSween was appointed as the non-resident chaplain of Mount St. Bernard College, the women's school affiliated with St. FX, and situated on the eastern side of the campus, where the great brownstone Cathedral of St. Ninian's piously—and at this time more or less success-fully—separated the men from the women. MacSween would be chaplain here for more than thirty years, and his duties included the saying of Mass every morning, and the counselling of the young women students who came to see him every evening.

The hours were long—especially after a full day in the classroom—but he always enjoyed the company of the sisters and the young women, and he believed that he was also doing some good, providing help to some of the troubled and often lonely students:

> I had to get up early every morning and also go over there every
> evening. I used to read handwriting over there. I'd find all kinds of
> misfits who wouldn't speak to anybody directly, but when I'd do their
> handwriting I'd see the trouble and question them a bit and have it
> come out. So I like to feel that I helped all kinds of girls over there.[1]

He came to place more importance on the handwriting than it actually deserved; but most of his colleagues and friends saw it for the successful ruse that it was—it got the young women to talk about their troubles. That he was popular as a counsellor is confirmed by the line of students that stretched far down the corridor late into the evening. While it is true that he used handwriting analysis as a means of getting the shy ones to be more forthcoming about their troubles, it was not the only reason he used it. Much of the time it was employed as a source of fun among

Fig. 32 Immaculata Hall, Mount Saint Bernard, 1956. Courtesy St. FX University Archives.

relatives and friends. Effie Duggan recalled that "we just loved it when he came and started his handwriting analysis. He loved doing that, too. We were probably thinking we were going to something like a fortune teller, because we'd get good news, and everything was nice about us."

In later life, there was something endearing, if incongruous, about this great intellect sitting gypsy-like with the paper equivalent of a crystal ball in an Antigonish or Cape Breton kitchen telling fortunes and predicting the futures of boys and girls, of women and men, and husbands and wives. He loved the role. His favourite times with these clairvoyant sessions concerned young married couples—more often than not former students—who submitted their writing for scrutiny. Without fail, MacSween would study the script, look up and then shake his head in sorrow followed by a slight grin breaking at the corners of his mouth: "This is the handwriting of an unmarried person, I don't think this is too good."

MacSween's counselling at the Mount was fully appreciated by the nuns who lived and worked there. Sister Helen Aboud recalled one evening when she

> was on the floor and this one girl really had an unfortunate thing happen. I settled her for the night and I said "Now, in the morning Father

MacSween will be in about half-past-six if you want to see him." And she went to see him, and that girl walked out of his office as if she was on cloud nine. So although he had this almost ferocious look about him, he was so gentle, and so kind, and so understanding.[2]

Sister Aboud's remark here, about the ferocious look that concealed an otherwise extraordinarily gentle and understanding man, highlights part of the complex persona that MacSween cultivated throughout his life. Without question, in the vast majority of cases, the ferocious look was indeed a fiction—and a comic one at that—but there were times when this look could be devastating, especially to vulnerable students in the classroom.

In the fall of 1954, MacSween met a woman at Mount St. Bernard who would become a lifelong friend and colleague. The Cape Breton-born-and-raised Margaret MacDonald carried the religious name of Sister St. Mary Philip, but she was known affectionately to her relatives and close friends by her childhood nickname of Marper—apparently her younger brother couldn't pronounce Margaret. By all accounts, Margaret MacDonald had much in common with MacSween: self-confident, highly intelligent, quick-witted and endowed with an infectious sense of humour. As Dean of Women she was also MacSween's boss and she would correct—and no doubt contradict—him when the situation called for it. Contradicting MacSween in discussion or argument, at least later in his life, had something imperial and comic about it. The refrain (for it did become

a refrain) "Are you contradict-ing me?" was employed almost exclusively among his friends. If the answer to the refrain was yes, and the speaker continued to contradict, MacSween would hold up his hand in the manner of a traffic cop or a king or a pontiff and say "stop" repeatedly until the culprit ceased or sur-rendered. The gesture may have been grand, even imperial, but

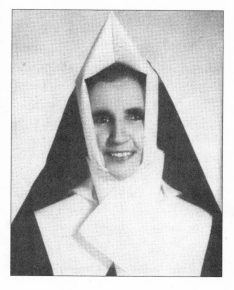

Fig. 33 Margaret MacDonald in the steepled habit of the CNDs, 1953. Courtesy St. FX University Archive.

the manner was good-natured and almost always comic. There was, as far
as I know, only one group that he did not employ this refrain or gesture
with and that was, naturally enough perhaps, his brothers. As the years
passed, in fact, MacSween engaged his bothers less and less in debate,
if only for the simple reason that they would almost always end on an
acrimonious note.

It was very different with Margaret MacDonald. This woman was
one of the best deans the college had known, and she was more than a
match for her new chaplain. The image of the tiny woman and giant man
walking the corridors and laughing together is one fondly remembered by
nuns, priests and students who shared their lives and company over the
years. For the nuns especially, the relationship between the man and the
woman, the dean and her chaplain, was unique. Helen Aboud recalled
how MacSween "would give [Margaret] books to read, poetry to read.
She would often say, I have this book Fr. MacSween gave me." Aboud also
remembered how alike their temperaments seemed, "she was an extremely
humorous, very, very, quiet person. You would never know she was around,
but I would say that she and Fr. MacSween were what you would call
kindred spirits, they really were." Agnes Cordeau also recalled the special
bond between the two of them, "She was Dean of Women and he was
chaplain, so they had that relationship, too, but I think it was even more
than that. They were just, ah—they had a beautiful relationship!"

Other sisters recalled that MacSween would join them for dinner on
Sundays and on special feast days, his humour and love of conversation
always in evidence:

> There would be much talk and laughter. Someone might bring up the
> blue whale. With that Father MacSween would take off happily about
> the blue whale, its ocean patterns, its known habitats and history, how it
> might disappear, the causes of its imminent extinction, and on and on.[3]

Eventually, MacSween's class sizes soon became large, very large, especially for English literature. He would often have more than 100 students
in several classes, including religion, which he taught in the old assembly
hall. His voice was not strong, not powerful like his brother Mike's, so he
learned a few techniques, a few tricks early on that helped him out. He
also learned a thing or two from his students:

> I remember talking to Frank German the first football coach we had
> in Canadian Football, he was from Notre Dame in Alberta. He was
> an old student when I had him. He seemed to be as old as I was. He
> was studying for his BEd and he took my course and one day I was
> talking to him and I said. "I'm kind of sorry Frank that you're in that

class because I know my voice isn't strong and I feel often that people aren't hearing me." "Oh," he said, "No, don't worry about that, we can hear you, but we can't hear the students. You question a student and we don't hear him." That put me very wise and after that I always insisted on repeating what the student would say or only asking those in the back rows. But I used to have a terrible class there, in the Assembly Hall. God, I'd come in and I'd see this sea of faces in front of me. There was always over a hundred. They gave me the old assembly hall because there was no classroom that would take that many.

The old Assembly Hall on the second floor of Xavier Hall held a couple of hundred people. Its windows looked out on the courtyard affectionately known as Confusion Square, and it was home to at least two saints: the university's patron, Francis Xavier, stood in one corner while a statue of the Blessed Virgin looked on from the other. Here MacSween taught the majority of his courses until the opening of Nicholson Hall, named for his uncle Doc Pat, in the late 1960s.

Fig. 34 Margaret "Marper" MacDonald at Mount Saint Bernard; the student to her left, Dawn Wolestenholme was in MacSween's creative writing class, 1956. Courtesy St. FX University Archive.

Patrick Walsh, a protege of MacSween's who eventually became a colleague and close friend, was an American from North Adams, Massachusetts. Young Patrick was part of the strong New England and "Boston States" Catholic connection that St. FX had recruited from and nourished for decades. He had come up to "X" to study Chemistry, and was doing so in his first year with one English elective. Because of his high average out of high school, Patrick was placed with forty other of the university's best students in a special English course, a class in literature, rather than grammar and composition. It was taught by a nun, a Sister St. Miriam, CND, a poet who'd been published in Joyce Kilmer's widely read *Anthology of Catholic Poetry*.[4] The professor's style in the classroom, however, as Pat Walsh recalled, was far from poetic:

> I could not understand what this woman was talking about. First of all, there was no joy in anything we did. For instance, we would be reading Chaucer and then we were to read an essay by E. K. Chambers in the library. She was a great academic in the purest sense of the word. We were to summarize what we read in the essay and hand it in. She came back the next day and she said, "You people are stupid. You know nothing about literature. You know nothing. Go back and do it again." So we did. Again "You're still stupid. Go back and do it again!" Here we are, and were supposed to be the top students—we were according to our marks—and we can't understand this professor. We can't understand what she's saying because she's using big words.[5]

Young Patrick squeaked through with the lowest mark of his life. Unable to sell his textbook, he considered "taking it out page by page and burning it." He resisted this, but was determined never to take an English class again. When he registered for his second year and tried to avoid taking English, Rev. Malcolm MacDonell insisted that he take Modern English—MacSween's course. There were more than a hundred in the class and Pat liked the anonymity; however, he was not impressed by the appearance of the professor: "In comes this great big man shuffling and I'm very skeptical and I'm saying to myself, God damned English class!" But MacSween soon convinced him that MacDonell had done him a favour:

> He walks over to the window and some student said something sarcastic and he spoke to the student and went and stood behind his desk. All of a sudden it came to me—he cut that student's head off, but the student didn't know it! I expected to see the kid's head fall off and roll on the floor! All of a sudden I realized that this guy is on some kind of wavelength that's different.

Pat Walsh, then, came to learn very quickly that every thing MacSween said, every thing that "came out of him, even the slightest throwaway remark, was loaded. There was never anything that the man uttered, that wasn't somehow electric, exciting, sharp in reflecting that intelligence in that mind at work, in that spirit of playfulness, the joy of language. All of that stuff, all of a sudden, electrified me. I was hooked."

Alistair MacLeod also recalled MacSween's style in the classroom during these years: "As a teacher he had a reputation for being very witty and very clever and also for being extremely intelligent and extremely well-read. I think there was something about him that made him very appealing to all of us." MacLeod remembered, too, that the classes "were unconventional and he was not chained to his lectern."[6]

One of MacSween's favourite classes was his religion class:

> Once I got going on religion the class was very popular. I got a terrific compliment one day from a fellow, he said, "I signed up for your course because I asked one of my buddies what he thought of your religion course, and he said, you'll never skip a class. It's too interesting." But then Fr. Greg [MacKinnon] came in and reformed the religion teaching and all the priests who didn't have degrees in theology were told not to teach religion anymore. I missed it too. I really missed it because it was a real forum.

It was in this same religion class that MacSween uttered one of his more famous witticisms. When asked by a student if the original sin in the Garden of Eden could have been sexual, MacSween replied, "What, with a snake!" Almost forty years later, Freeman Whitty, the student who had asked the question, remembered MacSween's response, "And this was at a time when the word 'sex' wasn't ever mentioned by a teacher in a classroom, even at university. If it was, you know, you'd have to go wash your mouth out. So he was an unorthodox man in the classroom that's for sure." MacSween himself recalled the remark in old age and was proud of it: "That was kind of inspired because I had no idea what I was going to say." Inevitably, there were times when this loaded wit would backfire on him, when having "no idea of what he was going to say" would cause pain or resentment. In many ways, he was like a great comic, a Lenny Bruce (whom he later admired) who could make you laugh or cut your head off with a single remark, as the young Pat Walsh had witnessed. Most—but by no means all—of the students who took his classes were aware of this; it was one of the reasons they sought him out in the first place. They quickly put a nickname on him: Moonbeam. It came from the 1950s *Lil Abner* cartoon character Moonbeam McSwine by Al Capp, and MacSween, naturally enough, did not like it.[7] It is hardly surprising, however, that a nickname would be bestowed upon MacSween, especially given the tradition of nicknames that existed in Cape Breton, which, after all, was where the vast majority of St. FX students and faculty came from. MacSween's sobriquet was well established by the late 1950s, but for subsequent generations the name lost its original reference and became associated instead with the professor's round and always gently smiling face. The metamorphosis seemed both just and fitting.

MacSween, then, seems rarely to have been caught without a reply—in or out of the classroom—but there was one incident that he liked to recall when he thought someone was being presumptuous or second-guessing another person. The United States Senate hearings of The House Committee on Un-American Activities (notoriously known as HUAC) were being broadcast, and MacSween was sitting in the priest's lounge area in Morrison Hall: "When Dr. Coady came in I said, 'McCarthy seems to be making some sense.' Well! Coady turned on me and said 'What the hell's the matter with your brains!'" Years after this incident, several of the priests were gathered around the television watching the World Series when Coady walked by again. MacSween remembered, "We thought we were going to get a blast, but when we told him what it was, he said, "Isn't it wonderful to think of all those people doing something innocent at the same time."

Besides his teaching, MacSween also helped students with the literary magazine *X-Writes*; Alistair MacLeod remembered:

> Oh, he was very good critically and very unselfish. We all had tremendous faith in his critical judgment. I recall some years after I had left St. FX, I was teaching at the Nova Scotia Teacher's College in Truro, and I had a little writing group.... And I remember not being quite certain of my critical judgments at the time, and I would come home to Inverness on the weekends, and take these poems and slide them under Father MacSween's door on Friday night, and then I'd pick them up on Sunday afternoon. And he would write comments about them. Some of these people are now rather well known. And I am impressed, looking back almost thirty years later, at how good his critical judgments were.[8]

Not long before *X-Writes*, MacSween had been involved in another "literary" production, as his long time colleague and friend Fr. Bauer recalled: "Well, I don't know when it happened, it must have been fairly early in his career, he got a paper out. Just one issue of it. It was kind of a takeoff on *The Casket*. And it was humorous, but some people didn't find it humorous. It was called *The Basket*. I know there was some disturbance about it, and people were not very happy with some of the things in it. It was like the students might do, a humorous issue." This satiric, comic and anarchic side of MacSween ran deep and it was no doubt another example of his artistic temperament. Although students sometimes felt the bite of his wit, MacSween would also intervene for them if he felt an injustice was being done: George Sanderson, a protege of MacSween's, recalled being deliberately humiliated in class by a professor-priest during the 1950s and when MacSween found out about it he quickly and publicly confronted the professor on his behalf.

*A*mong his autobiographical notes, MacSween once recorded a short profile of each member of his family: when he came to his sister Margaret, he wrote, "No natural gifts, spirit of forgiveness, spirit of goodness. Bringing home human dogs and doggish humans for supper." After his mother died, Margaret became the emotional centre of the family, and it was she and her husband, Archie MacEachern, who took in her adopted sister, Theresa, shortly after their marriage. Mike MacSween remembered his sister Margaret, as "the kindest person you would ever meet, no matter who she met on the highway, she would take them home." By all accounts, both Margaret and her husband Archie had a wonderful sense of humour, a sense of fun. Their son, John MacEachern, who later became Minister of Education for the province of Nova Scotia, recalled seeing his "father and Theresa dancing and crashing through the glass door."[9] Theresa remembered that notorious crash—she was being taught "the jitterbug." Archie MacEachern was fondly remembered by the young woman because he treated her with kindness and like an adult, often giving her cigarettes when she had none of her own. Margaret's husband, however, did not have a close relationship with the rest of the MacSween clan. He was, after all, the only brother-in-law, and Theresa Gallant remembers that Rod and the others did not visit often. A letter to Theresa, a few days before her wedding in Toronto in 1955, highlights how busy MacSween was and how out of touch he had become with his adopted sister. Dated July 5, 1955 the letter is written on the stationary of Holy Cross Church, Glace Bay:

> *I got quite a shock when I learned that you were to be married. You seem so young yet—but I know you're not. Your mind is old and very sturdy—and I'm sure that you've accepted a very fine young man. I've had no time to get you a good gift, one worthy of such a glorious occasion, and so I am sending you some money. Money is wonderful stuff—it makes everyone*

*happy and is very easy to send from one place to another. I hope to get you
something else after a space of time. Everybody is fine here. Pa is home
from the hospital after a cure of an erysipelas attack. I am taking penicillin
inhalations everyday for bronchitis (which is not serious), and every kid I
know has passed from one grade to a higher (not a lower) class. In two days
time I shall be teaching summer school in Sydney. (Didn't I give you a lot of
news in one paragraph?) I didn't receive your card at Christmas. You told
Margaret you sent one. Was I ever mad! No—I wasn't. I took your address
to write you a letter and forgot to do so. That's why I didn't find out about
the marriage until so late. I can't write anymore now. I hope you get this
before the wedding. We all love you very much even if we don't say so very
often. God bless you and the lucky man.*

Margaret MacSween was born immediately after her brother Rod so
she must have been his childhood companion for some time, and like all
older siblings he would have felt protective of her. The family photo of
the children taken by the Bras d' Or Lake in the summer of 1919 shows
Margaret sitting on her mother's knee. Like her older brother George,
Margaret would know the sorrow of losing young children—her baby
boy was struck by a neighbour's car. The accident was not fatal, but it was
sadly prophetic—the boy suffered a head injury, which was not serious,
but while in hospital it was discovered that he had leukemia. He was two-
and-a-half years old when he died. Margaret herself became ill shortly
after giving birth to her last child. Her brother Mike recalled that she was
never strong in health:

> She had this doctor who she idolized who delivered all her children.
> And I used to go out to see her once a week and I noticed the house
> was a shambles. She was sitting around going to sleep—she could
> hardly keep her eyes open. And I said, "What's wrong with you?
> There's something wrong with you!" "The doctor says it's my nerves."
> Well, I took that as gospel truth. One day her eyelid broke open and
> there was a crease that came down across her face here and burned it.
> So she thought there was something wrong with her eye so she went
> to an eye doctor. He said "There's nothing wrong with your eye but
> there is something wrong with your blood." So she went to another
> doctor, Dr. Joe, John O. MacNeill, Tubby they call him, and he told her
> your womb is infected. And then she went to the hospital and had a
> hysterectomy done and she was just ready to go home when the whole
> thing broke open and she caught one of these bugs that are in the
> hospital, and after struggling with it, and getting antibiotics, her heart
> gave out. So whenever I heard a doctor after that tell anybody that "It's
> your nerves" I said, "you're a God damned liar!"

Margaret MacSween died in 1956—she was thirty-nine years old. Her brother Rod had also been concerned about her health, as Mike recalled: "You see Rod told my sister that she shouldn't have any more children. So she told her husband and her husband went raging mad about it. It's only coming out now that women have some rights." While it was true that Rod did go see his sister about not having any more children, her son John disputes the fact that his father would have gone "raging mad." Hugh MacSween and his sons did not like Archie. He was a small, quiet, and humorous man who worked hard in the mines, but he was not ambitious about the material world. John MacEachern recalled that his family was very poor: "there were places where you could see out through the upstairs walls," but they were happy. The parents doted on the children and what wasn't there in material comfort was more than made up for with love and attention.

It was also at about this time that Hugh MacSween and his daughter, Catherine, decided to move away from Glace Bay for good. As his son, Murdock, recalled, "They took the notion of going to British Columbia—I don't know why—I wanted them to stay here and live with us, but they wouldn't." Hugh and his daughter were going west to be with his brother, a retired policeman, but when they got as far as Toronto, like so many other Cape Bretoners of the time, they decided to stay. For the next decade or so, then, MacSween would go to Toronto every year during the spring to visit his father, two brothers and his sister. In the beginning, most of these spring excursions were done in the company of Mick and Mary MacKinnon—his old friends from New Waterford. Eventually, Mary and Mick's own children moved to Toronto to find work, and when MacSween and the parents visited they would always stay with one or another of the children.

Fig. 35 Hugh MacSween in Toronto.
Courtesy Stewart Donovan.

When Fr. MacSween returned from these spring road trips to Toronto he always taught summer school: he looked forward to these classes because they were different from his regular courses both in subject matter, pace and especially in the kind of student they attracted. Most of those taking the summer courses, at this time, were teachers, mature men and women, mothers and fathers, who wanted to upgrade their licence and advance their teaching careers. A change of pace from his regular classes, he got to teach his beloved 18th-century literature, until a specialist in that field was eventually hired. That he should love this period of English history and culture is perhaps no surprise, given that it contained much that appealed to his own sensibility: it was an age of satire, of wit, and it heralded the birth of the novel and the Enlightenment—the advent of the modern age. It was also a neo-classical period that harkened back to Greece and Rome, two areas of history and culture that preoccupied him all his life.

In several biographies of the writer G. K. Chesterton, there is a picture of the famous English Catholic convert and apologist dressed up as Samuel Johnson, England's first great "man of letters." Of all the figures of the 18th century, Johnson is the one MacSween most brings to mind both in his physical size and in the nature of his intellect and personality. It was not, however, the author of the first English dictionary that the Cape Bretoner identified with and claimed as one of his heroes[10]—of which he had many—but rather the diminutive and deformed figure of Alexander Pope.[11]

In the fall of 1956, Pat Walsh pleaded with professor MacSween to hold a small discussion group in his rooms in Mockler Hall.[12] Eventually, George Sanderson joined the group and soon the evenings became "stimulating events" for the undergraduates, a place where life, politics and ideas were discussed: "To kick things off we'd read from *The Commonweal* magazine—this was strictly discussion, this was not the arts. I remember something would come up and Father would reach up and pull a book out here, and a book out there

Fig. 36 Pat Walsh at St. FX, 1957. Courtesy St. FX University Archives.

142

and everything was wide open." Pat recalled the sense of freedom the professor established: "You could say something and he'd listen. You know he didn't suffer fools gladly and I said some pretty stupid things there, but he was sincerely seeking to enlighten us."

The following year several of the students who got to know MacSween during the discussion group, and others who had an interest in writing, asked him if he would teach a course in creative writing. Because the course was not on the academic books of the university, MacSween was hesitant, but Pat Walsh and his fellow students persisted, "I said we don't care about credit, we want to write and we want you to teach us a course about writing." MacSween went to see the Dean Fr. Bauer, his old friend from grad school in Washington who told him to go ahead with the course, but there would be no question of receiving credit. MacSween did so and established what St. FX now claims as "the first [non-credit] creative writing course in Canada."

Some of the other students who took the course, and who would go on to become professors and writers themselves, included Sheldon Currie, professor of English at St. FX and author of *The Glace Bay Miners Museum* (adapted into the critically acclaimed film *Margaret's Museum*); Lyndon McIntyre, journalist, novelist and presenter of the hit CBC current affairs program, *The Fifth Estate*;[13] George Sanderson, professor of Philosophy at St. FX and long-time editor of *The Antigonish Review*; and Pat Walsh, a professor of English at St. FX, whose 1977 play, *Mad Shelley*, won in the Dominion Drama Festival. When three of these students—Walsh, Currie and Sanderson—graduated in 1958, MacSween

Fig. 37 George Sanderson at St. FX, 1957. Courtesy St. FX University Archives.

Fig. 38 Sheldon Currie at St. FX, class of 1958. Courtesy St. FX University Archives.

made sure to keep in contact with them, hoping one day that some of them might be able to return and teach at their alma mater.

cAlthough he was not getting much exercise in these years, MacSween was still in relatively good physical condition, and it was at this time that one of his students, Freeman Whitty, first got his professor interested in golf. MacSween took to the game with all his ability as a natural athlete, and within a year he had, astonishingly, won the Nova Scotia amateur title for his age at a tournament in New Glasgow. His natural athletic ability had clearly not left him, and he grew to love the game of golf, often encouraging his friends and colleagues to play with him. It would be the last sport that he would play and enjoy before his weight and arthritis finally became a handicap, a physical and psychological burden.

MacSween continued to travel in these years; long trips during the summers to New York, Boston and Toronto were still made with his New Waterford friends, Mick and Mary MacKinnon. During the school year, MacSween would also travel throughout the diocese saying Mass—Christmas and Easter, too, were always spent helping his brother, Mike, in the parishes of Louisbourg and New Victoria. Fr. MacSween's sermons—which he gave until he died—were always considered memorable, especially by those who were fortunate enough to hear them on a regular basis at the Mount, as Sister Helen Aboud remembered:

> They were short. He'd have three points, and he would tell us he had three points, and he would make those three points and that was it. You could always remember his homilies. I am sure there wasn't anybody who walked out of that chapel who couldn't tell you one, two, three, and we would say how many times do you go to other places and just try to remember what the theme was. And you couldn't remember the theme, but not with Fr. MacSween. He was well prepared, and always a good message. When the students filled the chapel, he would have a message that would stay with them. And they remember him to this day. When they come back for the Homecomings, they will tell you things that Fr. MacSween said. What he said wasn't the ordinary—well, of course it was ordinary—but it was the way he would phrase it.

His brother Murdock also recalled his talent as preacher: "He gave terrific sermons—quiet. Down here one time they had a do on and he was one of the speakers. He gave a sermon on the parish. I never realized before what it did—how it held the people together and the different organizations—the good that was created here."

There were always religious duties, some of which, however, were more pleasant than others. In February of 1956, for example, MacSween submitted the following report to his bishop:

> *On Friday, February 3, I was asked to accompany Father Gregory*
> *MacKinnon to the Parish Centre where a meeting of various groups*
> *was to decide the line of conduct for a campaign against indecent movies*
> *and posters. There was talk in the air that a boycott with picketing was*
> *contemplated. Our Vice-President, fearing the effect of such an action on*
> *our students instructed us to resist such a move.*

The report goes on to talk about a Father H. V. MacDonald who eventually verbally attacked MacSween because of his concern for the law and his call for moderation:

> *I found out that the CYO had invaded the rights of private citizens by*
> *covering up a poster. Thereupon, I spoke on the subject, pointing out that*
> *this was a misdemeanor and subject to prosecution. I had thought that*
> *the simple statement of these ideas would be enough to gain acquiescence,*
> *as I considered what I had said to be elementary. But the reaction was*
> *astonishing. First of all, Father MacDonald interrupted and heckled me*
> *while I spoke, as though his disregard for the law had been carried into*
> *the sphere of parliamentary procedure as well. I found this very annoying*
> *coming from a younger man and a priest.... Before I had time to insist on*
> *an answer and while the councilor still held the floor, Father MacDonald*
> *jumped to his feet and said loudly: "And now let us apologize to Father*
> *MacSween for covering up indecency."*[14]

That MacSween would have to battle the small town 1950s attitudes towards personal sexual freedom is perhaps no surprise. In later life, he recalled going to the doctor to get a prescription for contraception for a woman who needed help: the doctor, a Catholic, became indignant and at first wasn't going to give him the prescription—MacSween tore it out of his hand and said he would pick up the prescription himself. The doctor then apologized. Jack and Betty MacDonald had first put this woman in contact with MacSween:

> Well, she was only twenty-nine years old at the time, she already had
> eight children. We were trying to encourage her to talk to MacSween,
> because this is the way he would have talked to her, "Look, you've done
> your thing. I don't think the Lord expects more." Whereas 99 per cent
> of any other priests she would have talked to, well.... In the mid-1950s
> Father was very broad-minded in a religious way. There was beginning
> to be quite a rebellion going on amongst people. The very fact that we
> talked to Fr. MacSween about this meant that we were thinking the
> same way ourselves. We were in our early thirties then.

In his autobiographical notes from this time, MacSween writes: "Now the inclination to give up all the others for these: a sense of wasted time—but not wasted. All questions are at bottom theological or religious. The Necessary Odyssey. This can or should be yours."[15] Toward the end of his life, MacSween's knowledge of the world's religions was as profound and encyclopedic as a Mircea Eliade's or a Joseph Campbell's, and yet he still had a soft spot for what he called acts of simple faith—and if these acts sometimes had comic or absurd overtones, then all the better. It was at about this time, in the late 50s, that he went to visit his cousin, Sister Agnes Miriam, who was stationed in a convent in Herring Cove near Halifax. It had been a very dry summer—drought conditions existed throughout the Maritimes—and the Mother Superior of the convent had asked the younger nun if her cousin, the priest, would bless the well.[16] MacSween objected at first saying, "We don't do that nowadays." Then the elderly Mother Superior, who had grown up as a girl on a farm, appeared and begged him to bless the well, lamenting as she did so, "In the old days the priests would always bless the well, they would bless the farm, the animals and the crops—and now they won't bless anything!" Reluctantly, the skeptical professor-priest said he would bless the well. He was brought down to the basement by his cousin: "I went down these steep stairs, hit my head on a pipe and it wasn't even a well! It was a kind of electric pump or something." He blessed it in a cursory manner and left; about a year later, MacSween met his cousin in Cape Breton and asked her if she got water: "'Water!' she said, 'the floor came up and flooded the whole basement, it rained for days'!"[17]

ON the 28th of July 1959, at the age of 77, Moses Coady died at St. Martha's hospital in Antigonish. Coady's health had not been good in his last years, but he continued to make public appearances, appearances like the one Pat Walsh recalled as a first-year student five years earlier, in the fall of 1954:

> All the new students went into the auditorium under the Chapel and we got the usual introduction. Then they wheeled out this old fellow on to the stage with a gravelly voice—it was Coady. I had no idea who Moses Coady was or anything about him. This was my first day at St. FX and I was American all the way. Coady began to talk, and even though he was in his declining years, within ten minutes I had forgotten that I was American. He spoke about the fact that education was lifelong, that it was not degrees and graduations, and that in order to help one another we needed adult education; that we would have to

get together to solve our problems. He said, "If we do this, Canada will
be the great country of the second half of the twentieth century." And
I forgot I was an American because I believed what Coady was saying.

Coady worked and fought for his Extension Department and its goals of
adult education all his life. In his declining years, Extension received less
attention and funding from the administration than he would have liked.
Though he and his department continued to be of importance, Coady
himself had become a figure of legendary status—almost a figure of folklore. His work in the thirties, the mandate of adult education for poor
farmers and fisherman—co-operatives and credit unions—was radical, in
some respects revolutionary, especially given the conservative nature of
the people and the institutions he was dealing with: the Church's traditional laissez-faire attitude toward capitalism and the monopoly on wage
labour and markets held by big business. That organizations like co-ops
and credit unions—and adult education itself—slowly shifted into the
burgeoning middle class had less to do with Moses Coady himself—his
original vision, hopes and dreams—than it did with the changing demo-
graphics of Maritime life.[18] In his old age, Rod MacSween would often
evoke the memory of the great teacher whose biography he was once
asked to write:

> I got to know him. I'd be with him at dinner and supper. I never visited
> him as a friend, he was too old for me. I guess he was close to 80....
> Oh, yes, you couldn't help knowing that Coady was a great man. When
> he died John V. Campbell encouraged me to start writing his life, and
> I wasn't too anxious, because it means that you give up your life for say
> three years. And John V. said, "Well, try to," so I went up and asked
> his secretary if I could see his papers and letters, and she wouldn't let
> me see them. Just said, "No, no." And she was a good friend of mine,
> too. I think what was wrong was that she didn't have an order and she
> was frightened to let anybody find it out. I was wondering whether
> somebody in the Extension Department said, "Don't give those things
> to anybody. Somebody from the Extension is going to write his life."
> So I said, "Okay." His papers were all saved but nobody wrote a life on
> him.

We might wonder what R. J. MacSween's biography of Moses Coady
would have been like. Given his close relationship with Coady, the
reticence and guardedness of the religious community, friends and family—not to mention of MacSween himself in his writing—it is hard to
see how the one priest could have rendered an authentic or genuine "life"
of the other. MacSween's short tribute to Coady is noble but guarded. It

is interesting only insofar as it unintentionally highlights some important similarities between the two men, besides the obvious one of their Cape Breton and Catholic heritage:

> Everyone knew that there was a strong element of the physical in his nature. It was probably the source of much of his attraction. He loved food and talked about it constantly. His life was a long series of diets, pursued for longer or shorter periods of time, according to the need of the moment.... Along with this appetite for food was a love for the physically different. He looked back to his youth as to a golden age when he dwelt lion like among his fellows—swimming, skating, running, wrestling—breathing clean air and under a glorious sun. "How strong I was! I'd play all day, then come home like a hungry wolf. I would eat bread by the loaf and swallow oceans of milk." A contemporary of his assured me that this was the real young Coady.... When he was older, of course, he put aside these activities, but sometimes the urge would rise up again to pit himself against some external force. Once he and a friend were caught without conveyance in the village of Tracadie, about seventeen miles from Antigonish. Evening was coming on, yet he refused to ask anyone for assistance, and he and his friend proceeded to walk the seventeen miles.... On another occasion he ran into difficulties on the road to Margaree. It was Christmas time and he had agreed to be at the parish church for the midnight services. A blizzard struck but he set out in the midst of it, the road became impassable for the automobile.... Dr. Coady went on foot. At Margaree they had given up hope of his arrival when he appeared in the doorway like a huge snowman.... Shortly before he died, he spoke to me with his face radiant: "They're sending me some haddock from White Head—in a day or so." ...A day or so later I saw him pacing around the campus all by himself. "The haddock is coming today," he said. "I'm waiting here for it." In the evening I saw him crouched over a plate containing some haddock fillets which had probably been cooked according to his instructions. But he was old and very ill and the food he needed was not of this earth. It must not be thought that physical things dominated his life. His mind had an intense metaphysical strain which absorbed all things into his ambience. He was also very intelligent and capable of intuitive judgments of an amazing sureness. The two strains fed and supported each other, and in fact made him the unusual character that he was. Those who heard him speak of fish and potatoes may not have known that he often read Dante in the original and loved to be questioned about the meaning of different passages. Dante or haddock, it made no difference: both brought forth his wonderment and his praise.[19]

The image of the man who was instrumental in founding the Maritime Fisherman's Co-op eagerly awaiting a haddock that would do him little good is sad and moving. It would not be difficult to imagine what Coady would have thought about the extinction of the east coast fishery—the disappearance of a way of life in the small communities he had fought for all his life. The reference to his "intuitive judgments of an amazing sureness" apply equally well to the man who wrote the piece. Coady's love of Dante probably came from his early years in Rome, but like MacSween there was a strong strain of the autodidact in him as well. The love of food, too, was something both men shared in common, as was, sadly—and unsuccessfully for MacSween—the constant need for dieting.

In his last collection of poems, *Called From Darkness*, MacSween published what many might consider an appropriate memorial to the great teacher of Irish descent from the Margaree Valley. The poem is not addressed to Coady, but the first stanza of "where are they gone" surely must include his spirit:

> where are they gone
>> those souls I have admired
> they smiled at adversity
>> as they passed on to unknown countries
> they were lovingly prominent
>> in the landscape of forests and towns
> we could not even dream
>> without including them
> they stood in the centre
>> of our world of yes and no

MacSween would lose other people from his life in these years besides his mentor Dr. Coady. In the fall of 1959, his close friend at the Mount, Margaret MacDonald, was transferred to the Notre Dame Juniorate in Ottawa where she was to teach young women entering the sisterhood. She would be away from the university until 1971, and when she returned she did so to semi-retirement at her old college. During her years in Ottawa, MacSween never failed to visit her on his yearly trips to Ontario; they always enjoyed a meal at the Juniorate together and there would be much laughter, conversation and stories, as he brought a fellow religious and Cape Bretoner all the news, good wishes and blessings from down home.

In MacSween's first collection of poems, *the forgotten world* there is a poem entitled "the return":

I heard a friend was gone
beyond the Acheron
of listening
so much unsaid

heart thirsting
I wanted to call him back
across that boundary
for a final talk
I'd turn to him and say

don't hurry! just a minute
he'd smile a cynic's smile
with all his humour in it
I'd say don't smile

I want to speak before we part
all that is in my heart
he'd wait a while and say

what's in your heart today
and I'd begin the inventory
my ancient allegory
of shame and anger raging round
the broken tablets lying on the ground
and then he'd smile again as if to say

was I called from the dead
to hear this story that I knew
when I lived full of blood
the long days through

There is little doubt that the subject of the poem is MacSween's close friend, Dan E. MacDonald, who died in 1960. A slightly old-fashioned poem, in the style of W. B. Yeats's early work, was also written about "Fr. Danny" at this time. It is untitled and unpublished:

Before my friend slept in earth
I hardly knew he was my friend
He was the shadow on my way
From almost the dawn of day
When we met, we had a meal of memory
Every word made an echo in the other
I used to save—like a squirrel—the treasure

Of each day for our next meeting.
Now I look up as if to speak to him
And the thought of his eternal absence
Kills the gladness in my heart

Another good friend of Danny's, Hugh MacDonald, recalled how and when Danny died:

At Iona, on his way up to say Mass. Mass is at seven and he would always be there on time. So about twenty after seven the Superior said "we'd better go down." There was no answer to the phone calls that they were making, so she went down to the Glebe House and found him dead at the little gate near the road. Fr. Danny, for some reason, withdrew from society in the last year or two of his life. I really don't know why, but probably he was already having heart pains, and perhaps he didn't want to reveal them, because they ultimately showed up in his death"[20]

Dan E. MacDonald was 42 years old. There were always photographs in MacSween's rooms, mostly of graduates, students he had known and taught, but he only ever kept one picture on his bedside table, and that was Dan E. There is little doubt that the death affected him greatly. He had said—on more than one occasion—that it was the greatest shock of his life. Once again, Hugh MacDonald remembered the close friendship between Rod and Danny: "Father Danny would create an awful lot of humour—he was a little bit dramatic at times, but he understood Father Rod and Father Rod understood him. There was a communication there between them." George Sanderson, a long-time friend and protege of MacSween's, recalled his talking about the death of his friend Danny: "It definitely was a large thing in Father's life. He had Dan E's picture by his bed. He'd refer to Dan E as his best friend. His death crystallized for Father the tremendous pains of commitment, the suffering and denial, the finality of his own decision and the putting behind of all the aspirations that you'd normally have—the tremendous loneliness that encompasses the priests. This was a huge factor in Father's life: a continuous meditation on late night doubts."

IN many respects, it took MacSween a very short time to make the transition from the parish to the academy; much of this, of course, had to do with his success in the classroom, with the fact that he very quickly came to love the performance, the students, the audience. His reputation as a great teacher spread very quickly, and no doubt he received a boost from

it. His success of course was a double-edged sword: the more popular he became the more students he would get. Although he sometimes protested about his large classes, he also lamented losing the right to teach religion—his largest class. He willingly took on other projects as well, such as the literary magazine *X-Writes*, and the teaching of an overload non-credit course in creative writing. Add to this busy schedule his new work as chaplain at the Mount, the teaching of summer courses and his Feast-day trips to Cape Breton parishes to say Mass, and we begin to wonder where he found the time to read, let alone to write.

Naturally enough, as MacSween's career at St. FX began to thrive, other careers were ending: his uncle, Doc Pat, was sent—many believed exiled—to a large parish in Sydney, while his friend Sister Margaret was transferred from the Mount to Ottawa. And the legendary Moses Coady finally died. Coady's passing was the end of an era, not only in the history of the college, but for the Maritime region in general. There were also, as we have seen, private, personal and tragic losses for MacSween during these years—losses that would take him many years to recover from—the death of his sister Margaret began the decade for him, and the passing of his best friend from childhood and youth, Dan E. would end it. His guilt over Margaret was connected directly to his Church, if not his faith—he knew that if she had practised birth control her chances of living a longer life were beyond question. A few short years later, when Dan E died his lonely death at the foot of the hill of his church in Iona, his friend, Rod, must have gone to bed meditating, as George Sanderson observed, on the life he had chosen, on the lonely and increasingly conflicted nature of his profession.

Neither MacSween nor any other Catholic of liberal bent, could predict the radical changes that the next decade would bring, not only to the Church, but to the whole Catholic world view. For all their turmoil, however, the 1960s would be among the happiest and most productive times for MacSween: he would be given control of St. FXs English Department and, more importantly, he would finally have the time, space and encouragement to publish his poetry, fiction and critical prose.

VI   *C*hurch, State and School: Confronting the 1960s

*O*ne of the Catholic writers MacSween admired throughout his life was the 19th-century Englishman, John Henry Newman. When Catholic Ireland was granted a charter to found a university, they chose Newman, an English Catholic convert who had risen to the position of cardinal, to be its first Rector. The lectures he gave as president of the university were eventually published as *Discourses on the Scope and Nature of University Education*, but the book that has come down to us is *The Idea of a University*. In the last essay he published before he died, MacSween wrote at length on this English convert and apologist. Predictably enough, perhaps, MacSween was initially drawn to Newman because of his Catholicism, but it is fair to say that what he admired most in the famous prose stylist were his ideas and aphorisms on education: "An academical system without the personal influence of teachers upon pupils is an arctic winter. General culture of mind is the best aid to professional and scientific study. A university training is the great ordinary means to a great but ordinary end."[1] These three quotes on their own might form the basis of a liberal arts manifesto that MacSween and his mentors—Coady and Nicholson in particular—could easily have penned. And like these mentors, MacSween, too, would soon be in a position to leave a lasting impression, his personal stamp, as it were, on the nature of education at St. Francis Xavier. That this opportunity came as quickly and as unexpectedly as it did was as much a surprise to MacSween as it was to anyone else.

In December of 1962, Fr. Richard Bannon, who had become an icon on the St. FX campus retired as chair of the English Department, and Fr. Donald Campbell, Dean of Arts, appointed MacSween as the new

Chair. Moreover, Campbell gave MacSween the green light to hire as many faculty as he thought was necessary to cope with the university's increasing enrollment. The age of expansion and government funding had finally come to St. FX, as it had to every other institution of its kind, and professor MacSween had very definite plans—he knew exactly whom he wanted to hire and what he wanted to be taught. He had come a long way from a few years earlier, when Dr. Somers had twice strongly "suggested" that he go back to parish work. MacSween had resisted Somers, persevered and fought back, his response was defiant: "No, I said, I didn't want to come here in the first place, but now that I'm here I'm not leaving."[2]

Having survived his battle with President Somers, MacSween was now uniquely placed to implement his own ideas on education, teaching, scholarship and writing. Looking back from the embattled academic world of our present day, MacSween's position, his carte blanche, so to speak, to hire whomever he wished, might raise a few eyebrows: some in wonder, many in envy and more than a few in derision. From the outset, MacSween seems to have been determined to hire his former students, especially those recent graduates who had been interested in creative writing and who now had moved up and out in the world.

The first person MacSween called to offer a job to was his former student Pat Walsh. He had been to Pat and Jacqueline's wedding in Massachusetts in 1960 and he had made a trip to New York with them in 1961. Pat was teaching school in Boston and completing an MA at Boston College at the same time. He remembers getting a phone call in late December of 1962: "Pat, I've been named chairman. Fr. Bannon stepped down. I've got carte blanche to set up a department. You're coming to St. FX to teach English." Young Pat Walsh and MacSween had much in common, and not just their physical size, both men were over six feet in height and had to struggle with their weight, as Pat remembers, "I was six-foot-one when I showed up on campus as a student and I weighed 140 lbs, but by my third year I was 200 and heading up." Because of his size Pat remembered borrowing MacSween's shoes so he could go to the tri-service ball. And they shared other things besides shoes and shirt sizes: Pat's father had pitched at Columbia University with a young first baseman named Lou Gherig. "Duke" Walsh later signed to pitch for the New York Yankees—something MacSween himself would love to have done as a young man. So the student and professor talked pitching and baseball for hours at a time. Pat was also ambitious to write creatively, he had written a play about campus politics as a major paper for MacSween (the play was about his contemporaries at X, political figures, including Brian

Mulroney and Rick Cashin). The professor and his former student also shared, naturally enough, a love of literature and teaching:

> Why he wanted me back to teach was the fact that I caught on to loving the literature. I loved to read. I read everything. I think we shared that. I know the things I don't have—his keen retentiveness—I have to refresh myself every time I teach a story. I don't have the kind of sharp insights that can be as verbally felicitous as those he had. But we did have certain things together. He let me be me. He wasn't interested in making a little MacSween. He could accept my ability to perform, he could see the joy in it, and say "Hey, this is another way to reach students."

In the fall of 1963 another student of MacSween's, George Sanderson, also arrived on campus to teach, not in the English department but in Philosophy: "I got a letter from Father MacSween and he had been talking to Father Charlie R. [MacDonald] and mentioned my name and Father Charlie R. remembered me. So I wrote to him with a PS to Father MacSween and that was it. Things were done informally in those days. So I came in 1963. Gert was completing her MA thesis at the time."

Gertrude Sanderson, George's wife, would also become a close friend and protege of MacSween's. Her post-graduate work was in French and Spanish and she was soon hired to teach those subjects at St. FX. The third couple to arrive on campus, in the fall of 1964, was Sheldon Currie and his wife, Dawn Wolstenholme—both Dawn and Sheldon had been students in MacSween's creative writing class. Sheldon was a Cape Bretoner from Reserve who, like his mentor, came from a coal-mining family. Sheldon had taught at St. Thomas University in Chatham and was completing a PhD at the University of Alabama when MacSween contacted him about coming to St. FX. With the arrival of the Curries, MacSween had a group of former students whose ideas and outlook on education, scholarship, teaching and writing resembled his own. These young, energetic, witty and vivacious former students became a great source of companionship and stimulation for the middle-aged professor-priest, who was now ready to devote his considerable skills, knowledge and energy more directly to the art of writing.

Jacqueline Walsh recalled the atmosphere of the time, the parties, and the meals they regularly held at each other's homes: "Nobody had money

Fig. 39 Jacqueline Walsh, 1963. Courtesy Pat Walsh.

to go out so we would have supper parties frequently. Father would come as well. I think he enjoyed those evenings. It gave him a chance to relax, and he didn't have to watch what he was saying. We would sort of rotate every few weeks, or every month, depending on what people's schedules were."[3] Jackie Walsh remembered, too, that his visits often went in cycles: "He would come each night for a long period of time, and then I don't know what happened, but he just stopped. This would have been two or three years after we arrived. And then he went after Sheldon and Dawn the same way for quite a period of time, and then it was George and Gert. As far as I know it was just the three couples that he visited."[4]

Though they loved to see him visit, all three of these couples were busy raising families—some of them large families—and when "Father" MacSween, as he was always known to them, arrived everything would have to be dropped or put aside because company had come. MacSween, of course, especially in the early years, would be eager to discuss books, ideas and writing with these young people fresh from the outside world. And unlike his undergraduates, he could engage them on a higher plane about art, ideas and, above all, books, especially books he had just read. It was a heady and wonderful time for him: perhaps for the first time in his life he had an audience that fully appreciated and understood what drove and fuelled his imagination. It is no wonder he visited—some might say hounded—them day and night. He had brought a small vortex to Antigonish, a literary and art-house set, and he intended to milk them for all they were worth. Though he would never have voiced it, like his uncle Doc Pat, he too had expectations of people he had done favours for.

Understandably, then, there were times when it was a strain on the young couples as Currie, Walsh and George Sanderson all recalled. The Sandersons in particular felt the strain: "I can remember saying to Gert that it was like a parade to our house every night at 7:30 after he had finished his chaplaincy duties at the Mount. And he would come out on Sunday. And so we were seeing him for quite a few years on a seven-days-a-week basis. It was actually a little too much because at times we needed a bit of privacy. We liked Father an awful lot, but nevertheless, sometimes, we felt that we needed a little holiday."

Having the smallest family of the three couples must have made the Sanderson household more attractive to MacSween, as he could then be assured that he would receive attention, have a captive audience. But this was a bonus, rather than a reason, for the visits; of all of MacSween's proteges, George Sanderson was the closest to him in temperament. A brilliant conversationalist, Sanderson's curiosity and knowledge were eclectic, but above all, it was his sharp wit, love of puns and relish of situational humour (rather than jokes) that so appealed to MacSween. How similar they could be was illustrated by an anecdote Sanderson told not long after his mentor had died: he and MacSween had been discussing the size and habits of a species of bear, contradicting each other, neither yielding ground. Eventually, they went on to other topics and the evening ended. The next day the two men, after almost knocking one another over, burst into laughter as they reached for the same text on bears among the stacks of the Angus L. Macdonald Library. George Sanderson, like his mentor, was also iconoclastic when it came to bureaucracies and institutions. A typical quip by him—and one of MacSween's own favourites—happened during a meeting of a Senate Honourary Degrees Committee: Sanderson, having glanced at the list of candidates replied that, "The names on this list are so undistinguished that I expect to find my own among them."

Sanderson and MacSween also sparked one another's humour; a story MacSween loved to repeat happened in the faculty lounge where he and Sanderson were having coffee: MacSween saw a colleague approaching so he leaned over and asked Sanderson to back him up on whatever he said. The colleague asked MacSween if he had ever heard of one the most arcane of books, the *Digenes Akritas*—the only major literary work of the Byzantine Empire. MacSween replied that he had a copy of the epic poem, but a student had borrowed it. The professor was flabbergasted; he had never even seen a copy! MacSween then turned to Sanderson and said "George, you have copy. Loan him yours." Sanderson replied immediately: "I left it with my landlady in Louvain." As was the case with MacSween and his circle, a brilliant response often became a refrain. MacSween would use these refrains for comic and satiric effect, especially if one of his colleagues or fellow priests were attempting to put on airs, as the saying went. A fellow priest, for example, who worked for the Extension Department and travelled often and legitimately in the developing world, was heard to say within MacSween's earshot at lunch that "The last time I was in Hong Kong it was raining." MacSween, knowing the priest came from a Cape Breton background similar to his own would say: "The last time I was in Mabou it was raining, the last time I was in Meat Cove it was raining," and so on.

MacSween and Sanderson eventually became the closest of friends and it was MacSween who first got the young philosophy professor interested in what would become a lifelong passion—the ideas and writings of Marshall McLuhan.[5] In his later years, after MacSween's death,

Sanderson, who became editor of *The Antigonish Review*, reflected on his lifelong relationship with his mentor and friend:

> I think the thing that people most minded about MacSween, that we gradually adjusted to, was his tendency to correct and qualify and even dismiss the arguments that you might think were important. I think this was very good for me. He liked to have a responsive audience, and if you were sharp enough and had the energy you could get your little remarks in, which he liked very much. He liked sharp remarks even at his own expense. He didn't like anybody talking for more than a minute and a half. He resembles to me, McLuhan, when I met McLuhan a few times. In Father's case, he just knew so much—those fellows don't have the time. Everything I could say pretty much—even in philosophy—he had either read or read about.

MacSween had been writing reviews for *The Casket* newspaper for over ten years, but his first literary essay was not published until 1963, when he was 48 years old. It appeared in the inaugural issue of the university's alumni magazine, *Contemporary,* under the title "Ezra Pound: A Personal Estimate." On reflection, Pound was a natural choice for Rev. R. J. MacSween, as he came to sign himself in all his professional writings, later dropping the Rev. What first drew the young MacSween to the controversial American poet was not, surprisingly enough, Pound's encyclopedic mind, but rather his religious sensibility. MacSween recalled that he first became interested in the poet when, "I read those lines from the *Pisan Cantos* 'What thou lovest well remains, the rest is dross.'" Among his pages and pages of notes on the poet—always handwritten on foolscap or small scraps of paper—are the following quotations from Pound. They illustrate, among other things, a religious connection and preoccupation:

> The only vigorous feasts of the Church are grafted on to European roots, the sun, the grain, the harvest and Aphrodite.... From the crying of "Ligo" in Lithuania, down to the Greek archipelago, certain things are believed. Book instruction obscures them. The people in Rapallo rushing down to the sea on Easter morning or bringing their gardens of Adonis to church on the Thursday before, have not learned it in school. Neither have the peasant women <u>read</u> [MacSween's underlining] anything telling them to bring silk cocoons to church carefully concealed in their hands or under their aprons.[6]

Passages like this, handwritten by MacSween, highlight the paradox about culture that the professor-priest-poet always lived with. Like Pound, he was extremely bookish, and yet he understood that books by themselves could never create or sustain a living culture—all they could do was record it. In an interview in his old age, while discussing the possible disappearance of his Church, books happened to surface in the conversation: MacSween was caustic, "Whenever I hear a fellow talking about books I feel like spitting!" And yet, talk about books he did, especially in relation to his favourite poem "The Cantos of Ezra Pound":

> This is the greatest long poem of the century and the most controversial. It is the stumbling block for friends and enemies alike. It frightens away the badly-read man, and the busy man, and the man with Victorian habits of poetry, and the too-Western Western man, and the too-modern modern man. It bristles with quotations from Latin, Greek, Provencal, Spanish, French, German. It bristles with names of the great and of the small, of cultural heroes and of private acquaintances, of classical cities and of African villages. Worst of all, there is a peppering of Chinese written characters. And, finally, in the later Cantos, Egyptian hieroglyphics take their stately and esoteric stand.[7]

To write a simple essay on Pound for a general readership shows how well MacSween had absorbed and understood this complex and difficult poet. If further proof were needed, one would only have to look at his own copy of "The Cantos" from this time, so riddled with notes that it is difficult to see the original text. But perhaps the best indication of his mastery of this material was his ability—and insistence—on teaching "The Cantos" to undergraduates—which he began to do in the 1960s. In his notes from this time, MacSween lists forty topics for "Papers for Seminar." One of the students in the class was Joe Coffey, an undergraduate from Maine who would soon start up a newspaper in nearby Port Hawkesbury entitled *The Hawkesbury Sun*. The paper would eventually spark MacSween into writing journalism for the first time in his life; this experience, coupled with his essays for *Contemporary*, helped fuel his life-long ambition to found a literary magazine, a project that was realized in 1970 with the founding of *The Antigonish Review*.

The year MacSween published his first literary essay, 1963, was also the year, as Catholics of that generation will recall, of Vatican II, the 21st ecumenical council convened by Pope John XXIII. The "radical" nature of this council would change the role of the Church forever, and most Catholics believed that the changes were good and—to put it mildly— long overdue. For MacSween, the Council was a mixed blessing: the loss of the Latin Mass—the Church's one great art form—was something he would learn to accept (unlike his hero Evelyn Waugh), but the emancipation of the individual and the move toward ecumenism was something MacSween had longed for all his life; something he had envisioned from ·

the moment he first entered the priesthood more than two decades earlier. Almost four more years would pass, however, before Catholics would actually see the physical, the outward, examples of the Council's changes on the university's campus and in the wider community. The change that would eventually be most noticeable—because it was most dramatic—was among his female friends at the Mount and his other female friends in the kitchens of Morrison Hall.

If St. FX alumni turn to the pages of the annual yearbooks of the university, the *Xaverian*, between the years 1960 and 1970, it looks as if fifty—or perhaps a hundred years—have elapsed, and not simply a decade. Most noticeable are the nuns—the steeple-like headgear and chin-mounting-bibs and collars worn by the sisters at the Mount are gone (only Hollywood today in an attempt to be exotic and painfully nostalgic, insists that they are still with us); gone, too, is the slightly less medieval garb worn by the Sisters of St. Martha. And the students—the young people—who by 1969 finally *do* look like young people, have lost forever that fifties image which insisted that a seventeen-year-old teenager had to look like a thirty-year-old schoolteacher or banker. When we remember that *Rebel Without A Cause* was a story about a high school boy, it strikes us now as strange that the part should be played by James Dean—a young man who looked like he had been through the horrors of World War II, rather than the trauma of teen love and high school. That of course was the point. The repression of the fifties was about, among other things, sex and sexuality: the Kinsey report, women's liberation and the films of Fellini had come to the Maritimes too—the old paradigm was over. Philip Larkin, one of MacSween's favourite post-war poets, recorded the time-shift in his poem, *Annus Mirabilis*, the first stanza of which sardonically proclaims: "Sexual intercourse began/ In nineteen sixty-three/(Which was rather late for me)—/Between the end of the *Chatterley* ban/ And the Beatles' first LP."

When MacSween's fellow religious removed their habits in the late 60s it must have been an extraordinary moment for them, their families and their friends. When, for example, he went to visit his friend Marper, Sister Margaret, in Ottawa he would have seen, for the first time in his life, a religious who was also a woman. His own public transformation, his taking off of the collar, would not occur until somewhat later, and his emancipation—at least as regards public displays of affection—was still a good ways off as well. Gertrude Sanderson, a young woman in her twenties fresh from Paris, discovered this—to her surprise—on her first meeting with MacSween in 1963: "When George and I arrived, and when we met Father, we came with the European tradition of giving the person a peck on each cheek. I did that. Father said, 'Hold on, young woman.' And he pushed me back. That was in 1963, the day we both arrived here. My first visit in Antigonish."[8]

Fig. 40 Gertrude Sanderson, 1963. Courtesy St. FX University Archives.

Pushing back the intelligent, vivacious and pretty young professor was not the only sign of the priest's prudence and prudishness about his public persona in the small, middle-class town of Antigonish. George Sanderson recalled that when they lived on St. Ninian's street, "Father used to ask me to go down to the car with him when he was leaving because he didn't want to give the impression that he was visiting a single woman. I'd say goodnight to him there. The neighbours there—everybody—watched what everybody else did, and he was conscious of that. At first I didn't understand when he would say, "Let's go, George." And I'd walk down to the car and he'd drive off. But then I realized that he wanted to be seen with me, because there were priests who had reputations for doing what some priests do." It is easy to single out the puritanism of the small town, to see Antigonish as a "valley of squinting windows" in Brinsley McNamara's phrase, but we would do well to remember that the Hayes Code of censorship that dominated Hollywood movies was, after all, a Catholic-inspired code, kept in place through the influence of the Legion of Decency, among others.

Fig. 41 Margaret "Marper" MacDonald, post Vatican II. Courtesy St. FX University Archives.

IN 1961 "Doc" Pat Nicholson had returned to the campus after seven gruelling years in the busy parish of St. Joseph's in downtown Sydney. He was designated President Emeritus, and he took a room in the priests' residence in Morrison Hall overlooking Confusion Square. Ten years earlier he had often sat outside, on those long warm summer evenings Antigonish still enjoys, talking and joking with Moses Coady, "Doc" Dan McCormick and, of course, his nephew Rod MacSween. Doc Pat's final years were sad ones: he suffered from Alzheimer's and was eventually crippled by a series of strokes, seven altogether—the last claiming his life on November 4, 1965. Dolores Crawford, MacSween's niece, recalled being in the priest's dining room with her uncle Rod in 1989, just a year before he died:

> Father Rod talked about how bad Doc Pat was at the end. I remember sitting in Morrison Hall with Father Rod looking at an elevator door and him saying that every year the priests had this particular meeting: Doc Pat, as bad as he was, remembered that it was time for this meeting of the priests and the bishop, and he came down in this elevator—undressed in his underwear. Father Rod looked at the elevator—and he didn't plan to tell us this—but he did. He looked at the elevator and he was just shaking his head and saying his famous saying, "the poor fellow." No, he wasn't like a second father to him, Doc Pat was more like a first.

Doc Pat's nephew wrote him a tribute that was published in *Contemporary* and later picked up by the *Halifax Herald*. The article does not focus on his uncle's death but rather on his exile of seven years earlier, in 1954. Clearly, the nephew had not forgotten or forgiven the injustice done to his uncle: "He turned back to his place at the head table and began his meal again. The others muttered to themselves but there was no loud talk or laughter. It was an unusual day. Not often does a monument announce its removal from a scene which it had created. The old man at the head of the table had been powerful enough to give his character to the whole college."[9]

Doc Pat's grandparents had come to Cape Breton Island as adult immigrants from the Gaelic-speaking Hebrides off the coast of Scotland. There is a picture in the Xaverian yearbook for 1966 of Major MacLeod, first professor of Celtic Studies at St. FX, down on one knee playing the pipes for the remains of the man who had spent much of his life trying to preserve something of the lost culture, of that now forgotten world, of those first immigrant Nicholsons.

In his second collection of verse, *double shadows*, there is a poem entitled "the body" that captures something of what Rod MacSween must have felt about the passing of this uncle who had become a second father to him:

when a man dies
    we remember
    our failure of love
each jovial April
    we learn the life of frost
    that never ends

when a man dies
    our generous spirit stirs
    too late to be of use
we wash away
    our guilt with tears

we know the smell
    of his indignity
the iron mask
    of our solicitude

on the shore we join the lost
    who spoke too late
the badge of charity
    dead on our breasts

his biographer with liquid pen
    dots his life with islands
    green spots that hallow
    that long exile

too late the heart begins to whisper
    what it long denied
that human body
    rich with the blood of life
    was worthy our soul's
    entranced devotion

IN his poem "Annus Mirabilis," Philip Larkin does not mention that Vatican II took place in that same year of wonder, but there is little doubt that sexuality still preoccupied the Catholic Church, and especially its hierarchy. Five short years later, no practising Catholic of liberal mind could have guessed that the man who had helped the late John XXIII carry through the great reforms of Vatican II, Pope Paul VI, was going to do an about face on one of the most critical issues for practicing Catholics—the right to practise birth control, the right for women to use the pill. The notorious encyclical, *Humane Vitae*, was issued on July 29, 1968.

Looking back over the years, it is clear that the decline of the Catholic Church in the West was as inevitable as the decline of any other denomination, any other religious institution. The secular age had arrived in Europe and in Quebec, and it would arrive in Atlantic Canada as well. For priests of Rod MacSween's generation—and younger ones, too—it was a difficult time. There must have been a sense of loss, if not betrayal, for no one knew more clearly than MacSween that the sexual revolution and secularization had come to stay.

Politically, in the world outside the Church, it was a brutal time: the Vietnam war was at its most ferocious with the saturation bombings of Cambodia and Vietnam appearing nightly on living room televisions, not to mention the news of the My Lai massacre. Young St. FX graduates from New England who had been coming to the Catholic school for generations were fighting, killing and dying in the rice fields and jungles of Southeast Asia. A recent graduate, Richard Lane Cotter, BBA. 1967, was killed in action on February 10, 1969, in Quang Tri Province, Vietnam. He was twenty-three years old and his "In Memoriam" picture in the Xaverian yearbook for 1969 shows the handsome young man full of promise in his St. FX graduation gown.

With the world in such desperate shape, the Catholic Church—with its tradition of social justice and social action—was preoccupied instead with the matter of birth control, something that no one, or almost no one, in the West cared about anymore. In the same *Xaverian* yearbook that carried the photo of the recently killed young alumnus, there is a picture of a student in residence sitting in front of a wall covered with photos of beautiful women—models and movie stars—some of them are in bathing suits, some in bras, some topless, but covered up for the photo, the caption below the picture reads, "And now from the pages of the Pope's encyclical."[10]

In the October 1968 edition of *Contemporary*, Fr. Bernard MacDonald published an article entitled, "Says Blind Submission Not Required of Catholics." In the same issue of the magazine, Fr. Flanagan, an Irishman from Cork, wrote on (predictably enough, perhaps) "The Natural Law," while Rev. Roderick MacSween published an essay on a writer whose work had been prosecuted for obscenity: "A View of D. H. Lawrence: Prophet Preaching Liberation." Like all of MacSween's essays, it illustrates an easy command of the author's entire output, and he takes us through all of those weighty novels, the short stories, poetry, travel books and letters.

He concludes his essay with one of Lawrence's last novels, a controversial book about Christ, entitled *The Man Who Died*:

> For the first time in his stories he confronts Christ squarely, although he does not name him. It was only fitting that the meeting take place, for of all modern artists Lawrence is the most religious. Some may balk at accepting this statement but for Lawrence it was true. His attitude toward life was nothing if not religious.... The first part of this short novel is taken up with the agonized recovery of Christ from the grave into health. This part of the story is extremely beautiful.... Christ becomes the lover of a priestess of Isis, she becomes pregnant, Christ is chased from the scene by the forces of repression after expressing regret over the asceticism of his early life.[11]

The 1960s were manifest at St. FX, as at many other institutions of higher learning, with student unrest: a fire bomb damaged one of the buildings and a student strike, held during the 1971 spring term, forced the university to end the academic year early; final exams were written as take-homes. The students were protesting for something known then as "open housing," (i.e., co-ed visiting rights in male residences). George Sanderson recalled that MacSween "was very disappointed because he felt it was simply irresponsibility on their part." The grievances were not academic, but rather they had to do with students' "hearts desires" with "social things like open housing in residence." MacSween "just didn't like their demands." George recalled that he was "sympathetic to a lot of these things, but he was critical because he could more base motives behind the facades. Father couldn't stand phoniness; he didn't like the duplicity involved here. I have a feeling that his anger toward them was based upon disappointment in the shallowness of their motives."

There is little doubt that this was a challenging, tough and to a certain extent disappointing time for MacSween. He had been given a unique opportunity, the chance to influence directly the course, not only of his department, but also of the liberal arts in general at his school. And now just as his ideas and proteges were establishing themselves, taking root as it were, both the university and the Church—the two institutions that he lived by—seemed to be under siege. In his last collection of poems, published six years before he died, MacSween wrote a poem that harkens back to these years, to the sixties. The title of the poem is "treason," and it is a lyric that contains much anger and resentment, a poem about a lost world, a poem about betrayal:

when the young became dirty and savage
the aged surrendered their manners
   and the principles
     of arch and dome
when the young sang simple ditties

   according to blood
   and breathing
the aged threw away Palestrina
  the style of sense and balance
  the discipline of the parts
when the young grew tired of destruction

   the aged died
   without pageantry or ritual
they had beggared themselves
   in a cause
   of one day

It is possible to see this poem as reactionary, the cry of a frustrated conservative whose world has fallen apart—barbarians at the gate kind of stuff—but this would not be a fair reading. St. FX was not Kent State, and the students of '71 in Antigonish were not being beaten and shot like the students of '68 in Prague, Mexico City and Paris. The celebrated Mexican writer Octavio Paz quit his job as ambassador in protest at the killings in his city and returned home to fight for democracy; many Czech students were either scattered throughout the globe in exile or, like Vaclav Havel, playwright and first President of the Czech Republic, sent to prison to wait out the Cold War. And the students in Antigonish? They got the right to have female visitors (and possibly sex) in their dormitories. It seems comic now, a kind of undergraduate farce, something worthy of Monty Python, hardly worth the indignation that generated MacSween's poem. But the confrontation was real enough, and the issue—personal sexual freedom—was serious, especially in a rural Catholic world. More than one student at St. FX came from huge Catholic families, families whose mothers, if they survived (and we remember that MacSween's sister didn't), bore the suffering—physically and mentally—of generations of such sexual politics. If this symbolism or emblematic stance was missed by the students, it shouldn't have been missed by MacSween, a man and priest who spent his lifetime battling this particular obsession of his church.

What also disturbed *Father* MacSween about the whole affair, was how some of his colleagues and acquaintances had chosen to become "hip" overnight, as if they'd all gone through some sort of collective mid-life crisis, long hair and blue jeans their banners, instead of orange shirts and blue sports cars. The critic Terry Eagleton had similar (if more comic) reflections on the temper of the times: "Since they believed in anti-elitist spirit that nobody should be different from anyone else, they ended up doing themselves out of a job, like those radical 60s professors who ought logically to have sat at the back of their own classes and barracked."[12]

MacSween was too prescient not to know that his world was changing, and though he was better equipped than most to deal with this change, it remained a very challenging time for him. The pace and nature of the paradigm shift that was taking place was antithetical to the very conservative institutions and world that he inhabited. Not only modernity, but post-modernity had arrived in Antigonish and rural Cape Breton: its avant-garde was not led by Derrida, Marcuse, Godard or Foucault, but it was inspired by their subjects; gender, class and race, among other things, were asserting their political and cultural right to be part of the planet they inhabited. MacSween did not object to this right to be seen and heard—or to share the power for that matter—he did, however, perceive and predict an inevitable (and understandable) intolerance, a political and cultural backlash, against the institutions of "arch and dome"—and the grand narratives they represented. His Church, university and world view were under siege, and he would have to marshal some strong defences to try to protect what he believed was best, if not grand, about them.

IN his autobiographical notes 16 and 17, MacSween looks back on his seminary years with all the enthusiasm and romanticism of a young Wordsworth looking at revolutionary France: "A New World!! Music, Fathers, Doctors: the wonder of it!! From the inside!!"[13] It took him a long time to lose this shiny innocence, to have it scratched and shattered by experience; and as he lost it, he would, naturally, pay the inevitable price. Despite the coal-hard exterior he sometimes projected, the fierce look, and so on, there was a romantic if not an idealistic individual—especially in relation to his Church and university—hiding just beneath the surface. When MacSween finally grapples with the disappearance of this world—his world—the verse he writes is inevitably about loss, and the note, the tone it strikes is always elegiac and often tragic. It is this tone that would eventually lead the eminent Canadian critic and poet, Louis Dudek, to characterize R. J. MacSween as a tragic artist.

*A*lthough the secular age had clearly arrived in Canada by the 1960s, it was, ironically perhaps, in his role as Catholic priest that MacSween was chosen to judge a literary contest for the country's centenary celebrations in 1967. The two other judges were the poets Eli Mandel, who was Jewish, and Fred Cogswell, a Protestant and the editor of *The Fiddlehead*. Cogswell fondly recalled the time: "The meeting was a pleasant surprise to all three of us. It was probably the briefest and most harmonious one ever conducted under the auspices of the Canada Council. Each judge read out in turn the names of the winning entries in the order of his choice. All choices were identical. The first prize was awarded to Margaret Atwood for a manuscript later published as *The Animals in That Country*."[14]

MacSween's other literary activities in the 1960s included essays on the complete works of: Ezra Pound, Graham Greene, Hart Crane, T. S. Eliot, Ernest Hemingway, Dylan Thomas, Aldous Huxley, Morley Callaghan, Evelyn Waugh, William Faulkner, Norman Mailer, Ivy Compton-Burnett, and three Canadian poets—Bliss Carman, Charles G. D. Roberts and E. J. Pratt. All of these essays are mature pieces of criticism of a very high standard, and credit must go to the editors of *Contemporary* for having the wisdom and the foresight to seek them out in the first place. Some of these early essays would later be reworked for issues of *The Antigonish Review*, but the majority of them remain as they are—buried in a forgotten alumni magazine still awaiting recognition and a readership.

Some of these essays—especially those on Canadian writers—are significant in light of MacSween's own life and career as a writer, which was just beginning at this time. In the introduction to his essay on Morley Callaghan, written in the fall of 1965, MacSween addresses the often heartfelt subject of literary nationalism:

> There is a kind of literary nationalism which marshals a nation's writers as though they were heroes on parade. Writers are made to play their part in a game which adds nothing to their stature either as writers or as men. The critic who forgets to play this game runs the risk of branding himself as irreverent or traitorous, for he who lays his hand upon the idol of the tribe is liable to have the limb cut off.

MacSween goes on in the article to critique Callaghan's stories and novels; the critique, as with almost all of MacSween's earlier criticism, is absolute, universal and uncompromising:

> Nevertheless, Callaghan cannot be explained in simple terms. He has not achieved greatness but he has seen it very near. No man of his calibre has known so clearly the demands of art for simplicity, for the casualness

that hides effort, for the need to clothe the world's variety in order and purpose. All of these he saw and for all of these he reached. His failure to succeed may be the logical outcome of our Canadian provincialism. It is hard to say. At present his reputation is based squarely upon a handful of novels and a collection of short stories. The novels must make their way in a world that contains many great masterpieces in many languages. The short stories must stand without shame before the gaze of Chekhov and the early Hemingway.

MacSween is not a comforting critic for Canadian nationals to read in these early essays, and often he is not a reassuring one either. Canadians—like everyone else—are placed in an all or nothing contest where they must be judged only by the standards of the polymath, where even the author of *Axel's Castle*, writing on Callaghan, can't be trusted: "Probably it is this idea that struck the mind of Edmund Wilson and stirred him to praise for a neglected genius. To an extent he was right. The trouble arises when we go on to examine the structure more carefully."[15] It can be argued, quite easily of course, that this is criticism from a very old—and certainly no longer fashionable—paradigm—both patriarchal and hierarchical in the extreme; a world now mostly reserved for, and peopled by, neo-cons and defenders of great books.[16] I would argue, however, that while this is true of MacSween's early criticism—especially of Canadian literature—it is not all the truth; much of his support, or denial, of Canadian cultural nationalism is connected directly to his Catholic world view.

It is fascinating (and sometimes disturbing) to watch MacSween struggle with cultural nationalism, a nationalism for him that was increasingly in flux, as his culture—especially in the 1960s—was shifting rapidly and radically from a religious world view to an increasingly secular one. We might do well to remember that the Cape Breton Scot had been teaching and writing years before post-colonial critics and writers developed a theory and a language for deconstructing the imperialism (be it Roman Catholic or British) that had formed much of MacSween's culture in the first place. Canadian cultural nationalism and Canadian literary criticism was just emerging in the 1960s and 70s. What is interesting about MacSween is how he formed a way of writing and, to a lesser extent, teaching about Canadian literature while still living—or at least writing and thinking—outside its then nascent cultural identity. Like the writer Roy Campbell, MacSween too had colonial handicaps that would affect his writing, and his criticism, of Canadian literature.

In the 1971 spring issue of *The Antigonish Review*, MacSween reviewed a book about a fellow Cape Bretoner who also came from Glace

Bay; the review says much about MacSween's understanding of cultural nationalism:

> Hugh MacLennan is a rather ambiguous figure.... He has received more than his share of praise and honour. At the same time, there exists in the minds of many readers a doubt about his true worth.... Judgment concerning this writer boils down finally to one's attitude towards the world we inhabit. Do we live in Canada? Or in the English-speaking world? or in the whole world? Those who opt for a little Canada see MacLennan as a great writer; those who wish to live in a greater world accept with equanimity his rather small stature.... In spite of the occasional good chapter, MacLennan is found to be profoundly wanting in those things that elevate a novelist beyond the ordinary. His style seldom goes beyond good drab, he is painfully lacking in sophistication, his mind has not the metaphysical dimension which allows the novelist's matter to surge into universality. And yet he is a monument beyond the reach of all destruction, and there he will remain until some one else combines Canadianism with a greater art.[17]

It is somewhat painful for us now to read this candid criticism that is so divorced from the world, from the struggle of individual artists, and from an understanding of grim battles fought by a nascent literary culture in the giant shadows of Britain and America, not to mention the Russians, the classics and Bay Street. We might take some comfort from the fact that the passage probably tells us much more about MacSween than it does about his fellow Cape Bretoner. As a creative writer—and as a poet in particular—MacSween lived in isolation all his life. For the most part, it was a matter of choice, but his culture would certainly not have encouraged contact—we recall that the renunciation of the ego was central to the priesthood. MacSween, here seems unwilling to engage the importance to Canadian literature of a pioneering figure like Hugh McLennan. This, of course, is again partly due to his lack of any post-colonial theory to address what McLennan represented; what he was doing; why he was so important in the battle against cultural imperialism. To turn his own phrase back upon him, MacSween was painfully lacking in sophistication when it came to an understanding of cultural nationalism, post-colonialism and cultural imperialism. Furthermore, as a Catholic professor-priest—at least at this point in his career—MacSween was incapable of the necessary understanding precisely because his own cultural nationalism was so divergent and conflicted. How does a working-class priest, living in a Catholic rural paradigm, form a cultural identity in what was then an overwhelmingly British, Protestant country? It is not a moot question, and the raising of it helps explain, in part at least, MacSween's sometimes antagonistic, or as some saw it apathetic, attitude to nascent and established Canadian writers.

A classmate of mine, cramming for a poetry exam in the early 1970s at St. FX, once bitterly remarked, that if MacSween didn't like W. B. Yeats, how come "he taught so much of his God damn poetry?" It was a good question and, on reflection, I believe MacSween answered it, in part at least, in an essay he wrote on the Irishman in an early issue of *TAR*, where he said that Yeats was important for reasons other than poetry.[18] MacSween's willingness to grapple with the Irish cultural nationalism of Yeats and not with that of MacLennan, those "other considerations and other values," had to do in part with how he felt culturally as a Canadian and, of course, with how he was formed. MacSween's reluctance to engage Canadian cultural nationalism seems, on the surface at least, to have had more to do with his Catholicism than with anything else. W. B. Yeats was not a Catholic, but anyone who knows the famous Christmas dinner scene in *A Portrait of the Artist As A Young Man* or has seen the film *Michael Collins* or *In the Name of the Father*, doesn't need to be told that traditional Irish nationalism had something of a Catholic flavour to it.

Of the thirteen or so essays that MacSween wrote for *Contemporary*, only two are directly concerned with what were once called Catholic writers. And these two novelists are among the most significant writers in English of the twentieth century—Graham Greene and Evelyn Waugh. There is little doubt that MacSween was drawn to these two English converts, in the first instance, because they were Catholics; but his praise and criticism of them was based on his knowledge of good writing. The Catholic cultural world that MacSween grew up in was international in a way that it is difficult for a Canadian nationalist to grasp in this post-referendum, post-free trade world. The 1950s and 60s—especially in the United States—witnessed in its artistic community something close to an intellectual and religious revival. In an article on the advent and popularity of the Christian "thriller," Vince Passaro summed up the world that existed for these writers:

> [Flannery] O'Connor lived during a period of outstanding American Catholic intellectual life; she had the advantage of well-educated friends who believed as she did, and she had the support of a more influential world of religious intellectual journals than exists today. There was a kind of unheralded but deeply felt religious revival in fiction at the time, not just in Catholicism with J. F. Powers and a number of lesser writers at work within the fold, but in strongly influential Jewish writers as well:

Bernard Malumud and Isaac Bashevis Singer the most spiritual among them and Saul Bellow and Philip Roth the most culturally engaged.[19]

If there had been major Canadian Catholic writers MacSween would no doubt have embraced them as heroes (he did promote the Canadian Catholic Marshall McLuhan but he was a philosopher not a creative writer). The fact that most of the Catholic writers MacSween engaged and wrote about were English was both inevitable and, in some respects, unfortunate. Breaking from the paradigm of British Literature, English "high" culture, is much harder to do when there are figures in it that you strongly identify with because they share something of your culture, religion and, to a lesser extent, politics. V. S. Naipaul is a good example from the opposite point of view, where post-colonial scholars, writers and readers support him because of his art, yet can't abide his reactionary politics. From one point of view, Rod MacSween was culturally trapped by his heritage—as many of us were—caught, in a sense, among three Empires: Britain, America and the Holy Roman Catholic Church. The young woman whom MacSween helped award a prize to in 1967, Margaret Atwood, has written admirably on our cultural struggles with the first two of these empires. Few artists or critics of note—at least in English-speaking Canada—have grappled with the impact of the third. MacSween was no Kipling, nor was he ultramontane, but the historian in him—bolstered by the Catholic nationalist—firmly believed that the world, and the West in particular, would have been much worse off without the Church and the empires that it stood for.[20] In a poem entitled "the cathedral," published in his last collection, he made the impact of the Church, as he saw it, explicit in his opening stanza":

> without that stone hive
>   the iron men of Europe
>   would have eliminated
>   each other
> and left only silence
>   on the green continent

IN September 1968, Rod MacSween's father died in Toronto at the age of eighty-six. Hugh MacSween was waked and buried in Cape Breton, and his fifth son wrote a poem for him that later appeared in his first collection. It is entitled "eternal youth:"[21]

my father died
in his bed
his mind on heaven
his body lead
not my father

the man who died
my father lives
uncrucified

by pain or labour
cold disease
all that brought him
to his knees
his hands master
on the farms
calves cradled
in his arms

lambs tended
cattle fed
in the meadows
never dead

never dead
though my eyes
see the truth
my brain denies

his dead young features
bend to me
with a dream's
reality

father friend
man who died
eternal youth
uncrucified

Fig. 43 Hugh MacSween cutting wood in Cape Breton in the 1950s. Courtesy Stewart Donovan.

When Hugh MacSween died, the autopsy report showed that he was still in great physical condition for his age; his son Rod liked to recall that his father still "had the body of a young man." Unlike Hugh, Rod would not have good health for his middle or old age; as he approached his mid-fifties, he began to have trouble with an arthritic hip—the same hip problem that had crippled his mother and led to her early death. In a letter to a student named Loretta dated Nov 2, 1966, there is a reference, among other things, to this health:

> *I'm well except for rheumatism. Sometimes I can hardly walk. Generally I'm straight and vigorous. But days come when I crawl across the campus curled up like an 'n'. The boys and girls look at me in amazement, thinking that I'm looking for dimes on the ground! Give my regards to the rest of the family, some of whom have waited for letters from me for a long time. By the way, I do not remember you at all! Isn't that an awful thing to say! I know I did meet—was it three of you?—the same day a number of the Beaton girls. That's all I remember.[22]*

Besides the comic admission that he doesn't know the student, the letter is a good confirmation of how busy his life was; but despite this hectic pace, he still seems to have made time for family and friends. When, for example, his nephew John MacEachern arrived on campus, his uncle Rod took charge of him as if he were his own son. Naturally, MacSween would have felt much guilt about the death of his sister, especially when he looked at the face of the eighteen-year-old "boy," who looked so much like Margaret at that age. John remembered that his uncle took him shopping that first day and outfitted him with new clothes and footwear, and gave him spending money as well. John's relationship with his uncle remained strong over the years, despite the fact that "Father Rod did not like my own father." In later life, John recalled visiting the campus: "I was with someone when Father Rod passed in the car but he didn't acknowledge me when I waved." Later, when

Fig. 44 Playing golf in Antigonish with Fr. McKenna, 1970. Courtesy Stewart Donovan.

John went to visit his uncle in his office he asked why he had ignored him: "Oh," he said, "I thought your father was with you."

MacSween continued to play golf during these years, but his weight became an ever increasing burden to him, so much so that by the mid-1970s he would stop playing the game altogether; partly because he was embarrassed by his size, but also because his hip joint caused him so much pain. As a big man, he naturally enough had a great love of food, and especially of home cooking. In those later years, he would always spend Thanksgiving down in Cape Breton with his friends Marg and Ray Drohan. Marg remembered how he would eat a big home-cooked meal and then be invited out to his brother Mike's, where another meal would be provided and, though he would not want it, he would often eat in order not to seem ungrateful. This would happen not only on Thanksgiving but at Christmas and Easter as well: in Cape Breton, food—and plenty of it—is the first rule of hospitality, and MacSween had spent his lifetime living under this code. His willpower and his power of concentration were super human when it came to reading—he was a man who never had down time—but when it came to food he would surrender, partly no doubt because of the psychological comfort it provided in later years, when he spent more and more time on his own, alone.

Although his health problems began about this time, MacSween continued to work at an extraordinary rate: in the late sixties he was still chairing the department of English, counselling at the Mount, teaching three very large classes, and working as an unpaid collections librarian. By 1970 the Angus L. Macdonald library with its elegant Hall of Clans reading room and its Special Collections department was five years old—the library had changed greatly during these years. The beautiful new building had a large staff, including an official collections librarian, and there were now separate budgets for each department. MacSween continued to order books, to go through catalogues and make lists, even though many of them would never be purchased. He also continued to buy books of his own and his personal library was now somewhere between 15 and 20 thousand volumes.

At the end of the 1960s, St. FX underwent another major expansion to cope with increasing enrollment, and two aspects of this expansion would affect MacSween directly. The first concerned his own department of which he had been head since the retirement of Bannon in 1962. Like many other Canadian universities during this period, St. FX found itself, for better or worse, going outside the country—largely to Britain and

America—to hire qualified professors, academics with MAs or PhDs. In the mid-60s there was an increasing concern with image and competition in Canadian universities, not unlike today's student-as-consumer so encouraged by *Maclean's* magazine. George Sanderson recalls that "the university calendar became very important and you'd hear it mentioned about how many PhDs we had. There was all this talk about standards and how we rated with other universities. That was in the early 60s, then in the late 60s it really increased." MacSween's attitude toward post-secondary degrees in the arts, degrees like the PhD was made publicly explicit in an interview with Pat Walsh in 1980 where he said, "It's different in the sciences or in any course that requires a great deal of training. But in the matter of English Literature, I don't feel that you need a PhD at all. I think there is almost nothing in English that you can't learn by yourself. It may be good to have a well-trained professor give you a few courses, but I don't think you have to go through that drudgery so long as you like to work by yourself. And I like to."[23]

Throughout his life MacSween's philosophy of education remained fairly consistent. In the mid-to-late 60s he came under the influence of writers and philosophers of education such as Ivan Illich—who wrote of the necessity of deschooling society—and Maria Montessori, the radical Italian educator of young children. MacSween would eventually publish two essays on Montessori:

> Her classroom showed where her heart lay. The doorknobs, the tables, the cupboards, the windows were all ordered with the child's size in mind. No more reaching for door knobs, climbing on to chairs, fighting with windows, being frustrated by bathroom facilities for her children. She felt with them as though she too were a child. Her whole plan was to entice from hiding the secret forces that lived within the mind. She arranged a series of projects that would arouse the child's creativity.... Progress was demanded of no one as each decided his own. The hungry mind cried out for food: when it was satisfied, education was at an end in one particular area. This was a matter that could not be decided by any external rule. Each mind has its own rules. Maria watched and saw her children grow as a gardener sees his plants arise form the soil.... She knew however that it would be a long time before her views were accepted, probably a hundred years. She was right.... Some vast effort must be made to make her ideas operative if society is ever going to be rid of the mass of hostilities generated in the schools.[24]

MacSween published other essays and reviews on teachers and teaching, both at the elementary and post-secondary level. Several of these—especially those concerning the university written for the *Hawkesbury Sun*—give the impression of being turned out very quickly; they are responses to the moment, and the moment was the late 1960s. Some of the titles are alarmist, "The University is Going" and "Should the University Be Abolished?" being the most eye-catching. These articles contain passages that are by turns comic, sad and prophetic:

> It could be that the radicals are not radical enough and have in the depths of their minds a notion of a new university which is actually the old one with the furniture shifted around a bit, the father out of his comfortable chair sitting on the piano stool, and the son with his feet up smoking papa's cigars. It's a wonderful idea.... The confrontation of students with faculty, the struggle for advantage that seems to be only a step towards a further struggle, the dissatisfaction with teachers and methods, the grasping for complete sexual freedom in campus dormitories, the injection of politics into academic matters, the violence shown by radicals for the average moderate student—all these are signs that the academic body is preparing for death, not for reformation.... Msgr. Illich of Cuernavaca has explained how to teach any subject by an intense tutorial system.... It would not require large classrooms, dormitories and libraries.... As we come into an age where computers accelerate the processing of knowledge and where everyone may possess the equivalent of a huge national library in his home, we should see that the centralization that those buildings take for granted is an outmoded concept, developed in an age of cumbrous communication. For the first time in history the learning of the world can come to our homes.[25]

Clearly, MacSween felt passionately about these issues and, on the surface at least, he thought universities might not recover the status he once felt they had. Clearly written in the heat of the moment, the passage still reveals many of MacSween's attitudes of the time; what is especially interesting—and some might say naïve in the extreme—is his notion that "academic matters" are non-political. And his utopian hope for the computer contradicts Cardinal Newman's adage that "an academical system without the personal influence of teachers upon pupils is an arctic winter." MacSween, of course, was not alone in his despair about the state of the university; many others felt the same way, including Hugh MacLennan, who published an article in *The Halifax Chronicle-Herald* entitled "Universities must act or outraged public will."[26]

In the interview with Pat Walsh, MacSween expressed some dismay at how large his university had become, about the difficulty of knowing students when a campus gets too big, where students become numbers. It is now an old debate. The size of the small college where he first came to teach in 1948 was brought home to him in 1970 when he received a form letter telling him he was no longer Chair of his department. George Sanderson remembered that it was a "terrible shock" for his mentor, a shock because he felt betrayed: "betrayed by the way it was done." Sanderson recalled, too, that

> Father felt like this, "If they had come to me and said we think it's time that someone else should do it, I would have said, Okay. And I would have given my advice about it." But this was not done. He got a letter in the mail telling him he was no longer Chair of the department. It grew out of the conflict or dispute between the new fellows hired from England.

Pat Walsh, long-time professor and secretary of the English Department, recalled the hiring of the five British professors in 1969:

> Joe D. Campbell and Father Bauer went overseas and they interviewed these guys and they hired five men and brought them back. Five British guys in one whack! They had gone to London and put an ad in the paper and interviewed. They selected these guys and all five came.

On reflection, it has a sad (and almost comic) colonial feel to it: two provincial, Canadian, Nova Scotia priests visiting London to seek out someone to teach their mostly Catholic Cape Breton students. It is almost worthy of Dickens, but it is more accurately described as an academic example of what the Australian art critic, Robert Hughes, famously called the cultural cringe: If it or they are any good they can't be from here.

Four of the five hired were, of course, English Catholics, and one was a priest who would edit the first couple of issues of *The Antigonish Review*. Though MacSween initially supported—and pushed for—these hirings, he soon came to regret having done so.[27] Looking back at his colonial heritage, his championing of English Catholic converts and his love of the canon of English literature, the tradition it represented, it comes as no surprise that he would back such an extraordinary decision in the first place. Catholic institutions continued the policy hiring of Catholics—of various nationalities and cultures—long after the paradigm had shifted. George Sanderson recalls that for MacSween it was a very difficult time:

> Father didn't say a lot but he was obviously very upset by it [losing the position of Chair]. We were very upset by it. There was no need for it, the department was doing very well, but there had been a new administration brought in. Father was so upset by it because there had been no hinting about it. He didn't think of himself being in the same category of not having the PhD. He knew it was important for others,

but didn't place himself in the same category because he was a priest and had been there for so long.

By 1970 MacSween was a formidable presence on the St. FX campus: a popular teacher of tremendous wit and erudition; a respected counsellor at Mount St. Bernard; a forceful spokesman for his fellow priests; and, finally, a professor with a strong following of former students who were now themselves respected professors and supportive colleagues.[28] Given these strengths, then, his demotion from the departmental position of Chair—because he didn't have a PhD—was a considerable shock. Jacqueline Walsh recalled,

> It hurt him deeply. I found he kind of withdrew from everything after that. Before that he knew what was going on, who was doing what, in all the departments. He had a feel for everything. He was a fighter for what he wanted and I think after that he just withdrew and didn't want to become involved. I don't know what his motivation was, but that's the feeling I got—that he withdrew his presence.

It is at this time, too, that the university's other area of expansion—its buildings—had a direct impact on MacSween's life. A new residence called MacIsaac House was built on the southwest side of the campus near the Trans-Canada Highway. Although the system of prefecting was no longer the responsibility of the priests, several of them were asked if they wanted to take up rooms in these residences. Rod MacSween and his good friend, George Kehoe, did so immediately, Kehoe on the ground floor of MacIssac Residence, and MacSween on the floor above. The move, George Sanderson recalled, was a very good one:

> He didn't want to move exactly, they invited him, but it doubled the area of his living space and the number of books he could buy! It was an easier set-up. He had a little stove in it and a fridge. I would say that apartment made a big difference to his life. It gave him a new focus. It was like a little coach house—he could entertain there.

The "coach house" referred to by George Sanderson was where Marshall McLuhan taught and entertained at the University of Toronto. It is a good comparison, but those that know the St. FX of these years realize that MacIsaac residence, relatively quiet in the first years of its existence, soon became known as "the zoo," a place of wild parties and heavy drinking. An irony not lost on MacSween's friends, colleagues and students, was the knowledge that this gifted intellectual lived under such conditions. By all accounts, he did not mind them and in general the students went their way and the "old" professor-priest went his. When their stereos

Fig. 45 MacSween outside his rooms in MacIsaac Residence, 1970. Courtesy Stewart Donovan.

blasted "Stairway to Heaven" to the point of rocking his door, MacSween's response, if he responded at all, would be to simply turn up his television or the classical music he so often listened to; the noise never seemed to bother him to any great degree. Sheldon Currie, in a tribute to MacSween after his death, recalled "When he lived in an apartment in residence in MacIsaac House, students pinned a name plate on his door. They called him, Big Mac."[29]

MacSween's two terms as chair of the English department carried him through the 1960s and, as we have seen, they were both vital and challenging times for him. His activities as a teacher, writer and administrator are complex, compelling and sometimes contradictory. On the one hand he hired his former students because of their interest in creative writing and their anti-academic bent (the fact that they are all practising Catholics does not enter the question because at the time it was a given); on the other hand, he refused to let a Canadian literature course—proposed by the historian, Raymond MacLean—on the books of the department even as he judges the writing of Margaret Atwood in a literary contest. Furthermore, his pro-scholar and anti-academic stance—the terms scholar and academic were mutually exclusive for him—collapsed when it came to hiring five academic English (English) professors, four of whom were Catholic.

With the too-easy benefit of hindsight—and available theory, both post-colonial and otherwise—it is possible to understand and clarify some of MacSween's positions. His cultural nationalism, as we have seen, was deeply connected with his Catholic ideology; this proved both a handicap and a source of strength. He wished to nurture creative writing (i.e., Canadian writing) but he was also trapped—like many another colonial—in the old paradigm of British Literature, culture, canons and attitudes. Because of his strong identification with the university as an institution, he pays a personal price when he is demoted from the only administrative position he has ever held; and yet, it is this demotion that eventually frees up the writer and editor.

MacSween was fifty-five years old in 1970. A year after he lost his position as chair he founded a magazine, published his first and most ambitious collection of poems, started a novel and published numerous short stories, poems, reviews and essays. Losing his position— his place at the helm in the department—was painful for the teacher, educator, counsellor, and administrator, but it would be overwhelmingly beneficial for R. J. MacSween the poet, fiction writer, critic and editor.

VII

*T*he Forgotten World

*I*n October of 1971 MacSween published his first collection of poems, *the forgotten world*.[1] He was fifty-six years old. The poems were brought out locally with the financial help of the university and the editorial help and encouragement of friends such as Gertrude Sanderson, Pat Walsh and George Sanderson. It was Gertrude Sanderson—perhaps more than anyone else—who persuaded MacSween to publish his poetry: "I think I said to Father one night he was visiting that you should bring the pieces down and I'll type them and when you see them typed you can decide. All the poems in *the forgotten world* were there. In fact he was embarrassed because he said that some of them were very old poems."

It is not easy to date these poems, some of them may be as early as the 1950s, but the majority appear to have been written in the mid- to late sixties. MacSween himself confirmed Gertrude Sanderson's role in bringing the poems to press: "Gert typed out my poems and encouraged me to print them. She deserves a lot of credit for that, and she did all the proofreading for the magazine from the very beginning."[2] With the exception of the last title in the collection, "The Death of Ecclesia," the poems are written in lyric or short narrative form and are generally confined to one or two pages. Meditative in tone, much of the range and subject matter of this collection, and MacSween's other published work, was first characterized by Louis Dudek in his seminal essay on MacSween, "In the Tragic Mode":

> Now we begin to see the nature of this poetry. It is concerned with a
> variety of great themes and baffling questions: one can list about fifty
> topics of primary importance that are treated in the poems. I will just

proffer a good handful to give some idea of the scope and range of these: (1) The menace of technological progress, (2) the necessary return to ancient mythologies, (3) the meaning of poverty and asceticism, (4) the blindness of business culture, (5) the failure of communication between people, (6) the dying of the church in our time, (7) of Satan in the world (8) the nature of nature before the coming of man (9) heresies old and new, (10) Greek skepticism, (11) art as seduction, as self-projection, as aestheticism, etc., (12) regulations as chains on freedom, (13) poetry and barbarism, (14) Communism, Leninism, (15) the problems of old age, (16) chance as a process of nature, (17) the defects of education, (18) the world under God's eye, (19) each man's nature as a prison, (20) the suffering that is in the world, (21) the end of things; and so on, and so on."

After listing and commenting on many of these themes, Dudek goes on to insist, "that this kind of poetry leads to a recovery of the tragic sense. The degradation of all social and spiritual value in a civilization results in a deprivation for which only the simplest speech can be adequate, and in which a sense of the tragic loss is a perpetual burden one bears."[3] Dudek's listing of the above themes, and his critique and categorization of MacSween's poetry as tragic, provides a passageway into the poet's world. While this tragic awareness, this tragic stance, never completely disappears, it does become transformed—especially in the final collection and in his last unpublished poems—into something possessed of both equanimity and transcendence. Dudek was too shrewd a critic not to notice this, and in his essay he spoke of MacSween's confession of faith, of his despair, but also of his "radical return."

In *the forgotten world* collection, however, the poet-priest is a long way from radical return; though many themes that Dudek mentions are present here, almost all of them are subservient to what is the central focus of the collection: "the dying of the Church in our time." There is, as Dudek pointed out, "a deep sustaining unity of thought" in these poems, but there is also much rage, and at times an almost overwhelming tide of despair. If nothing else, *the forgotten world* can be read as one of the most profound, disturbing—and unique—spiritual autobiographies of the twentieth century. For those who knew MacSween personally, reading this often harrowing collection can indeed be painful: there are many instances, for example, when his own personal despair emerges and the reader is left contemplating the tremendous cost paid by this individual—by this poet-priest—for his belief, loyalty and obedience to his faith, culture and Church.

There are many poems in *the forgotten world* that chart the spiritual struggle MacSween had with the world and with himself. Eventually, a pattern emerges that enables us to discern what are essentially three approaches to grappling with the death of the Church in his time. The first and easiest to comprehend are those poems that explicitly state the theme—poems that concern themselves with the world overtly and directly. These include: "travelers should fear," "waiting," "the cave," "messages," "our garden," "the forgotten world," "the quality of art," "he will send fire, "obdurate mysteries," "the heretics," "in an early country," "the holy ones," "chasms," "squares of death," "the hermit" and, finally—and most explicitly—"the death of Ecclesia." Despite the pitfalls of simple reductionism—especially when dealing with poetry that is intellectual—it is fair to see these works as lyric notes on the advent of the modern secular world—they both lament and critique the end of the Christian era.

A common theme in this group is a wished-for return to the distant past or, at the very least, to a land beyond the reach of the urban and electronic imperative. Thus, in "waiting" the reader is enjoined to "smash television/cut wires, close roads/ curtail extra desires/ for food and clothing" all of this is done, we learn in the final stanza, so that we can "develop new rituals/to remind us of God." Similarly, "the cave" embraces a retreat from the world into "the dark chamber/a cave in the rock /where heretic and rebel/ have foraged for food." "Our garden" decries how we have destroyed our Eden with "acid air" and "carried our God/ into this furnace" until God is nothing more than a "withered man/a leather idol/fallen to one side." The solution once again is both physical and metaphysical flight, "we must drop all our belongings/and move to another land" and once we have arrived in this new land "we will rediscover our history." History here means the revivification, or rebirth, of God, of Christianity and, fundamentally, of the Church. This wish for a return to the past is not a wish bred out of simple nostalgia, nor is it the frustrated view of the reactionary; MacSween was no meliorist, but he did acknowledge some . progression in history.

"the forgotten world," the poem MacSween chose for the title of his collection, is somewhat less direct, but no less insistent on its message; it is a subtle and deceptively tranquil poem that beautifully describes—and to some extent envies—the natural world, the world of the animal kingdom:

> strange to be an animal
> to startle at a falling star

above to see the gigantic wheel of heaven
   creeping around the roof of night
to see without thought or comment
   this primeval wonder
      of order and silence

In the final stanza, the poet remarks, without comment, how the animal both feels and doesn't feel and how it is "unmoved/ by time and death." The poem is deliberately ambiguous, and we might wonder what MacSween is recording here: possibly the price that has been paid for our enlightenment, for the knowledge of good and evil; or, even simpler perhaps, the cost that accompanies our capacity for thought. Terry Eagleton has remarked that "to see the world aright is to see it in the light of its contingency. And this means seeing it in the shadow of its own potential non-being."[4] In a poem entitled "the fish," the brain, the intellect, is seen as a pitiful courier when "asked to carry into eternity/ the load of our suffering." This conflict between feeling and intellect is constant in the poetry; it is also a struggle that is never resolved.

Because of their public stance, these poems about the condition of the world and, more specifically, about the condition of the sacred and religious world, are easier for the reader to contemplate, to meditate upon than those poems of a more personal nature. We might wonder here if MacSween, consciously or not, felt that the solutions he was proposing were hopelessly utopian and ineffectual. In the poem "finality," for instance, the poet acknowledges and accepts the reality of the present world:

but to that past there's no return
   we could curse at the injustice
      of it all
   we're wounded to the heart
      by finality
our hearts rebel

In a poem entitled "questions and answers" the poet continues this dialogue with himself, admitting a helplessness but still persisting: "the answers I know/defenseless as they are/would turn me to the world/to challenge the world."

MacSween's heart does eventually "rebel" and, for a time at least, he collapses—there is a free fall that is also, paradoxically, a kind of desperate hanging on. The despair he experiences is partly brought on by his tragic vision of the world—a world in which his Church and his religion are slowly dissipating, fading out and becoming irrelevant. But we cannot help but suspect that the real forces behind his despair are personal, familial and Freudian—the fear of loneliness, ageing and death. But whatever their final inspiration, the poems that make up this group are numerous and compelling, and they include such works as, "when we wake" which ends with the poet, "spitting and coughing" to his "usual morning"; while in "bitter gall, sweet honey" the professor-priest confesses:

> I go back to my room
>   from under the quiet stars
>   a weaver to his loom
> and weave a bitter poem
>   to stop the drops that slide
>   from the spear-thrust in my side

The personal despair continues in poems like "the late spring" where the poet sadly acknowledges that:

> there are times
> when waking is torment
> turning from bed
> the sheets creased like ropes
> in my hands

MacSween's personal suffering in these years is given voice by this group of poems, and they make up a substantial part of *the forgotten world*. Most of them are powerful, if grim, meditations that explore questions most of us refuse to confront—let alone meditate on—until the end is upon us. It is more than a little disturbing to see this poet-priest, who dedicated so much of his life to helping and comforting others in times of stress and suffering, so ruthlessly examine and question his own self-worth without, it seems, anyone to turn to for comfort or counsel. To be somewhat cold, literary and aesthetic about it, many of these poems remind us of the sonnets of John Donne and, more recently, the last, haunting and despairing poems of Hopkins, sonnets MacSween knew all too well and taught throughout his life.

Once or twice in the collection poems do surface against this pervasive tide of despair, poems like "the fountain":

I am placed in a dark cell
I know silence and loneliness
darkness is normal
   if the eyes are closed

I have always shunned the peaks
   hid in the valleys
   the silent caves

there is a fountain in my head
   leaping with light
it will never stop
   even if my heart be still

this fountain sings God's name
   but makes no sound
I cannot feel it
if it should stop
   my life would end

The second stanza of this poem is as explicit as MacSween ever gets about his career, his life as artist, intellectual and priest. And while it is true that he shunned the peaks and lived away from fame and recognition, it is also a fact that he had little chance for these anyway. His choices were limited and circumscribed, but to a large extent they were also preordained. The poem's declaration of the importance of his faith both explains his life in the valleys and silent caves—his rooms and libraries—and acts, as well, as a small but crucial signpost of hope. There is a danger in reading too much into this lyric (and a few others like it), and we risk glibness if we see the poem and its declaration as healing and sustaining in a collection that is so often fraught with a deep and pervasive despair.[5]

Finally, MacSween's attempts to come to terms with the death of Ecclesia, the death of his church, in poems that are not, ostensibly at least, directly concerned with the subject. In poems such as "Vico," and "silence," historical figures are evoked as the poet-priest considers the lives of famous men for very specific and familiar ends. In "silence," for instance, we read about Beethoven in old age when his "music spoke with feigned assurance/within a wild complaint/ against time and death." The last two stanzas of the poem have a confessional feel to them, as if MacSween is speaking of himself:

and he himself unsure
   forcing the depths of memory
   to yield him just one chord
   that would restore his heaven
   bring back to plangent skies
   and planets spinning
   their praise of God forever

his dreaming was his own
   in a hollow land
   where steps were velvet
a vegetable land of textures
   and pains
   monotonous with light
when he died the only change
   was that his rage
   had ended

There is less identification with "Vico," but battling the world and time remain a constant: the old Italian philosopher is portrayed as "a fugitive figure/alarmed by time/ the rain of the past/pattering upon his back."

There are, of course, as Louis Dudek first pointed out, many other thematic concerns in MacSween's first collection: "from the jeweled garden" for instance—written almost fifty years ago—is prophetic of our present relationship with the animal world:

the world robs me of the lion
   the golden plague
   alive on the savannahs
no more the elephant
   shall trumpet
   among the thorn trees
nor the hippopotamus snort
   in the muddy rivers
the whale dies alone
   in an oily roll
   in the splayed spaces
   of the vast water
we are being robbed of friends

The poem is a form of protest verse, lines written out of desperation because of the state of things—the constant degradation of the planet, the destruction of the natural world. There is also a disturbing, if inevitable, element of the apocalyptic and post-apocalyptic in MacSween's verse—it is clearly meant as a warning, as a lesson. It is the poet as prophet pleading with us to clean up our act before it is too late, and like so many of the poems in *the forgotten world* it is an attack upon the triumph of materialism and the late-20th-century capitalism that Marx had hoped would exhaust itself.

In a review of Ted Hughes's collection of poems, *Crow,* MacSween acknowledged the break, the rift, between the poets of the 50s and 60s and their modern mentors: "Hughes has always appealed to the reader who is sick of the antiseptic cerebration of many modern poets whose intellectualism comes close to being a denial of life."[6] MacSween's relationship with the great moderns is complex and, on the surface at least, appears contradictory: he admired the poetry of Pound and Eliot—he taught them until he retired—and yet his own verse leans more towards the style—though not the content—of Hughes and his slightly more famous contemporary, Larkin. Above all, the verse seems to have its greatest affinity with writers such as Zbigniew Herbert, Czeslaw Milosz and Joseph Brodsky. Milosz's poems have been described as modest yet profound meditations on the fate of humanity and culture, and his best-known work, *The Captive Mind* (1953), is a meditation on the spiritual condition of modern man under communist totalitarianism.

Louis Dudek, a second generation Polish-Canadian and fluent speaker of Polish, may have had Milosz in mind when he first noted the characteristics of MacSween's verse, but whatever the affinities, it is clear from poems like "the forgotten world" that MacSween's gift is for meditative yet explicit verse. Though the language and the diction are often commonplace, the word selection is precise and the important questions about the grand narratives are always addressed.

In the same issue of *TAR* that published "forgotten world" MacSween reviewed an anthology of British poetry and took the occasion to make a few statements about the art of verse. It is a kind of mini-manifesto and he may have consciously wanted this in the first issue of his magazine both as an encouragement and warning to his readers and writers:

> One thing stands out: there is among most of these poets an inadequate dedication to the work at hand. There is, instead, an inordinate dedication to themselves as the enlighteners of the present. One gets the impression that the modern world is busy producing poets who are not truly interested in poetry; this judgment may be severe but I believe it is accurate. It is not enough to be young, it is not enough to know four letter words, it is not enough to have experiences. These are common

to all. What is necessary is a grasp upon the art of arranging words for the expression of truth and feeling. Behind all modern movements looms the gigantic shadow of Ezra Pound. His presence may not be acknowledged but it cannot be denied. The fierce individualism of his life can be duplicated by many; by itself this may be only a form of self-indulgence. But how many can duplicate the labours of his early training? It is known how he sucked the vital matter from his early studies, how he sat at the feet of those he considered his masters, how he traveled to learn new languages and literatures, how he responded to every living spark in every darkened corner of his world. This humility before the task at hand is what the young poets have to learn. Their master was and is the eternal student of the unknown.[7]

It is an interesting passage and an uncharacteristically polemical one for MacSween. Although a generous critic, he was exacting, and the style of poetry and prose that most appealed to him had its roots, its beginnings, in the classical tradition. A champion of free verse, he also saw the need for formalism; so in the classroom he would praise the lyrical flamboyance, the adjectival brilliance of a Dylan Thomas, but it was not the style he most admired or chose to write himself. Similarly, he would teach almost all of Gerard Manley Hopkins, including "The Wreck of the Deutschland" marvelling at passages such as the famous, "I am soft sift/ In an hourglass," but Hopkins would be criticized because he often overdid his sprung rhythm, straying too far from the cadences of human speech.

There are, of course, great risks with the kind of poetry MacSween wrote—the poetry of plain statement—and in his review of Ted Hughes' *Crow* he noted some of these risks himself. One evident danger is that plainness can become all, so that all you may be left with is banality, or, in one of MacSween's own favourite coinages, an "obviousity." In prose, too, as in poetry, MacSween championed simplicity, and so Hemingway was one of his favourite models for the nature of good prose:

> It is many things, but it has at least this quality: transparency. It does not make a screen between mind and mind. It carries the reader with a subtle authority along a train of thought or narrative. Above all, it lacks idiosyncrasy.[8]

MacSween read *Ulysses* diligently, but without affection—he always had a love/ hate relationship with Joyce. More than a little of this was related to the Irishman's anti-clerical stance, but part of it was the question of style, or rather styles. (This feeling of love and hate did not abate with the years, as late as 1987 he quoted passages to me over the phone from an article by Martin Amis. Amis was kicking at Joyce for being spoiled by money, for being the teacher's pet; MacSween, with more than a little delight, agreed, but then he quoted with reverence a passage singled out by Amis: "The heaventree of stars hung with humid nightblue fruit.")

Terry Eagleton, among others, has written about the flamboyant prose tradition found in the Irish. In *Heathcliffe and the Great Hunger*, he singles out *Finnegan's Wake* as a great post-colonial text, a book that both enriches the English language and stems its corrupting imperial influence; it is "the non-Irish speaking Irish author's way of being unintelligible to the British." For Eagleton, the Irish Joyce appropriated the English language for his own non-English ends, and "In thus estranging the English language in the eyes of its proprietors, he struck a blow on behalf of all of his gagged and humiliated [Gaelic] ancestors."[9] MacSween's new world Scots heritage—insofar as it is relevant—was a culturally and politically assimilated one; he did not, as his life and work illustrate, think in terms of ancient or modern culture and politics. There are many reasons for this, but the underlying and simple one is that his Catholicism was the main source of his culture. MacSween's religion made him aware from very early on in his life that he had a specific cultural place and voice in the world. It can be argued, of course, that there is a fear of being provincial or parochial in his writing; that never having really left home, having hid in the valleys and caves, he was reluctant to write in the tradition of high realism, or even naturalism, that his background (and sometimes his subject) so clearly demanded. Reluctant, too, perhaps to render the world he came from—the world of his neighbours, family and friends—in the language and idiom of the parish. The writings of Patrick Kavanagh and Seamus Heaney, of Alden Nowlan and David Adams Richards and, especially of Alistair MacLeod, are all old- and new-world examples of how successful, appealing and authentic this kind of writing can be.

It is an old debate as to what comes first: writing about home or writing about the outside world. The Irish novelist George Moore once remarked how "art must be parochial in the beginning to be cosmopolitan in the end." His fellow countryman Thomas Kettle saw things differently: "My only counsel to Ireland is that, in order to become deeply Irish, she must become European." We remember too that one of the tragic heroes of Yeats's great poem "Easter 1916" was Thomas MacDonagh—an English professor whose last class at University College, Dublin, before he joined the ranks of the Rising to shoot at British Tommies, was devoted to his beloved Jane Austen. Of course each colony, or former colony, of British cultural imperialism reacts differently, and there is always the individual talent that is both a part of and separate from the tradition—especially when the tradition is fledgling.[10] The scholar MacSween, for whatever reasons, very quickly outpaced the artist, and that this happened very early on, at a time when young MacSween decided to become—like so many who suffer from the cultural cringe—Derek Walcott's ideal reader:

> One could abandon writing
> for the slow-burning signals
> of the great, to be, instead,
> their ideal reader, ruminative,
> voracious, making the love of masterpieces
> superior to attempting
> to repeat or outdo them,
> and be the greatest reader in the world.[11]

How many schoolteachers could post this manifesto on their walls? Walcott, of course, is writing from a post-colonial perspective, a position that artist and critic MacSween would not appreciate until much later in his life. As we have seen, in discussing his criticism of Canadian writers, MacSween was handicapped, to a certain extent, by the very Catholic culture that gave him the opportunity, if not the will and desire, to write and teach in the first place. The suppression of the ego, of the self, the acceptance of the status quo, the belief in the literature of empire—British, American, or Roman—and, finally, his almost complete isolation as a poet and writer, all combined to limit and, in many respects, determine the kind of artist he became. But even with these limitations, the quality and quantity—especially of his poetry—is still remarkable, especially given the conscious and unconscious battles he had to wage with himself, his colleagues and his culture.

Admittedly, it is hard to place MacSween in an either-or context: on one hand, he always came across, first and foremost, as an intellectual of enormous intensity, range and sagacity; the writer—or perhaps more specifically, the intuitive artist—always came second to the scholar and reader; but on the other hand, he also always insisted, like his hero Ezra Pound, that creative writing was a much more important endeavour—a far greater achievement and calling—than any critical, historical, scholarly or philosophical work. The man and artist contained contradictions. Eventually, the artist—especially the poet—recovers control from the scholar/reader, putting him firmly in the back seat, but never quite kicking him out of the car entirely. The artist could hardly leave the intellectual by the roadside, not after having come so far with him, and having learned and endured so much.

Rod MacSween, the reader, felt as much at home in the Gotham Book Mart in New York as he did in the kitchens of Cape Breton, but in his art these two worlds would never meet or merge, at least not in any recognizable or meaningful way. The unique cultural world he came from would be left for others to record. That two of the first Cape Breton writers to record their culture with authentic artistic voices, were also MacSween's two best creative-writing students—Alistair MacLeod and Sheldon Currie—is something he surely must have reflected upon. In MacLeod's stories and his award-winning novel, *No Great Mischief,* we find a fidelity to Cape Breton's heritage in the everyday poetic details of the life itself. Here is a passage from "The Boat," his first story to gain wide recognition:

> The most important room in our house was one of those oblong old-fashioned kitchens heated by a wood and coal-burning stove. Behind the stove was a box of kindlings and beside it a coal scuttle. A heavy wooden table with leaves that expanded or reduced its dimensions stood in the middle of the floor. There were five wooden homemade chairs which had been chipped and hacked by a variety of knives. Against the east wall, opposite the stove, there was a couch which sagged in the middle and had a cushion for a pillow, and above it a shelf which contained matches, tobacco, pencils, odd fish hooks, bits of twine, and a tin can filled with bills and receipts. The south wall was dominated by a window which faced the sea and on the north there was a five-foot board which bore a variety of clothes hooks and the burdens of each. Beneath the board there was a jumble of odd footwear, mostly of rubber. There was also, on this wall, a barometer, a map of the marine area and a shelf which held a tiny radio. The kitchen was shared by all of us and was a buffer zone between the immaculate order of the other rooms and the disruptive chaos of the single room that was my father's.

This describes a kitchen MacSween would have known or visited often in White Point, Beaver Cove, Ingonish, Glace Bay or New Waterford; it is also one he would never have thought of recording, of placing in his memory for the background of his art. It is arguable that MacSween was deracinated, cut off from a living Gaelic heritage, a tradition he was encouraged to abandon if he wanted to escape the working-class culture of his childhood and youth. We have seen, too, that part of the price of "getting out," of becoming a priest, meant that he would embrace "high culture" and that he would not be able to look back at his own world to draw out a single line of beauty. When he does try to write about his ancestors, to make contact with the past (as MacLeod so successfully does) the connection is weak, the images are vague, and the voice indistinct and unremarkable. MacSween himself acknowledged his inability to write this way, and the one poem he wrote about these people—his ancestors—he believed was "not very good." He was grateful but disappointed that Lesley Choice had chosen it for his *Cape Breton Collection*. He understood that Lesley was looking for more than local colour, but he also knew that he was not the writer to provide it; it was not his style, nor, in many respects, did he regard it as his culture. The poem is entitled "long swords" and I quote it in full not because of what it says about the battles of the Celts, but rather because of how it reflects on MacSween's own battles at the time of writing, his continuing wars with the university administration, his colleagues and the wider world:

> the Celts had long swords
> for duel and for battle
> we can imagine their stance
> > legs wide apart
> > braced firmly
> > like an overeager golfer
> we can see the muscles strain
> > agony on the face
> left arm in the shield
> > right arm swinging at the avenger
> > at a shrinking enemy
>
> it was not so with warriors
> > who fought at close quarters
> > and aimed at complete destruction
> the Roman sword was short
> > could annihilate ten
> > to the Celt's one
> the Roman stopped the long sword
> > with the shield's edge
> > then stabbed quickly
> > for the face
> his equipment was developed
> > from the gladiator's
> in the arena warm with blood and sweat
> he learned all the tricks
> > whereby man can survive
> > against enemies
> > as skilled and as desperate
> > as himself

and so it is with everyone
    of his type and caliber
at a distance they are helpless to destroy
      but close at hand
      they can extract one's life
      without delay or bungling
      and in their hands
      the knives
      can scarcely be seen

On the surface the poem deals with one of MacSween's life-long loves: his study of the classical world and, in particular, the Roman Empire. The first stanza is, I think, unintentionally comic: the Celts playing a round of golf could be the inspiration for a Gary Larson cartoon, or at least a scene from Monty Python. It then becomes even funnier when we remember that, yes, indeed, they—the Scots—did invent golf. There's not much comfort for the Celtophile in the second stanza either, where MacSween's Roman heroes quickly win the day over his beloved ancestors. There is, however, nothing funny about the third stanza, which seems out of place in the poem. It risks cliché of course (as does the whole poem) with its *Et tu Brute*, but it hints at how betrayed he must have felt by his colleagues, some of whom were good friends, not at his demotion in the English department, but rather at their insistence that the world of the university as he had known it was now over. The college too, it seems, without his really fully accepting it, was becoming a part of the forgotten world.

Fig. 47 MacSween in his office on the fourth floor of Nicholson Tower, 1972. Note the picture of the poet, Ezra Pound, in the background. Courtesy Stewart Donovan.

The reception of the *forgotten world* collection by MacSween's family, friends, colleagues and students was mixed. Some, including his fellow priests and nuns, found the poetry difficult, sombre and depressing; many of them, not unfairly, were looking for the comfort and realism of the old kitchens, for a connection with their past; nostalgia, like humour, helps us take the tragedy on board, even though there is the risk that we might ignore the suffering entirely. Looking back, it is easy for those who knew MacSween to understand the hostile and indifferent reaction his collection received: it was hard, if not impossible, to link the man—celebratory, humorous and upbeat—with the often despairing verse that dominates the collection.[12]

The critic George Steiner, reflecting on the present age—the era of mass media, the death of the book, the decline in educational standards, the need for silence in a world gone mad with noise—remarked that the Dark Ages of the medieval and pre-medieval period probably weren't as dark as we've portrayed them to be. MacSween has a lot in common with Steiner, and he expresses similar sentiments in a poem like "waiting":

> we're gathering into cells
>   a few to each group
> we'll close our eyes to weather
>   the colours of artificial things
> we'll raise walls of crude stone
>   the real walls inside us
> for now we feel
>   that we alone matter
> ears closed to the rush
>   and scurry outside

As the poem continues we are encouraged to "send no letters" and to "read only the few books/ we happen to own." We are also told to "write no new books" partly, it seems, because there will be "no time in the evening" and also because "outage" has come: "the sun our only light." This "outage" is no act of nature, no ice storm, tornado or El Niño, but rather the active blackout sought by what will be a new generation of Luddites. The narrator, as it turns out, is against technology for a specific reason: not because it will take his job away, but rather because it is responsible for his loss of contact with God, with the eternal—the poem is another direct attack on the culture of materialism. The brilliant and notorious German existentialist philosopher, Martin Heidegger, in response to the state of the world, famously said, shortly before he died, that "only a god can save us now." MacSween, unlike Heidegger, always had faith, but many of his poems reflect a similar concern about technology, about materialism, about those who do not reflect on their being and non-being and finally, about those who feel the need to continually question the concept of "progress."

One of the most surprisingly influential writers in English of the last few decades has been the British travel-writer Bruce Chatwin. Chatwin died young, at forty-seven, of AIDS. His masterwork, *The Songlines*, is a book about the Aboriginal people of Australia and its central theme is "the nature of human restlessness." There are many parallels between Chatwin's work and MacSween's, not least of which is their call for a return to a new asceticism if the planet is to survive. In the opening of *The Songlines,* Chatwin has a sympathetic and poetic portrait of an aboriginal Catholic priest, a man of God who is also a man of the people, a man of his tribe. He is a figure who would have appealed to MacSween, though as a man of action he has more in common with MacSween's mentor, Moses Coady, than with the poet. I mention Chatwin only to highlight the prophetic and contemporary nature of MacSween's verse. Chatwin of course went from world-famous art critic to iconoclast: a man who favoured the nomads who walked in the shadow of the pyramids to the great piles of stones themselves. He hated empires and all that they stood for. MacSween's position, like George Steiner's, is different: without civilization there is no art, no literature, no painting, sculpture, architecture or cinema. The great cities, in Chatwin's view, are killing us, and the great empires—the Church not least among them—continue to crush the voices of the "other."[13]

The "other" of course includes women. MacSween dedicated much of his life to serving women as both students and nuns, but his poetry, like Steiner's criticism, belongs firmly in the classic and often patriarchal tradition. MacSween was not unaware of the women's movement, and one of his favourite writers was the novelist, Ivy Compton-Burnett, a lesbian. She was not, however, a lesbian writer, someone who consciously spoke and wrote of her sexuality the way, for example, the poet Adrienne Rich so clearly does. By and large, the poetry contained in *the forgotten world* is more public than private; it is, as Dudek has shown, a poetry concerned with the tradition, with grand narratives; a poetry that concentrates too on "civilization," its triumph, costs, contradictions and at times its potentially apocalyptic end.

MacSween spent the vast majority of his life in obscurity, an artist hiding in the valleys and caves, and although much of this was not of his choosing, some of it clearly was. In a poem entitled "the quality of art" he shuns those who "drop the names of poets/ and music makers." In a world where everyone is now an "artist" his choice is one of self-imposed exile:

> it would be good to return
> to a little colony
>   deserted even by music
> to dig in the earth
>   and fondle worms
>   would be a blessing

to fight with a stubborn root
to watch trout swim for shelter
  beneath the brownish bank
  would be heaven
rather these than have an incestuous
  drawing together
  into streets and rooms
  where the air vibrates with
  the voices of the dead
  and the living speak
  a dead tongue

MacSween's poetry first received national recognition in *The Globe and Mail*[14] on June 8, 1985. Louis Dudek, who reviewed his book, *Called From Darkness*, later wrote two in-depth articles on MacSween's poetry and fiction. The first was published in the Jesuit magazine *Compass* in July of 1992, two years after MacSween's death, and then both articles appeared in a collection of essays later that year.[15] Dudek's acknowledgement of MacSween's work is significant. One of this country's best poets—and arguably one Canada's best literary critics—Dudek's is no small voice. The critic Bruce Powe, in his collection of essays, *A Climate Charged*[16] once singled out Dudek for high praise, calling him our best literary critic—it is an assessment that MacSween would have agreed with.[17]

In MacSween's poetry, especially his later work, Dudek found a sensibility very much attuned to his own, a mind that asked the great questions in simple and straightforward language—as "straight as the Greeks" in Dudek's phrase. To be sure, there are many differences between the two men: Dudek, grew up in the urban and sophisticated worlds of Montreal and New York, in touch with the famous writers and critics of his time (including Lionel Trilling, his old teacher), and he is responsible for promoting many of our finest poets—Irving Layton and Leonard Cohen not the least among them. But both men were polymaths, extremely well-read in many fields besides history and literature. One of these shared fields is the domain of science: "So Father MacSween, in his first book of poetry, *the forgotten world* (1971), takes up the question at the heart of science, the concept of matter, and its difficult or impossible relation to life and the light of the spirit." Dudek then quotes from "obdurate mysteries":

tortured by excursions
  into realms of light
we turn

to the obdurate mysteries
of matter
these rebuff us with a darkness
equal to the smother of light

there is a kind of happiness
in turning away from light
it has long enticed us
with unfulfilled promises
we begin to despise the birds
who fly only short spaces
but continue to fly

we turn to matter
the home from which we came
in that long done darkness
of the beginning
we should like to stamp our feet
with disapproval
of that obnoxious parent
who sent us out in the primeval dawn
to bring back God

Poems like these are clearly provocative; they ask the epic questions in the simplest language without expectation of an answer. And these are the same questions posed so often by Einstein and his disciples—figures like Stephen Hawking. Another of MacSween's scientific poems, and one that has a special relevance for us in this antibiotic world of AIDS and SARS, is his prophetic "viruses":

viruses should not be considered too long
they inhabit an ancestor world
which we have passed long ago
now we hate to look back
into that chasm
containing many answers
as though a vast underworld
were suddenly revealed
to our startled eyes
as though stones had intelligence
and water analytical power
and all the solidities of life
had puffed and heaved and blown away

their very simplicity is their power
like the soul they are simple things
hence powerful in unity
powerful in being what they are
hence they will resist destruction
and gorge themselves at our expense

to them we oppose
  our bitter complexity
    of mind and body
the earth too has produced this plant
  cathedral of flesh and bone
and flung it upward
  through millennia of effort
    from its teeming surface
it rings with bells and prayers
  contradictions and curses
    searching for the unity
      that sings in every cell

we are vulnerable
  as a beaten army
our captain defeated and betrayed
we stumble in the long night
  die in the morning

Despite its somewhat bleak ending, the poem is a good example of MacSween's achieved style: in lyric form the poem condenses millennia—the material of the epic—into the briefest of moments. The poem is, in fact, a brief history of time, a snapshot of our short stay amid the stars. There is a similar poem by Robert Frost, one of MacSween's favourites, called "The Bear" that contains the lines: "The telescope at one end of his beat, / And at the other end the microscope, / Two instruments of nearly equal hope, / And in conjunction given quite a spread." "Their very simplicity is their power" might be the motto to place above all of MacSween's verse, but what accompanies this simplicity is the range of his poetry, its broad arch that encompasses so much thought, time and space.

By any standard, *the forgotten world* is a remarkable first collection of poems: its consistent tone, the sweep of its subject matter, its handling of classic and modern verse forms—all of this signals a mature, confident and compelling voice. The collection has a unity of purpose and a uniqueness of character unseen in Canadian literature, both because of its subject matter and because of its author—a Roman Catholic priest. The book, then, among other things, records the beginnings of a spiritual journey: MacSween was not, in any traditional sense, a confessional poet, but there is certainly a confessional dimension to his work. Indeed, readers—friends, colleagues and relatives mostly—often complained about the preoccupation with death and dying, with the suffering and despair so often found in the poems. Their complaints were not unfounded. If MacSween had put some of his humour in these poems, especially the cutting and ironic humour he was known for, the sardonic humour we associate with poetry of this nature—poetry by Hardy, Housman or his beloved Larkin—his fans and friends might have been better able to take on board the verse and the suffering it records. But looking back at who MacSween was in the late 1950s and 60s and, more importantly perhaps, where he had come from, is it any wonder that this poetry would record what it does? It is important to remember, too, that *the forgotten world* is the beginning of MacSween's poetic journey and not its end; in the years and collections to follow, the voice will become more confident and less despairing until, at the end, the poet-priest achieves a serene equanimity in matters of the spirit. While striving for this Confucian-like balance and this Zen composure, MacSween demonstrates a profound willingness to reconcile himself with the world, even as he battles it, grieves for it and inevitably transcends it, in order that it may, like all things material, be left behind.

VIII   *T*he Antigonish Review

*T*hough he was no longer chair of his department, MacSween continued to teach a full course load to very large classes; and he would do so until he turned 65 years old. In an interview with his colleague and former student, Pat Walsh, MacSween spoke about what he felt constituted a good professor:[1]

> Well, first of all, I think he should try to make his subject loved by the students. He can't be dull, and he can't have views on life in general that do not elevate the life of the student, do not increase his spiritual vitality. In every aspect of life his views must inspire and incline towards spiritual freedom. And if he hasn't got these, it makes no difference what his learning may be because he will be a failure as a professor. The actual matter of what is taught in the classroom is no mystery. It can be assimilated by any energetic person. This is dangerous ground, of course. Anyway, the teacher needs broadness of vision, a vision that to some degree resembles the visions of the great writers he deals with. He can't go into the classroom and talk like a dolt about writers who aren't and weren't dolts. He can't teach like a reactionary about writers who are always forward-looking, and he can't teach with cruelty in dealing with writers who always taught kindness, generosity and so on. So, it's a big order, but most of that order is not concerned with literature alone.

MacSween's style in the classroom could be broadly described as a version of the Socratic question-and-answer, with the touch of a stand-up comedian—in other words it was driven and defined by humour. In the interview with Walsh, he also spoke about the immense enjoyment he got from teaching; he also addressed his use of humour:

The most satisfaction is teaching. I don't know if anybody realizes how much fun I get out of a class. In fact, it's the nearest thing to a Charlie Chaplin show. We do so much laughing that—well, I'll give you an example. I walked into the last class one year, it must be ten years ago now—and I saw a student in the back row whom I hadn't seen before. I thought he had been skipping class all year and had come to the very last one, so I told him to get out. He went out. He waited for me after class and he said, "I'm not in your class at all, but I was in the class next door and all year long we were listening to this class laughing, so I decided I'd come in to find out what it was all about, and you kicked me out." That was Professor Joseph; he now teaches at the College of Cape Breton.

MacSween's humour in the classroom was made up of several elements: wit, the quick and often cutting remark, the nickname/foil/ straight man/woman and, finally, his reliance on the absurd. The first of these elements could be very funny, and often students would join in: once, for example, while discussing the seven deadly sins in relation to a poem, a young woman at the front of the class asked in credulous tones if lust were a sin? MacSween looked up at the class and asked, "Did you hear that? She doesn't believe lust is a sin." A football player at the back of the room immediately asked if he could have her phone number. Students knew they were running a risk in his class, they might be chosen to play the straight man/woman, but it was a risk most of them were willing to take. The list of students who wanted to get into his classes, but couldn't be accommodated, was almost as long as, if not longer than, the list of those who did. Sometimes of course his humour, his wit, betrayed him, and he said things he later regretted to students who were shy or vulnerable. He spoke about one of these regrettable slips of the tongue in his old age:[2]

A big guy with a shock of red hair, very red. I knew him in New Waterford as a Boy Scout cub and I liked him. So a number of years later the boy grew up and he came to St. FX and was very friendly. Whenever I met him I recognized him right away. This day I'm teaching and you know how hard that modern poetry is, to explain those poems. I was grinding away at some poem trying to explain it and I look down and this fellow has his book open but he's not looking at it. So I said why aren't you reading your book. And he said I've no glasses. And I said to the class (I knew what he meant), but I said to the class, "Look at this [his name] he grew up in New Waterford, he went school, he was in school for about 12 years, he came to college, he's been in college now 2 years and he can't read without glasses and he has no glasses." And he said, "Oh, Father, I don't mean that, I have two pair in my room." And I said "One for each head." Don't forget the big red head—the big shock of red hair. He took it all right there, I thought. But that was, say, October and at Xmas time after I returned from New Waterford or wherever I was, [the student] knocked at my door and he comes in. He was coming from New Glasgow and he called in (he had left my class shortly after that two-headed episode and he got a job in New Glasgow), and he told me how much he minded that remark. Probably because he'd been made fun of in school for his red hair.

Similar incidents occurred throughout his teaching years, a more recent one concerning another student who appeared not to be paying attention in class:

I asked the student if he'd had his breakfast because I thought he was biting his nails. He was a superior student and superior around the campus. He came to my office and was furious with me for accusing him of that dirty habit. And I said to him, did you tell anybody else about this? Yeah, I told all my friends about it. I said, that's a shame, because in 20 or 30 years when they remember you, all they'll remember is that I accused you of eating your fingernails because you'd had no breakfast. They won't remember another thing about you, so try your best to play this down. I'm sorry that you made such a fuss over it. It threw him right back on his heels. He came in to blame me, then he started to apologize. I was half serious, you know, that's the kind of thing that people would remember. I was sorry though, and I discovered later on why he was so mad because he was such a high-class student.

And I had a young woman in class years ago, a MacDonald from downtown, her average was always in the 90s and lo and behold I suddenly get her in religion class. It must have been some special arrangement—she was the only woman there. Next to her was Kyte Gillis who is now Fr. Kyte Gillis. Anyway, Kyte Gillis and she wouldn't stop talking and I wanted to call him up and put him in the front row for that, but I couldn't because I didn't know his name, so I had to pick on her—the perfect student! So I said [students name], I've stood enough of this. Come up here and sit in the front row. And [the student] who was the perfect student, to be shamed in front of everyone, and she came up blushing red and just astonished that anyone would accuse her. Oh, I often had to pick on the wrong person in class because I didn't know their name.

By all accounts, MacSween mellowed with age, but there can be little doubt that incidents such as the ones described above left a lasting impression on the undergraduates. It was an attempt to keep order, to control the large class, but it came at a price. Anecdotes still persist: not many years ago a former student of my own struck up a conversation with a fellow Maritimer he had met in a bar in downtown Toronto. Noticing his fellow Maritimer's X ring, MacSween's named soon surfaced, the former X man was not impressed: "the man was an autocrat."[3]

There is no denying the presence of wounded students, but they seem very much to have been the exception, rather than the rule. More typical of MacSween's legacy in the classroom, of his quips and nicknames, was his story of the student with long legs in the front row:

> You know, you see flies on tables and they're going like this with their front legs. So I called him "the fly." And about a year later I was going across the square to my car and I met this guy. "Hello Father," he said. "Hello," I said, "Do I know you?" "I'm the fly," he said. He didn't mind the name. He liked it.

Whether or not "the fly" was a Cape Bretoner, MacSween certainly was and the tradition of nick-naming almost everyone continued unabated in Cape Breton long after his death.

MacSween also loved it when a student would catch him out; it didn't happen very often, I only remember one occasion: we were reviewing Melville's masterpiece "Bartleby the Scrivener" and MacSween asked a student if he would summarize the plot; the student replied in the famous refrain of Bartleby himself: "I would prefer not to." MacSween loved it and (jokingly) said, even though it was September, that the student had just passed the course. It could also be hazardous to venture an insight as I, personally experienced: asked what we thought of Yeats's "The Lake Isle of Innisfree," I replied that the poem seemed escapist—MacSween quickly turned on me and demanded, "Is that written in your book?" An indignant young man, I replied with a rather surly no. There were risks. But the humour, the absurd, the laughter were all used for the serious business of teaching, as, again, he told Pat Wash:

> I expect them to be pleased with what we're doing. No, I expect them to be wide-awake, and that's the purpose of the fun. And I mustn't exaggerate this. It's all spontaneous, spur-of-the-moment stuff. It keeps them alive. But then as for the literature and its effect upon them, first of all, I try to make them see the joy of it all, that there is a pleasure in doing a poem, but not pleasure that gives a laugh, but a kind of passive enjoyment in seeing something well done. The same pleasure that you get from watching a horse gallop or a deer go across a pasture. They are both fine works, well-organized works. The poem is well-organized too, it's beautifully put together, and there's an aesthetic enjoyment in the reading of it. As for the subject matter of the poems and the stor-

ies; it should always be something that hits you vitally. It should touch life; it should teach life. You should always have to stop and say, "My God, that's true." And so long as you get the aesthetic pleasure from it, plus the idea that these things are not toys but pointers to thoughts and emotions, to the vital areas of life, then you've got it.

MacSween took other risks in the classroom, too: when he taught Philip Larkin's signature poem "This Be the Verse" or Ezra Pound's fertility "Canto XXXIX," he usually approached a student before class—male or female—and asked them if they would mind reading the poem aloud. He always insisted that poetry should be read aloud. Larkin's poem begins with the lines: "They fuck you up your mom and dad" while Pound's contained the lines: "Girls talked there of fucking, beasts talked there of eating." Inevitably, the class would break up in laughter and while MacSween tried to keep a straight face, it was all but impossible. For a Catholic priest to present these poems and analyze the use and purpose of language in artistic writing in a small Nova Scotia town in the 1960s and 70s was daring and unconventional, to say the least.

MacSween's other favourite classroom texts besides poems were collections of short stories and novellas. He admired the Russian tradition of narrative so much—in particular Tolstoy, Dostoevski and Chekov—that he often put a supplementary text of their writing on the course. When Malcolm Muggeridge, the English journalist and authority on Dostoevski, received an honourary degree from St. FX in the 1980s he was greatly impressed by MacSween's knowledge and insights into his favourite writer.[4]

IN 1974, a fellow Cape Bretoner who had grown up a few streets away from MacSween, the Hollywood director Daniel Petrie, received an honourary degree from St. FX. Petrie, in his convocation address, urged the undergraduates to take part in the media revolution. MacSween was a student of Marshall McLuhan, and like him he had an optimistic side about the nature and possibilities of mass media. In the 1970s, however, MacSween, now in his late fifties, turned all of his energies towards print, towards writing and the promotion of fellow writers. The classroom was there to provide the audience that he needed—the human contact that helped to nourish and sustain him—but his focus in these years was, as it had always been, on the written word.

MacSween published two more volumes of poetry in the 1970s: *double shadows* (1973) and *the secret city* (1977). The themes that Louis Dudek highlighted in *the forgotten world* continue to be explored, but the voice is more subdued, the verse even subtler: the title of the collection comes from a poem entitled "eclipse." A total eclipse of the sun took place in the mid-1970s, and one of the best places for viewing it was Antigonish. The singer, Carly Simon, bestowed a pop fame on the event with her hit song "You're So Vain" addressed, as fans will remember, to another famous pop star, her ex-husband, James Taylor—who flew his new jet to Nova Scotia to watch the sun disappear. Father MacSween was also observing the rare mid-summer-day darkness:

> the eclipsed sun is dark
> its perimeter blazes in a crown of fire
> the leaves have double shadows
> the air is cold
> birds tremble and lament
>   in the thick branches
> in our minds anxious dreams flourish
>   beyond understanding

Once again, as with the forgotten world, the theme of the end of the world, of apocalypse, emerges:

> that fateful dark will come again
>   perhaps too late
>   for us to learn from darkness
>   of a great light
>   that creatured us
>   far in the long ago

In poems like this MacSween is clearly attempting to reconcile science and faith, while in poems like "streak of light," the poet-priest reaffirms his own faith:

> within myself a shudder of light
>   an arc that is my own
> it can never be taken from me
> it would remain
>   even if the sun went out

This affirmation of faith is heartening in *double shadows*, as the poetry—once again, like *the forgotten world*—still proclaims the essentially tragic nature of the human condition. And while there is still no humour here, there are, thankfully, more moments of stillness and beauty: moments where the poet-priest is more accepting of the world, even though he is still a long way from being reconciled to it. In poems like "the fern" brief glimpses are given of a pristine summer woods, as yet uncontaminated, where the poet guides us and

> we walk among the ferns
> in summer weather
> over the black floor
> and the green feather

In the stanzas of the "wild rose," too, we discover with the poet how,

> the old poets have lied
> it is too strange and sweet
> for all their songs

> I reach my hand among the thorns
> the old poets have lied
> they are too many and too sharp
> for all their tears

There is still much reaching amid the thorns in *double shadows*, and the theme of despair inaugurated in *the forgotten world* is intensified in this collection and made more personal. If some readers are uncertain as to whether or not MacSween went through a period of depression when writing his first collection of poems, there can be little doubt that *double shadows* records one. The first and last poems in the volume seem to evoke a personal crisis, and convey a tragic sense of loneliness, loss and, ultimately, failure:

> death will come to betray
> > my steady vigilance
> render inane
> > my life-long deference

> as I watch at the cliff's edge
> > suppressing anger
> challenging the pledge
> > of the grim marauder

> my labouring heart cannot
> > comfort my ghost
> as it waits a sad spirit
> > in its igloo of frost

I see again adolescence
the middle span
I stretch farther my senses
to where I began

clouds darken lights falter
my soul goes down
the stone close to the water
will soon drown

"the day's harvest" is even bleaker than "the stone," both in its details and in its subdued and all but defeated stance:

I stride the pavements
speaking to masks
and gargoyles
glancing at the cold clouds
feeling the freezing rain

after evening meal
there is darkness
the roof hides the stars
books are clouds
that hide me from the moon
and other wheels of night

sleep calls with its vague ghosts
the sea swirls around me
its sighing life
I close my eyes
clasping in my arms
the harvest of my day
a breast of sighs

Few of MacSween's poems are so personal and so sad. It is not improbable, as Dudek and others have suggested, that MacSween was suffering from clinical depression at this time, a depression partly brought on by the decline of his church, the loss of his position at the university and finally and most critically by his advancing age and deteriorating health. Regarding this last factor, MacSween had an almost pathological fear of doctors, a fear that went so far as to drive him to borrowing other peoples' prescriptions for penicillin. It is well known, too, that many priests and nuns—especially of his generation—feared doctors and hospitals because of the loss of privacy and the personal, physical exposure.

It was at about the time that these poems were being written that MacSween was tested and operated on for a small melanoma. His close friend, Pat Walsh, remembered that he seemed to take it in stride. He was in fact much more relaxed than his friends, as Pat recalled: "I realized for the first time in my life that he was going to die. And if a mind like Father's is subject to death what hope is there for the rest of us." Perhaps MacSween did feel he did not have long to live; if productivity is a measure of the fear of death, then the professor-priest was certainly battling the clock. Consider this: between 1971 and 1977 he publishes three collections of poetry, a volume of short stories, a novel, dozens of reviews and essays and 24 issues of *The Antigonish Review*; he also wrote, beginning in 1968, and battled—battled is *le mot juste*—to have three more novel manuscripts published.[5] We remember, too, that MacSween was teaching three full courses—usually averaging seventy to a hundred students per class—plus summer school, and counselling at Mount St. Bernard; and—last but not least—reading books, many, many books. Even if you use the argument that priests have no family life, and hence lots of time to themselves, it is still a staggering amount of work for a man who was also often out visiting his friends and relations.

IN 1974 MacSween began correspondence and a friendship with a relative that was to be unlike any other he had had in his life. Dolores Crawford, as we recall from chapter one, was Rod MacSween's niece, the only daughter of his eldest brother, Joe. He had not seen or heard from her since she was sixteen: "He told me," Dolores recalled, "that he came to my graduation, but I don't remember him being there, but that's how elusive he was. You know, he would come in, stand at the back and then leave." In 1974, Dolores was thirty-three years old, both her parents were dead, and she was a nurse, married with two children and living in Edmonton. At this point in her life, Dolores wanted

Fig. 48 MacSween in his office 1977. Courtesy Pat Walsh.

to know more about her past, about her people, her family. Her uncle was delighted to hear from her and wrote a detailed two-page letter telling her so in December 1974: "I was pleased to hear from you. What a surprise! I would have answered sooner—but didn't know how. You want to get family background, but where is it?"[6] The letter goes on to describe what he knows of his family origins. It ends with him saying, "I don't think I'll travel as far as Alberta. I'm not curious—and I have too many things to do here, But...." The letter is warm and heartfelt and it clearly invites this mysterious young woman from his past to continue contact. The correspondence would continue for the rest of his life, and a warm and intimate friendship would develop. These relatively late letters between MacSween and his niece are the only substantial correspondence of his that survives, so they are interesting and important both as examples of his epistolary style and as a record of his more private life as it was then being lived.

In October of 1977, MacSween sent his niece copies of his poetry and prose, explaining some of the background of his only published novel; his love of the pun is evident in the address:

Dear Dollars,

Here I am again—and this time on my own completely, pushed to writing by nothing but the memory of your last letter. I'm glad you liked "Furiously Wrinkled."

After telling his niece the story of his Aunt Mary, MacSween ends the letter with a reference to his own life and health,

I'll be sending you another book of poetry this winter—I think! If I gather some money together. I have only a few years to go—I'm 62 and close to retirement. The College gives me grants for books, generally about half the cost, otherwise I would print nothing, so every year I try to get something out before it's too late. I have 2 other novels written but unpublished. They're a bit longer than "F.W."—and then I have a new short novel from last summer. That's a lot to have on hand! I'm well, I suffer from arthritis occasionally, sometimes so badly that I'm unable to walk. But it always passes away. I'm fine so far this year. I suffer also from the MacSween disease—overweight—but it doesn't seem to kill any of us. So—I have nothing to complain of."[7]

Eventually, Dolores Crawford would tell her uncle her own story, about her struggles through childhood and youth, and she would seek answers from "Father Rod" about why her parents—and her father in particular—was the way he was.

In 1979 Dolores got the chance to meet her uncle for the first time in more than twenty-five years: he remembered when she was born and she remembered her first meeting with him at the age of ten:

> I went and asked him if he wanted a soft drink and he said yes he wanted ginger ale and I said oh, we don't have any ginger ale and he said well what did you ask me for then. I never wanted to see him again, not because I hated him, but because I feared him. That he was going to embarrass me. I was probably ten or eleven, very vulnerable and very much wanting to please, wanting some communication with him—and that was it. That was the communication and nothing more. I got something from him when I graduated from high school, and something when I graduated from nursing, and I still have it. But I made no overt move to have any relationship with him until I wrote him a letter in 1974, looking for information on the family tree. And that was the beginning of communication. I was thirty-three. I was tough then. I'd been around the block a few times.[8]

Even with her age and toughness, Dolores knew that getting to know her uncle was not going to be easy; the MacSweens were not known for their gentleness or intimacy: "I always give Father Mike a hug when I'm leaving, but not coming in—he won't have it. He says you're just going to knock me over. He didn't want the hug, but he was going to get it anyway. He didn't mind putting his arms around us to take pictures, but that was it, no warmth there. There was no warmth like that between my mother and father—not at all. I never saw affection between the grandparents either—never!"[9]

Besides the undemonstrative nature of the MacSween's, Dolores also had to deal with the tribal Catholicism of "home," as she recalled on one of her visits back east:

> I had been away from the church for decades, and when we were in Antigonish the first time, the children were five and ten, Father took us to the convent. Sister Gregory, our cousin, was there, and there were some of the nuns who had been in Glace Bay at St. Joe's, when I trained there. So we were having dinner with them and I'm just dying a thousand deaths, you have to know. I felt so…. I was just nervous. One of the sisters comes in and says, "And now where are you living?" and I said Sherwood Park and she got excited and she said "You have our Father Albert there." I didn't know Father Albert from first base. I just gasped, we do? And I just smiled. Then she turned to my daughter who was just ten and said, "Well, you must have made your first communion with Father Albert?" And Heather just looked at me like "gulp." And Father Rod saw that and I never told him, but I could just

see his little eyes going back and forth between us, and my husband just eating. And I was like, I'm not going to be able to eat another bite, so what am I going to do. And he jumped right in and said "How about those Eskimos?" and immediately Sister knew, and she started talking about the Eskimos and the Oilers and I'm looking at my plate going, ah, thank you. I didn't talk about it after that with him. He didn't mention it, and I didn't mention it. And it wasn't until several years later when I was back there, and my daughter was eighteen now, that I said, by the way, eight years ago this is what was happening. He just laughed.

The relationship, then, after some initial caution, eventually flourished:

> When I first met him it was a very strange kind of meeting, he talked a lot, and he talked a lot to my husband. I don't believe we talked about family at all. He was making contact with the children and all his books fascinated them. I was quite cautious with him. I didn't know him, it was kind of like shadow boxing or sparring. And I remember staying physically away from him on the other side of the room, and the other side of the table.

Dolores also recalled that "he didn't hug me the first visit but, oh!, he did the second time! Yes, and it was very strange for me. Very strange for me! And I thought, oh, I don't know if I like this or not. I would say to him, I don't think I come from the kissing side of the family."

Many warm and intimate letters soon passed between the uncle and the niece. In December of 1980, he is complaining about his health, he was now sixty-five years old but still teaching and editing *The Antigonish Review*:

> *"I do feel that I'm in terrible shape and haven't the energy to start exercising again. The start is the hard part. When I was younger, I could start at any time—in the spring or the summer—and feel okay. But now the*

Fig. 49 Dolores and her husband Bill in MacSween's rooms. Courtesy Dolores Crawford.

first day of golf kills me. I've been sedentary too long. I must do something though."

He continues to talk about himself and though he tries to avoid self-pity, there is a tone of sadness to the letter:

Just sitting around in my room, trying to do some work and finding it very hard. I fall asleep very easily now during the day if I'm quiet too long, just like my father. After he passed age fifty or so, he seemed to sleep all the time. Now I'm sixty-five and well into the age of sleep. Thursday I got my first old-age pension cheque. Talk about rolling in money!

There is little doubt, then, that his age was bothering him, but he never dwells on it, partly no doubt because the university still expected him to perform like a young man: "I was told that I would be teaching 1 course + the magazine. Then I was asked if I would go back to three courses—as I was needed. I agreed on two courses. It will be nice to have even a partial rest." The last part of the letter concerns his grandfather, but he is worried that he may have already told his niece the story, and again his age comes up: "I'm afraid that I may have told you, and if I were to repeat myself, I would indeed be sixty-five. I had never heard a word of it growing up. Strange how little parents tell their children. And the children are starved for stories of the past."

In January of 1981 MacSween writes again, marvelling at his niece's ability to write beautiful letters, but seeing it clearly as a natural gift of the MacSween clan. "It's strange how the love of reading and writing accompanies the clan everywhere. Murdoch in Glace Bay is the same. And Father Mike. And George. And poor Pat. And here are you, popping up in the West, taking English courses and writing with the greatest ease."[10] It is interesting and curious how these letters to his niece finally bring out the side of his heritage—the clannish, tribal, historical side—that he spent a life time trying to exorcise from his writing and professional life. There are several other points of specific interest in the letter, one concerns the private interpretation of poetry:

"Be sure to tell Stephen that a student should be able to give his own opinion (even in an exam), provided that he also gives the teacher's, he proves that he is learning and that he has prepared for the exam. But then he may exercise his own imagination and produce his own answer to the puzzle. However, unless he's a great genius, he will be unable to equal the age and learning of the teacher—and consequently will be labouring under a tremendous disadvantage. I find that the college kids often give little bits of insight that expand or modify my own; but left to themselves, they would do very little. Let them not be in a hurry—they will be old soon!"

Another interesting point in the letter concerns Dolores and her decision to go back to nursing:

> *I think you were wise to get a job. It will keep you lively—at least during some crucial years.... I hope work at the Nursing Home doesn't get you down. It's strange to think that the saints found such places the porch of heaven, the place where we truly prepare ourselves for the other world. The poor patients who rebel against their state don't see (and would I?) that they are situated above us all.*

Finally, MacSween speaks about his own poetry and that of another poet who has recently died:

> *"I'll be sending you another magazine in a day or so. It has a poem by me on that very subject (my poems, of course, are often above my own reach)—that we experience so much of the harshness of life although we are capable of inhabiting the realm of love and hope. A poor Chinese woman, Cheng Chia, is in for the second time. Her poems are lovely but sad—she was dying. Yesterday she died.[11] She brought her poetry to me week after week until we had gone over it all. I didn't advert to the fact that we had become good friends—I found out when they moved away to Singapore and then Halifax."[12]*

MacSween's poem referred to in the letter was "the unexplored":

> in the heart
>   are unexplored areas
>   vast tracts of space
>   that could hold the world
> indeed we wonder at them
>   all our lives
>
> there is always regret
>   at so much death
>   where life should reign
> our greatest joy is a fraction
>   of what our lives should be
>
> fear an awful spirit
>   expands to the mind's borders
> sorrow a deadly wind
>   blows into all crannies of our being
> longing a sigh
>   touches from end to end
>   of body and soul

before we die we shall explore
the far tundras of fear and pain
but not the Indies
of our hopes and desires

IN 1977 MacSween's youngest brother Patrick died in Toronto at the age of fifty-seven. His life had been one of much suffering, in and out of hospitals, for many years. He had lost several of his toes from frostbite the year before, and he was dead for about three days when they finally found him kneeling at the side of his bed in his rooming house. Pat Walsh drove MacSween to the funeral; there were few mourners. Pat MacSween had suffered much during World War II, but MacSween had told his niece Dolores that there was evidence of a disorder from very early on when he was a boy, which the war no doubt intensified. John MacEachern, his nephew, recalled his one meeting with Pat: "He was always reading. So I asked him what he was reading at the moment. He said Kafka, a German writer." Unlike his brothers, Pat, according to John and others, was different; he never put himself forward; he was quiet, shy and reserved.

MacSween had not been to see his family in sometime. His father had died in 1968, and he had not made the trip to Toronto in four or five years. He knew he was losing contact with his family: "I went up to Pat's funeral and I saw all these people grown up. Children grown up, my nephews and nieces looking old, and I said, My God, I'd better start going back." The next year, young Mick MacKinnon, the son of MacSween's old friend from New Waterford, began driving him to Toronto once again.

*IN*terviewed for the local paper in 1986, MacSween was quoted as saying, "I consider *The Antigonish Review* to be the most important part of my career."[13] It is a revealing statement from a man who was a priest, social worker, counsellor, professor, critic and poet. Public statements, especially in the press, aren't always to be taken at face value, but MacSween clearly regarded the magazine he founded as an important achievement. "Little magazines," as they are known in the business, are generally collaborative efforts, especially the ones that depend upon volunteer labour. MacSween had a group of writers and editors he could depend upon, most of them were his former students, including George Sanderson, Gertrude Sanderson, Pat Walsh, Sheldon Currie, James Taylor and Kevin O'Brien.[14] MacSween stated that his ambition, when he became chair of the English department, "was to bring into the department people who longed to write, and I thought that if we could get, say, seven or eight who were oriented that way, we would have a good nucleus for the magazine which I intended to start later on."[15] Most little magazines, however, usually express the vision of one person, the editor, and MacSween clearly had a particular point of view for *The Antigonish Review*.[16] In his interview with Pat Walsh in 1980 he reflected on his founding of the review:

> I had the notion from the time I came here; I was very interested in these little magazines, many received through the Gotham Book Mart and through seeing them advertised in magazines. I had begun to collect many of them early in my career. It seemed to me that this was about the only way we could break into what you'd call the world of culture. In this region we haven't the wealth or population to break into that world. But we could start a little magazine with a small outlay of cash, and everybody knows how to write—not write well—but everybody knows how to write, and with a little bit of finesse we could get a group here who thought as I did. It wasn't a question of achieving fame—but of producing a good magazine. When I was very busy, in the first part of my career here, I knew it couldn't be undertaken, but later on things began to look up.[17]

Given his long-standing desire to found a magazine, it is all the more surprising that he would choose someone other than himself to be the review's first editor. But this is exactly what he did: Reverend Brocard Sewell, an Englishman who belonged to the Order of the Black Friars, and the founding editor of *The Aylesford Review*, was brought in to do the job. MacSween spoke about Sewell's appointment: "I actually appointed him myself. I put him in charge of everything. I felt it was mean not to do so, since he had experience as an editor already. But I think I made a mistake because it cut me off from the rest of the editors."

In a letter written to Father Sewell in February of 1971, MacSween was more specific and less apologetic about his mistake:

> *I asked you not to publish "bad" work from your friends in England.... Moreover, we find that you seek outside support for your views among those who had nothing to do with founding the magazine. The word "academic" is seldom used without pejorative intent, in writing and in printing. To approve a thing as academic would be a kind of joke to our culture heroes. In this matter of academic publication, there are ten thousand universities which can beat us at that game. To be different is our only salvation. I am amazed that a man without a degree and who has lived on the outside of academic affairs would allow himself to be caught in that sterile activity. I do admit that it is an activity which has its own attraction, comparable to that of crossword puzzles, and there are always*

those on the sidelines who mistake it for true learning. Nevertheless, it is those outside of academe to whom we must go for creative insights in criticism. They are without exception those who have earned their rank in the first place in the creative field. I am for them to the utmost of my ability. I am not against criticism—their style of criticism—but I am against academic criticism, the product of establishments.... I simply took for granted that you would realize these matters much more clearly than I could. I know now that I was mistaken.... There is nothing "popular," in your sense of the word, in my plea of lighter criticism and the acceptance of good literature.... I do appreciate what you have done. Nevertheless, you definitely look towards your English readers rather than to the great bulk of our subscribers. I would be very happy if the English readers like the magazine, but they have many others to choose from, whereas our community has almost nothing.[18]

It is an important letter in that it highlights MacSween's lifelong battle with "academics"; his fierce desire to have a cultural magazine of wide reach; and his equally fierce support of creative writers and artists. The letter, too, is a good example of MacSween's cool but combative style, only once or twice would he write this way for the magazine, and then only to answer an attack on a favourite writer who had been slandered or unfairly treated. Finally, the letter highlights MacSween's commitment to Canadian writers and artists; when he was Chair of the English department he often resisted courses that were strictly Canadian in content, even though he taught Canadian writers in his Modern British and American course. There is little doubt, however, about the magazine's direction; MacSween's policy was to publish Atlantic Canadians first, but only if the work was equal to that of contributions from outside the region. As the years went by, *TAR*, as it came to be known, got more and more contributions from "away" and the editor, whose own tastes were so eclectic, clearly relished the cosmopolitan character that slowly developed in the pages of the review.

MacSween had to fight other battles besides editorial ones with Brocard Sewell. Though his good friends and fellows priests in the administration, Msgr. Malcolm MacLellan and Fr. Malcolm MacDonell, supported *TAR* and understood its worth, there were others in the corridors of power who were less supportive of culture and the arts. In a letter dated December 17, 1971 to his friend Malcolm MacDonell, President of St. FX at the time, MacSween spoke of his battles with faculty and administration: "As regards the faculty in general, we are faced with indifference (in a few cases, hostility) and with a surprising lack of creativity. The cultural level is not high. All of this means that we have only ourselves to fall back on in case of need." His tone of disappointment moves to one of anger when he speaks about his battles with the Dean of Arts:

> *I think that the President should appoint the Editor, and not the Dean of Arts. He has no judgment in such matters. His letter to me last year stated that he appointed me—which is not true. Our agreement was that the President appoint the Editor, but (if he wanted it so) through the Dean of Arts. Moreover I do not see why it should be for the period of one year.*

It is interesting that he wrote two versions of the next section of the letter—both fully illustrate his scorn and contempt for power. He was a man who made enemies, and he knew that having all the right enemies meant you were doing "something" with your life: "This matter I regard as a kind of insult, as if the Dean of Arts were capable of judging whether or not I was successful. It smacks of the love of power, a sin into which every bureaucrat falls sooner or later." His second version is somewhat more tempered and judicious, but equally fierce in its indignation: "I do not think my character and competence are in doubt and that I should be controlled, as though I were a child, by others who know much less than I do, and who have still to prove themselves in many areas of life." The end of MacSween's letter could have come from "The Dunciad" of his beloved Alexander Pope, a poem which became more and more relevant to his life as time went on: "Anyway the magazine is one of our few bright spots. There are not many. Envy, stupidity and pedantry are having their long day." Their day would indeed be long as MacSween's battles for the magazine continued into the seventies: a letter to the Canada Council illustrates the nature and intensity of the struggle:

> *I am answering your enquiry concerning continuing help from the University for* The Antigonish Review. *The trouble lies in the fact that the university administration is asking a similar question of me concerning the Canada Council. They are paying bills at the moment in the expectation that they will be repaid. They have only our assurance to go on: that we have the kind of magazine that merits help, and that merit will be recognized. Those who run the Administration at the moment, and who are busy making what they consider necessary retrenchments, are a chemist and a teacher of business procedures. Need I say more? They have already written to me to say the magazine will be judged (?) by its ability to elicit help from outside sources; no other criterion of judgment was mentioned.*[19]

Brocard Sewell edited four issues of *The Antigonish Review* before he stepped down. They are excellent issues of their kind and include several well-known and soon-to-be-famous English writers—including Angela Carter and Penelope Shuttle—they also include at least one major

Canadian poet, Alden Nowlan. But for all their quality, there is little doubt that the issues were directed at a British audience, and a very specific one at that—those interested in the England of the 1890s and the work of a group of writers known as the Aesthetes and Decadents, figures such as Oscar Wilde and Aubrey Beardsley. MacSween of course was present in all four issues, represented by excellent poems including "the forgotten world," but his real presence as a force for the magazine is in his book reviews and essays. In these first four volumes he reviews eleven books besides contributing an essay on Graham Greene and a half-dozen or so poems. The number and titles of the books under review show his broad reading and highlight his attitude toward little magazines—their purpose and function in the general culture of a country.[20]

MacSween took over the editorship of the review for the spring issue of 1971, and both the content and the format of the magazine reflect this change at the helm. The cover banished completely its previous academic look, with a delicate and airy array of colourful daisies designed by Pat Walsh. The academic articles on long dead figures from the 1890s and earlier were replaced by the avant-garde and the controversial: the figure of choice for the spring of 1971 was the French writer, Ferdinand Celine and his masterpiece *Rigodon*. The issue also contained several heavyweight poets, critics and prose writers from Upper Canada including Louis Dudek, Dorothy Livesay, George Bowering and MacSween's former student, Alistair MacLeod.[21] Scattered throughout the text are quotes from Ezra Pound and, more importantly, illustrations, lots and lots of illustrations. MacSween, as George Sanderson[22] later acknowledged, fully absorbed McLuhan's message about breaking up the print to allow the eye—now so accustomed to the image—to enter the text at almost any point. There were, of course, as always, contributions from MacSween, including six book reviews. Beneath his name there is a telling, if by now predictable, quote: "Artists first, then, if necessary, professors and parsons. Scholarship is but a hand-maid to the arts." The quote is from Ezra Pound to Harriet Munro, editor of *Poetry*; the date is 1915.

By the third issue, then, MacSween had truly made his impression upon *TAR*. As with all little magazines (unless they are designated as specifically fiction or non-fiction) the majority of contributions come from poets. This can present

Fig. 51 Bela Egyedi cover for TAR *16.*

a problem in terms of variety unless you have writers you can rely upon to supply fiction, reviews and articles. The editors of *TAR* contributed on a regular basis: George Sanderson provided reviews and occasional fiction (Sanderson was also instrumental in the magazine's design and layout, eventually obtaining the art work of the Hungarian émigré, Bela Egyedi, whose covers, paintings and sketches would become a hallmark of later issues); Sheldon Currie wrote fiction, articles and reviews and published his now internationally renowned story "The Glace Bay Miner's Museum" in *TAR* 24; Pat Walsh wrote stories and articles and produced most of the magazine's early art work. Walsh also worked as a contributing editor in the early seventies: a doctoral student in Ireland, he obtained the work of several major Irish writers including: Thomas Kinsella, Seamus Deane and Brian Moore. Gertrude Sanderson, professor of French and Spanish, was instrumental in establishing and maintaining the magazine's interest in translation: these early issues contained the work of the now-famous Quebec poet, Gaston Miron, who Sanderson herself translated. It was also a policy of *TAR* to always have both languages represented.

As editor, then, MacSween was lucky: his colleagues and collaborators play down their actual contribution, insisting that the ideas originally came from the editor, but MacSween always acknowledged their contribution and he knew the magazine could not have been what it was without them. Issue number 7, however, MacSween's third issue as editor, is a good example of how he himself could step in and fill the pages that needed filling. There are six reviews by MacSween on books by and about Jerzy Kosinsky, Dorothy Parker, Mary de Rachewiltz, Roberston Davies and this review of Nadezhda Mandelstam:

> This book is like a phoenix arising from the dead ashes of Mandelstam's memory. It is fearless and human, and it preserves the man for the benefit of future ages. Not only did she keep his memory alive, but also she memorized hundreds of lines of his poetry so that it could not be destroyed by the police. A tiresome occupation, after he was gone she went over the poems constantly as she moved about, fixing them in her memory until the moment of freedom would come.... The most awful thing about this book is the evidence for the servile way in which most of the population accepted the rule of Stalin. Not only did they accept it, they warmly embraced it. As a condemned man embraces the headsman. Once a person felt the vengeance of the State, he found himself a pariah among his familiars. Only rarely did another have the courage to help and sympathize. But although such heroes were rare, they were plentiful enough to raise our spirits as we read. The loyalty of Anna Akmatova, a well known poet, is indeed a brightness in this history.

Almost all of MacSween's reviews have this sweep, style and insight. Issue 7 also contained the first of two essays he would pen on one of his favourite writers, the modern English novelist Ivy Compton-Burnett:

Below the surface the passions live their secret life and pride and its attendant devils shake the individual and shatter the group. For she has chosen for her sphere of action the most entrancing and the most dangerous of all human institutions—the family.... The family is the natural domain of the tyrant. Its bonds are bonds of steel. No one can wholly escape its net. In addition to blood relationship, Ivy Compton-Burnett's families are joined together by financial want. The weak cling to the strong, gratefully or ungratefully; the strong (that is, often, the wealthy) exercise power over the weak, sometimes with kindness more often with savagery. In any case, a tyrant emerges and governs the other defenceless people with fantastic thoroughness.... But it is children who make up the author's suffering chorus, generally. Children are more dependent than grownups and there are many ways in which their dependence can be made to endure.... No others suffer so long and so silently as these and with so little hope. They may pass into adulthood without achieving one jot of liberty. It is no wonder, then, that they speak like a Greek chorus. Their voices chirping like those of old men, weary with the experience of frustrations borne without hope. Here are their voices in a typical sequence from Mother and Son:

"So it is true that comedy and tragedy are mingled," said Adrian
"Really it is all tragedy," said his sister. "Comedy is a very wicked way of looking at it, when it is not our own."
"Yes, life is all tragedy," said Francis. "It would be tragic to see its comic side."

Here is another passage from the same novel:
"I don't think we are as bad as Francis thinks we are," said Adrian.
"Perhaps we are sound at heart. That is said of people who are unusually unpleasant."
"Why is it said of them?"
"Well, they are clearly sound nowhere else, and we cannot see the heart."

Their creator passes on to them the seething passions of their elders and also the sharp wit that goes with a very hopeless kind of mental agony. They are all cynics before their time.[23]

MacSween would write again on Burnett in issue 24, and it is interesting to compare and contrast the two essays because of the subtle but remarkable changes in style. Although he wrote and published very competent fiction (to damn him with faint praise), MacSween's gifts as a writer were

fundamentally in poetry and criticism. Part of the strength of his criticism lay, unquestionably, in his vast reading and remarkable powers of
retention. Martin Amis, reviewing Gore Vidal's collection, *United States*,
remarked that the ex-patriot American was the master of the droll stroll;
it is a shrewd observation, and could easily be applied to MacSween. Like
Vidal, MacSween's fiction may not survive the journey out, but there is
little doubt that his poetry and criticism will be "new," in Ezra Pound's
special coinage, for a long time to come:

> Ivy Compton-Burnett seems to be one of the undoubted classics to have
> emerged from the modern period. A classic, as time goes by, seems more
> and more to have upon it the mark of the individual who made it. It may
> be called "an expression of its time" or some such phrase that denotes
> some inexorable product of the *Zeitgeist*, but its enduring character is
> that of the author who wrote it. Nothing more true could be said of Ivy
> Compton-Burnett, for there seems to be an exact harmony between
> the awful world of her fiction and the dry intense nature of the life she
> lived…. The mother was a more troubled person, she lived beyond the
> death of the father, and she became quite a burden to young Ivy. She,
> too, does not exhibit sufficient disturbance to set in disarray the growing
> spirit of Ivy, although who can know what weight an adult can lean
> against the frail mind of a young girl. We are inclined to think that
> Ivy's character was hers alone, that she was born with the potentiality to
> be dry, rational and severe, and that however much she was swayed by
> events, she remained true to herself alone until the end.[24]

There is much in this extract—and in the previous one—that could be
equally applied to MacSween, as he too was born with the potential to be
humorous, rational and severe—especially in his poetry.

The list of writers who appear in *TAR* over the years quickly became
a who's who of Canadian literature: David Adams Richards published
his first fiction in *TAR* 9 in the Spring of 1972; he was nineteen years
old and his story was called, prophetically, "The Promise." In the notes on
contributors, MacSween had written simply that "David Adams Richards
is a young writer of great promise." Carol Shields, then living in Ottawa,
appeared in issue 17 in the spring of 74 and the Montreal poet, Peter Van
Toorn appeared regularly. Marshall McLuhan, Louis Dudek and Hugh
Kenner all appeared in the seventies with articles on the high modern-
ists—T. S. Eliot and Ezra Pound in particular. While he was delighted to
have contributions from these major (or soon to be major) figures, they
were not of primary concern, as he explained to Pat Walsh in 1980:

> To get the best writers in Canada, or better, in the English-speaking
> world, we'd have to be in a position to pay all our contributors in cash

or else at least be in a large centre like Toronto. Personally, I'm not very anxious to get the writers that are considered important. Say, the best ten writers in Canada or the best fifty in the States—I'm not anxious to get those people at all.... Those people crowd out the lesser known writers, they write a great deal and they dominate in a few of our magazines. You'll see them all the time in the Tamarack Review, and when they're in they are well represented. They might have ten poems in one issue. I'd rather give five people two poems.[25]

MacSween, as we have seen then, was an extremely discriminating and generous critic. In all of his criticism there are only two attacks and both of these are in defence of writers he greatly admired. The first is a major essay, one of three he was to write on the English novelist Evelyn Waugh. As we have already seen, MacSween had a soft spot for the hard but comic Waugh, both because of his Catholicism and his brilliant style as a satirist. When Christopher Sykes' biography of Waugh appeared, MacSween was quick to jump to the novelist's defense:

Although it was written by a man who was Waugh's personal friend, it fails in sympathy and enthusiasm; it never gives one the feeling that a labour of love has been accomplished or that it was a privilege to have known intimately one of the best novelists of the century. It could be that Sykes is simply incapable of rising to the level of his subject, and if this be so, he is not to blame; but there are certain emotions of which we are all capable, notably that of gratitude for those who enrich the world with art and humour. It could be admitted that Sykes had a difficult subject, one which prevented a full measure of sympathy; and to this we would reply that the commission should be given to someone else. It is now too late to do this. The book is before us, the most potent factor in the future evaluation of Waugh's character. It is all a matter of emphasis; Sykes says many fine things about Waugh, but every one of those is balanced by something vicious. Is that fair? At first notice, yes. But the evil that men do lives after them, and gives an unbalanced picture of what they were. The question to be answered is: What kind of man was Waugh? Was he a villain or was he a stumbling sinner trying his best in a difficult world? The latter is true according to his family and his friends. Those most vicious in attack did not know him.[26]

The Cape Breton priest's love and defense of Waugh is directly connected to what I have referred to throughout this book as MacSween's Catholic cultural nationalism. Waugh's allegiance, his loyalty to the Catholic "state," to the Church (or at least to the pre-Vatican II Church) was uncompromising—and very different indeed from MacSween's own attitude towards Rome. On the major theologian Hans Küng, for instance, Waugh notoriously (and comically) said, "In a happier time he would have been burned." Of course, Waugh was also fond of asking his outraged friends to imagine how much nastier he would have been had he not been Catholic.[27] MacSween's other favorite English Catholic writer, Graham Greene, was a different matter—though a good friend of Waugh's, Greene was also great defender of theologians like Küng, and he was the opposite of Waugh in political matters.

While it is true that MacSween missed the beauty of the Latin Mass, he was, as we have seen, clearly in the camp of Greene rather than Waugh. MacSween's politics were a curious and at times contradictory combination of both the left and the right—Waugh and Greene, no doubt would both have felt at home in his presence. It is dangerous to overplay the religious card with MacSween, as he in no way fits the orthodox mould. In issue 29 of *TAR*, for example, he wrote a review on François Mauriac, where he highlighted the modern French Catholic writer's preoccupation with Jansenism: "The world has almost turned its back completely on this religious aberration, once considered standard Old Testament Christianity." Furthermore, MacSween loved and often quoted Celine's characterization of Mauriac as a Praying Mantis. As mentioned earlier, the older MacSween got, the broader and more encompassing became his religious vision, and this vision was part of his natural progression on his journey from the *politique* to the *mystique*.

The breadth and scope of MacSween's religious vision is well represented in his review essays on the expatriate Romanian religious historian, Mircea Eliade:

> It is indeed a fact that Eliade inspires curiosity about himself; some of it may come from the mystery of his name, some from his origins, some from the esoteric nature of his particular study—the history of religions. This matter is very strange, for he has always laboured to keep himself out of his writings. It is difficult to know from them whether or not he is a believer, and if he is, what elements he would appropriate for himself from the numberless strands of belief collected and described.... Nevertheless, Eliade says that the sacred (which for him is the truly "real") has not been destroyed but remains underneath the various shapes modern life throws up in order to express itself. The sacred is camouflaged by these forms. We still have not learned to profit in a real way from the technology that dominates our lives. Other great ages of change have enriched us; this age has impoverished us.... In this matter we see Eliade's optimism, which is remarkable in that it sees hope in the very monster we had thought would destroy us. He has sent us back to the Stone Age for our rejuvenation; he may send us into the future for the same purpose.[28]

The other writer that MacSween promoted and at times defended was also, like Greene and Waugh, a Catholic and an Englishman—the only difference was that he was born in 1688. MacSween's admiration for this 18th-century writer is notable in that his championing of the modern era in literature is so thorough and all encompassing that it seems to leave little room for any other period of literature. With a few exceptions, the writers he wrote about are almost all from this era, his era; but MacSween always had a special place in his heart for the writers of 18th century. The Age of Reason, the Enlightenment, the Neoclassical Age, whatever you choose to call it, had a great appeal for him. It was a time when writing and printing truly came of age, an era when artists and critics held social standing—and a time, too, in western history when their views mattered. Wasn't John Dryden almost beaten to death for a pamphlet he'd written? Didn't Daniel Defoe get put in the stocks for a similar act? And hadn't Jonathan Swift been investigated for the *Drapier Letters*? The vitality of a time when print was pre-eminent and religion could get you killed, could not fail to attract the mind of a MacSween. Catholic nationalism, in both its cultural and political manifestations, was alive and well; so, too, as Linda Colley and others have shown, was the nationalism of the Protestant nation. MacSween's hero from this time, then, could not be the man he had penned a poem about, the man who most resembled him in shape, mind and vision, Samuel Johnson, because Johnson, as we all know, was a Protestant; no, the professor-priest's hero was a fellow Catholic—the diminutive, handicapped, elf-like genius, Alexander Pope:

> And so Pope after years of rejection, after years of suffering hatred and calumny at the hands of a rather vile crowd of enemies, turned on them and wrote "The Dunciad," the epic of dunces…. Pope was definitely out to make the dunces suffer, and no wonder! What mattered was whether he could transcend the occasion, forcing his artistic sense to govern his resentment and to fix the dunces in a framework of action. Like his friend Swift, Pope had always felt that the values of European civilization were in danger—and he had included the dunces in that threat. Now the whole matter crystallized as in his imagination he saw not the vast and cloudy dangers which ordinarily confront civilizations but the Queen of Dullness.[29]

What inspired this passionate defence of a figure long dead? One who, it might be argued has, with the exception of a few devoted readers and scholars, publicly been reduced to cliché: "Fools rush in where angels fear to tread," et al. Having risked entry into "The Dunciad," it seems that while MacSween's apologia rests on Pope's art and vision, it was his

Catholicism, the fact that one of his kind was being slandered over the centuries that motivated him to defend the great satirist and translator of Homer. MacSween's cultural Catholicism, his "nationalism" ran deep, and to say that his defence of Pope is tribal at its core is not to belittle his criticism, but rather to seek the source of its passion. It is also fair to point out that "The Dunciad" had a particular relevance for MacSween, for a man of such diverse talents who had fought many battles over the years and who now—as his poetry often tragically records—felt he, too, had lost his battles to dunces and the Queen of Dullness.

It is fascinating to see MacSween draw on his vast scholarship when he chooses to marshal an argument such as this one for Alexander Pope; but more often than not, MacSween preferred Pound's phrase, that scholarship was but a handmaid to the arts, and so he loved it when a figure such as Jorge Luis Borges made it manifest in his fiction:

> An even more pronounced mark of his work is the learned allusion. Ordinarily fiction, especially short fiction, eschews the burden of learning. But Borges, the linguist, the reader in a number of literatures, and also the researcher into the exotic and esoteric, was not to be denied. Sometimes his stories are like scholarly treatises in which he handles with loving care the different strands that make up the history of some remarkable idea. He quotes abundantly, he cites catalogues of authorities (some real, some fictional), he introduces famous names, and even the names of friends, to bolster the reality of his narration. Only at the end do we perceive that scholarship, for the first time, has become the slave of fiction and serves its will.[30]

MacSween's interest in Borges' fiction was more than passing, more than the interest of the reader or professor; like the great master, MacSween was ambitious to write short stories that were also moral fables—commentaries on the times and world he lived in. As with almost all of MacSween's work, Louis Dudek was the first to give a critical introduction to the fiction. Dudek entitled his article "Blighted Lives," a title which accurately sums up the central concerns of *The Burnt Forest and Other Stories* (1975) and *Furiously Wrinkled* (1976). The stories are plot-driven, which might seem odd for MacSween, given his dislike of writers whose only strength was often their plots; writers like the American, O. Henry, for instance. Similarly, MacSween had a preference for Chekov over Maupassant because of the Russian's more persistent pursuit of character. But there is much more than plot in the *Burnt Forest* collection, as Dudek first noticed: "Stories are written to tell us something about the world, not about ourselves; and MacSween's stories are highly impersonal, all of them. They have their purpose as moral parables, and it is as such that they work their powerful effects." Dudek's article is both a testament to the readability of the stories and to his own unwavering strength as one of our finest literary critics:

> I can only comment briefly on a few of these stories, those which have moved me most, although every story in *The Burnt Forest*, as well as the novel *Furiously Wrinkled*, is superbly worked out and is satisfying in detail. One of the finest, and bound to prove one of the most popular, is "The Portrait," about a man who sees a picture by "a disciple of the elder Breughel" which he believes resembles himself. The portrait, however, is entitled "The Idiot." I suppose it is because each one of us fears that he (or she) may be found out, that in some secret way we know we are insufficient, dull-witted, absurd, and will eventually end in that state, that this story has a surprising appeal and hold on the reader. It is a small masterpiece.[31]

Although the stories are indeed highly impersonal, we know that at least one of them came from MacSween's younger brother Pat.[32] "The Scream" is about a man who returns from a hospital to his one-room shack in the woods to find another man living there. The man, Flint, is a misanthrope, who hates his fellow humans because he is able to hear the suffering of all that is not human, all the other creatures of the earth who seem to be tortured by humanity. When, for example, Mr. Nelson, the owner of the shack, catches and skins some eels for his supper, Flint turns on him insisting that he can hear the eels—and all other creatures—scream: "Don't you know it's suffering, you heel? Don't you know it's alive! For God's sake, man, how can you do a thing like that?" At the end of the story, Flint refuses to help Nelson when he is stricken with another heart attack, scattering his pills on the floor because he stepped on an insect and showed no remorse. Dudek suggests that the story presents a Christian dilemma: "He will not listen to the cry of a dying man, because he is obsessed with the scream of dying insects. And yet his obsession is also compelling: it is the suffering of a world in which 'the very air is made of pain.'" Apparently, Pat MacSween was assailed with similar feelings during one of his many battles with depression and mental illness.

Another story that presents a Christian dilemma, and one that could also have a personal connection is "Another Desperate Cry." The story concerns a man, Gerald, who is drawn toward those who need help, yet his own projects remain forever unfinished:

> First it had been his sister, who had called to him for aid all the way across the country. He had gone and helped her but at the cost of his own job. Later on it was his mother, then a close friend then his fiancée who later on gave him up, and a score of others.[33]

Finally, Gerald plans a trip to Europe, but his housekeeper of long-standing has died. Nervous about his home, he asks his aunt, who lives alone in Vancouver, to come and housesit for him, all at his expense. The aunt we soon learn has never been to Europe, but she knows Spanish fluently and is well versed in art and architecture, especially the work of the modern master, Gaudi, of whom she has "read every book and article ever written about." Gerald is astonished at her knowledge and fluency—so much greater than his own. Once again he feels unworthy and sends his aunt to Europe in his place. Dudek suggests that the character

> "might just as well have been—perhaps was, in some first conception—a priest of the cloth; with his housekeeper, his kindnesses, his character is very much that of a man of religion. Yet there is also a slightly amused perhaps ironic resentment—at his being used in the interests of 'Heaven' to his own dismay."

D. H. Lawrence once remarked of St. Francis of Assisi, that the great danger for the saint was the total surrender of ego. MacSween was no saint, and he certainly didn't surrender his ego, though the story participates in the criticism.

Another story about the risks inherent in the Christian life, the life of service, is "Weariness." This is the story of Tom Curtain, a lawyer and a do-gooder who is loved by everyone in the town. After his years of charity work he one day discovers that he is exhausted. In gratitude for all he has done for the town, the local organizations raise money to send him on a world cruise. Tom stays longer than he had planned on his trip because he has been doing missionary work, or its equivalent, on some of his stops in India and Southeast Asia. Those who sent him on his journey are now glad he is gone, as his irrepressible goodness has created the "Weariness" of the title. When he returns, they are disheartened and ostracize him from their circle. He ends up a bitter man who sticks "grimly to his work and has no time for anything else." Dudek suggests that this story, like "Another Desperate Cry," "is a somewhat ironic view of excessive helpfulness, which can often become meddling kindness. At any rate an excess of Christian virtue is seen in somewhat satiric and humorous terms."[34]

It is interesting to speculate on these stories about Christians and people of the cloth in an age that was becoming increasingly secular. Did Doc Pat, his brother, Fr. Mike, and countless other friends and relatives such as Fr. Dan R., Sister Margaret and Sister Gregory give too much to their religion? What was too much? As the years passed, MacSween would see plenty of resentment and ingratitude meted out to his colleagues in the cloth, some of it deserved—by his own admission—but most of it not. In an interview shortly before he died, Fr. Malcolm MacLellan, who was president of St. FX when MacSween founded *TAR*, spoke about "Rod's integrity"; when the university administration had tried to reduce MacLellan's pension, "Rod had stood up and fought for me."[35] What, perhaps most fundamentally, we also see being worked out in these stories is MacSween's own slow but inevitable abandonment of his Catholic "nationalism," his traditional—and at times overwhelming—identification with his church and religion.

Predictably enough perhaps, at least three of the stories in *The Burnt Forest* collection are concerned with death. In "When Foundations Shake" MacSween seems to be answering his readers and critics about his preoccupation with the subject: Alexis Houghton witnesses the death throes of an old man at a railway station in the 21st century; he is disturbed by the indifference of his fellow citizens, but a passing stranger advises caution:

> All hostility was suddenly turned away from the dying man to him. Never before in his life had he felt so many hostile glances. He turned and walked to the other end of the platform. The tall dark man followed. "You mustn't remind people of death. It disturbs them. Everything has been removed from their lives that could remind them of death. Sick people are whisked away immediately;

In his interview with Pat Walsh in 1980, MacSween also addressed the subject of death in his work:

> Well, I think death is a great and terrifying thing. If you don't realize that, you're not alive. We're all heading towards death as fast as we can go. And it doesn't take away any of our love of life. If anything it intensifies it. Even if you do enjoy life a great deal, the enjoyment doesn't, in any way, take away the power of death. But, I think, an amateur poet, as I am (I was even more the amateur in the early days) only writes when he is moved by something unusual—and he's generally moved by death, the death of somebody else, or the sickness of someone else, or disappointment, or a feeling of depression in his own life. So, if he writes in that way, he'll end up with a collection of poems with the emphasis heavily slanted towards depressing things like death.... But I think everybody thinks about death a great deal but only the poet writes about it. His next-door neighbour, who perhaps never wrote a laundry list, thinks about death just as much as the poet does.[36]

Although he does indeed write about this subject, MacSween was clearly overstating the case. After all, only three of the stories in *The Burnt Forest* collection deal directly with death, though it must be admitted that the others are indeed sombre, even when they contain moments of wry humour. Some of MacSween's colleagues felt that—the priest, professor and especially the artist—had become trapped behind the persona that he and others had constructed for him; for those who knew MacSween intimately, this was clearly not the case; and for those who didn't know him well, they need only read both his criticism and his poetry to see how much he continued to grow, develop and change. If anything, MacSween is a much more radical being—a much freer spirit—in his old age than at any other time in his life.

Not long after the publication of *The Burnt Forest*, MacSween abandoned the short story and novel form altogether and devoted his remaining years exclusively to writing poetry and criticism. We must remember that this collection of stories was published in MacSween's sixtieth year. Indeed, because of his productivity and energy, we are constantly forced to recall that this is not a young man's life, nor is it a particularly healthy man's life.

double shadows and the *secret city* were the last two volumes of poetry that MacSween published in the 1970s. Most of these poems, like his short stories, appeared in the pages of *TAR*, with the exception of the poems published in *the forgotten world*, all of which were written before 1970; MacSween's method of composition was to write the poems and then publish them in *TAR*. There is very little rewriting in these years, and almost none in his last works. The poetry in these collections, then, like the poems in *the forgotten world* continue to illustrate a broad range of subject matter and a distinctive style. "ghosts" and "siberia" are indicative of the collection as whole, and both poems share much in common, even though they, oddly enough, link rural Nova Scotia with the forbidding tundra of then Soviet Russia:

> the skeptic would dismiss
>   ghosts from the house
> those quavering spirits
>   having no power
>   over the adult mind
>
> why then did men create them
>   in the shadows of mansions
>   and monasteries
> perhaps they wanted to send down

into memory
all the pain and regret
that gathers in a house

when no man bothers
to remove iniquity
a ghost rises from nothing
to redress the balance

a house is still mind
no wind moves
to disturb the dust
spiders spread their webs
from chair to floor
from corner to window
there are no sounds
the dust floats
such stillness is not right
in a house where blood
calls to God
innocent victims
hold up their lily hands
for help
a ghost must rise on the moonlit floor
to ask the vengeance of those
who come in later years

now in the dim mansion
of a quiet brain
phantoms slip like
shadows
chains make a psychic
tremble
in the ears of the listener
vacant faces once drained
by pain and violence
gibber in the falling
dust
and ask to be believed
because of their
perfect rightness

The poem, in many respects, has more in common with the Henry James of *The Turn of the Screw* than it does with the research of the folklorist, Helen Creighton. There are other works that come to mind as well, the Irish poet Derek Mahon's "A Garage in Co. Cork" and closer still, "A Disused Shed in County Wexford," where mushrooms hidden and crammed in the dark represent "all the pain and regret" of ghosts of ages, these lost people whose "vacant faces once drained/ by pain and violence" want us to "remove iniquity" "to redress the balance."

Throughout his life, MacSween had a special place in his heart for Russia and Russian literature (at one point, looking for the feel of language, he actually studied enough Russian on his own to struggle through some poems). As we have seen, in the classroom, he taught his favourites: Gogol, Chekov, Dostoyevski, Tolstoi, Turgenev, and he also wrote several reviews on modern Russian writers. In *TAR* 45 MacSween wrote about Varlam Shalamov, a man who suffered in the Gulags at the same time as Solzhenitsyn: "The material is the same as we find in the Gulag accounts, but fashioned with greater art and, as fiction, more viable in the precarious Russian environment.... He has learned well the lessons of Chekov, his master, but Chekov never faced the open horror of these stories." Earlier, MacSween had written on other Russians including, Pasternak:

> Pasternak is a giant figure in twentieth century letters, not only because of his acknowledged literary skill but because he is a witness to the finest values of civilization in the face of a vicious tyranny. Everything learned about such a man is precious to us, and indeed everything that we learn of him only elevates him in our estimation. Such a judgment cannot be made for everyone. Gladkov deserves our gratitude for offering himself as a minor kind of Boswell to Pasternak's Johnson. Our complaint is that he is not Boswellian enough, but we must be satisfied with what he gives.[37]

There is no doubt that MacSween's attitude towards the Soviet Union was shaped by the Cold War ethos he spent much of his adult life living in. In Don Delillo's novel, *Underworld*, an unofficial history of the last fifty years, the Catholic Church has its dark place amid the mushroom clouds of Nevada and in the bays of the B52s. As in the United States, the Catholic villages and schools of Nova Scotia had their own brand of Cold War hysteria. And in the Ireland of Neil Jordan's film, *Butcher Boy*, the Virgin Mary hangs alongside the portrait of JFK. These two Catholic icons were also worshipped and very much at home in the Catholic Cape Breton of my own childhood. Like many Catholic priests, MacSween bought the Cold War package, but when he finally brought it home and opened it up it wasn't the persecution of the Church by the Godless red atheists that he found inside, but rather the suffering of his beloved writers. In his later years, MacSween founded a local chapter of Amnesty International in his town and he faithfully recruited people, sent donations and kept up on the literature. It was all of a piece, of course, and the spirit of it can be found in poems like "siberia," the second stanza of which begins:

> see them walk by
> their voices and walks agree
> eyes cry in the ragged flesh
> wrinkles run up and down
>> the devastated map of Siberia
> there is the Yenisei river
> and there the Ob
> there is the desert of Gobi
> there is the Lake Baikal of a mouth
> and the plains where Gengis Khan
>> roamed with his Golden Horde
> even in this century death came into all the
>> valleys and meadows
> ghosts haunt that country
>> no one will forget
>> the horror of this age

the secret city, published in 1977, was MacSween's third volume of verse. The volume as a whole is not as sustained, not as strong as *double shadows*, the poetry is—I hesitate to use the word with MacSween—lighter. In other words, his depression is, thankfully, gone; he seems to have written out and ridden out the dark night of the soul—left it behind perhaps in the more sombre and demanding pages of *double shadows*. There is a different tone, then, in the secret city, we find it in poems like "harmonies" where the poet acknowledges that he hears harmonies "shooting into the spaces of each day/mystery everywhere." Unlike the pages of *double shadows* and *the forgotten world*, when the poet sleeps here, it is to a "run of chords/ sounding in the soul's abyss," and he wakes, not to despair, but to wonder, and perhaps even enlightenment:

> but precious beyond telling
> the distillation of all hopes
> what the heart longs for
>> far beyond the mind's seeing
>> the broken scraps
>> of a perfect thing

In "silence," a somewhat old-fashioned rhyming poem (inversions and all) MacSween seems to admit where he has been emotionally: "if silence were in me/ I could capture a great song/ a turn of the tide in my life/ away from sadness and wrong." There is a tranquility, then, in the *secret city*, the poet-priest finally seems to be at ease, or at least more at ease, with the world he lives in and the world he has made—a place of books, knowledge, memories and, of course, solitude. Naturally, he still lashes out in indignation at the ever-present mediocrity; in poems like "the prince of this world" he mentions, in passing, that the prince's "illiterates write books/ teach in the university" nothing more than "blind astronomers/ who analyze the sky." The prince could be Satan or simply a personification of mediocrity. More importantly, perhaps, is the fact that the university is now a target of satire in his verse; it highlights that he has made, or at least is in the process of making, an important break, a separation from the institution. Later, in poems like "Jerome" we will see him make the same break, create a similar distance, between himself and his church. Despite these flashes of the old anger and indignation, the general tone of *the secret city* is not satirical, but quietly and profoundly meditative and reflective—there are many moments of wonder, renewal and hope.

MacSween once said, in reference to Wallace Stevens, that the writers who do not travel are often our most exotic. MacSween himself travelled very little in his lifetime, and then not very far: south to Washington and west to Toronto. He relied instead on his books and imagination to take him on the great and distant journeys; we see some of his hunger for travel and the exotic in poems like "night visitors" where "we meet nomad and camel/ horse soldiers of Ghengis Khan/ antelopes flying before the wind." The poem is old-fashioned in style, but it has a boyish sense of mystery and wonder to it, and in the final stanzas we are told "if we but follow/ we will come to a hidden land/ where all our fears will end."

For all his size there was also something hobbit-like about MacSween, something boyish and curious that survived in the man, a capacity for wonder that existed despite his knowledge of the wider and darker world, especially the world found in the pages and activities of Amnesty International. In one of his memoir pieces published in *The Casket*, MacSween spoke about his love of the mysterious, the arcane: "Certainly in my early days the world was a more mysterious place than it is now. There was something in the air that said that everything was suffused with the supernatural, the ghostly, the magical and along with these the fortuitous, the lucky, the unexpected. It was all one thing—this world threaded through with mystery of many kinds. It was not a matter of being watched by God; there were also the evil spirits and the guardian angels—and far away over the hills and the lakes, there were wizards and witches...." The passage would not look out of place in the pages of Tolkien.

Besides the standard fare of geographic magazines, he read the travel books of Waugh, Robert Byron, Jan Morris, Bruce Chatwin, Dervla Murphy and many others. Like Tolkien's hero, Bilbo Baggins, MacSween also loved maps, his office and rooms bulged with them, especially historical maps. He loved Tolkien's *Hobbit*, too, and was delighted that the mind of a professor had produced it. He had a similar love for C. S. Lewis and his Narnia tales (with, of course, the added affection for a Catholic English apologist), but his great favorite in this genre was Kenneth Grahame's *The Wind in the Willows*, of which he had many editions. And his favorite passage was the sea rat's parody of the wandering Odysseus.

Given his immense library it comes as no surprise to find a poem like "to read again" in *the secret city*. The opening stanza of which proclaims:

> I'm going to read again
> the books I've read before
> take down from my shelves
> the dog-eared texts
> once the inspiration
> of my youth

Fig. 50 MacSween's grandniece, Heather Crawford, in his rooms at MacIsaac Residence. Courtesy Dolores Crawford.

This poem, and many others in the collection, affirms the youth of MacSween's mind, its fervent curiosity—its capacity for wonder, and its hunger for knowledge. In the title poem, the poet insists that he is "peopled like a city/ with many inhabitants." These inhabitants seem to come from literature as well as life, though it is "those I have loved" that he wishes to bring back to "full life."

If MacSween had not founded *The Antigonish Review* it is doubtful that he would have published more than one volume of poetry in his lifetime—indeed, he may not even have published that. It is impossible, then, to overstate the importance of the magazine for him as an artist, and as a person. His contributions to *TAR* in its first decade were formative and sustaining, and it is his writing—above all else—that established the quarterly's tone and quality. *TAR* served MacSween well in several ways: it gave him a public forum for his poetry and fiction, and it became the perfect vehicle for his ideas on writers and writing; it also allowed him—for the first time in his life—to write about the books and authors that mattered to him. One of the realities of undergraduate teaching is its perennial adolescence; the knowledge shared with the young must be, for the vast majority, general and accessible—hence the perennial complaint about standards. Few scholars, especially at undergraduate schools, get to use their research, their reading in the classroom. The audience for *TAR* would never be large, but it would be sophisticated from its inception. What is more, once the institutional side of MacSween's world shrank—beginning with the Church and then the university—*TAR* became increasingly important to him until, finally, the professor, and to a lesser extent, the priest, inevitably stepped into the background and gave the field over completely to the editor, writer and reader.

IX   *C*alled From Darkness

*O*n April 12, 1981 MacSween wrote to his adopted younger sister, Theresa. The school year had just ended and his spirits were good:

> *I'm watching a baseball game with one eye, and writing to you with the other (using a pen too!). I think both can be managed. It's a very miserable kind of Sunday. The weather has been lovely up till now, but today is cold and windy. Classes are over, and we're waiting for the exams to start. I have one on Holy Thursday—then I'll run down to C.B. [Cape Breton] to help Fr. Mike. He wants me earlier, but the matter is out of my hands. I'll come back Monday and have another exam later. Then graduation. As you must know I'm semi-retired. It hasn't made much difference. I teach 2 courses instead of 3. I resigned as editor of our review and was kept on as Poetry Editor. I hope to have more time to myself now. It's not good to retire completely, but it's not good to have too many things to do. Everybody I know is well except a few that I shall not mention. I'm glad you had a good anniversary. I enjoyed it, despite a bit of guilt about not attending.*

Though he is still teaching two six-credit courses—with more than sixty students in each—and functioning as poetry editor of the review, MacSween regards himself as being semi-retired. Two months after writing this letter, he celebrated his 40th anniversary as a priest with two classmates from his diocese—one of them his long-time friend, Joe Marinelli. The three jubilarians concelebrated Mass with Bishop Power in the St. FX chapel before a large congregation while an article in *The Casket* spoke about MacSween's long career as priest, professor and writer—he was reaching milestones. On his 25th anniversary he had been made a full professor, but the honour, as he told Pat Walsh, did not impress him. A year earlier, Pat had published his long interview with his mentor and colleague in the summer edition of the *Alumni News,* an interview that delighted many of his former students, who sent letters congratulating him on his career as teacher, writer and editor. The next issue of the *Alumni News* was a memorial one for Fr. R. V. Bannon, who died on October 19, 1980, aged eighty. MacSween wrote a tribute for his old English teacher and former colleague, remembering how "he recited poetry as though he were eating something delectable, savouring each syllable while the class gloated along with him." MacSween also recalled the man:

> For many years he played golf every summer day. Nobody who has seen him in action could ever forget the fierceness with which he struck at the ball. And if he messed it up, nobody could forget the anger that flashed from him, warm enough to scorch the grass. But then, inevitably, would follow the humorous remark in which fun and vexation blended. And so it was in everything—in the way he prayed or said Mass, in the way he ate and drank, in the way he crossed the street or read a book. An unusual man, rich in character, rich in eccentricity, who taught us all and who gave us the gift of his spirit.[1]

The sentiments are genuine; MacSween thought highly of Bannon though he never forgot the cold shoulder he received from the older priest and English professor when he first arrived on campus.[2] They never became close, perhaps because they had too much in common, but whatever their differences MacSween always admired the fierce spirit of the Irishman. Bannon's specialty was Shakespeare; though no Anglophile,[3] he clearly, like James Tyrone of *Long Days Journey Into Night,* claimed the English playwright as one of his own, and could quote entire passages of the bard. In 1972 a scholarship was established in Bannon's name by the alumni association, and in the Homecoming program for that year there was a write-up that included one of his poems: "I used to tell them it was a translation from the Roman poet Martial." The version Bannon gave the alumni office was sanitized, cleaned up for the more con-servative alumni audience, but in MacSween's copy of the program, the edited version was crossed out in pen and the original written in the margins:

> I did not send my son to college
> to put him in the way of knowledge
> I exercised a parent's right
> to put the bastard out of sight[4]

Fig. 52 Richard Bannon in his youth. Courtesy St. FX University Archaives.

It could be Bannon's father speaking about young Richard, but the poem cuts both ways, indicting home and institution with equal force. MacSween loved it because it captured, as nothing else could, the rebel and iconoclast buried deep down in Dick Bannon, a man long hidden—from all but his fellow priests and family—under the fading black robes of his youth.

IN February of 1982 MacSween wrote again to his sister, Theresa:

> *I was down, as usual, at Father Mike's—my 34th time to be with him at that time. He's still talking about retirement [he is 68] but has no definite plans yet. He's the oldest active priest in the diocese now. There are a few older who help on Sunday but none who are in pastorates. I've heard from George a few times and from Catherine. And Murdoch gave me a run-down on what he saw during his Christmas visit. I'm all right myself—although when you're old and overweight, you never feel quite well. So I plug along from day to day, and the days go very fast. It's hard to believe that were heading down hill towards spring and summer again. We must do the best we can as long as we are still alive. I send regards to Ivan and to Brian and his wife, and to the girl who likes horses. Long may they reign! And the best to you, Theresa, all things heaped up, pressed down and running over.*

This letter, and the previous one, describes the lifestyle MacSween was leading when I met him in the fall of 1982. I had been away from home, from Cape Breton, for more than six years at graduate schools, one year in Ottawa and five in Dublin. MacSween still had his office on the fourth floor of Nicholson Tower, and although I had not seen him since 1976, he greeted me very warmly with that gentle grin of his saying "Well, look at the Irishman!" A partial dig, on reflection, at my acquired Dublin accent, but also, no doubt, at the fact that like him, I was a Cape Bretoner whose maternal grandfather's first language was Scots Gaelic. I was cautious and nervous around the monument, as he had once called his uncle Doc Pat, whose tower he now occupied, and I half suspected he would test me to see if graduate school had "contaminated" me—as it had almost everyone else he had known. University College Dublin was different from most North American graduate schools in that its students were often taught by creative writers and critics rather than by standardbred academics. Knowing MacSween would know this, I quickly dropped the names of John McGahern, Seamus Heaney, Denis Donaghue, Tom Kilroy and Seamus Deane, but before I had finished, or half finished, scattering my list, MacSween quietly intervened, tilting his huge head slightly sideways, he asked softly "What about Evelyn Waugh?" I wanted to say he didn't teach me or he's not Irish, but I didn't dare, and replied instead that, "Well, seven comic masterpieces is not bad." He repeated it immediately, and I realized, to my good fortune, that he had not heard it put quite that way before—or if he had, he'd forgotten it. Either way, I had earned a cup of coffee in the faculty lounge through the help of Sean O'Faolain, whose phrase I had borrowed but failed to footnote. (Later, much later, I found *The Vanishing Hero* on his bookshelves, he had read it when if first came out in 1957, the phrase I'd "quoted" underlined.)

The sixth floor of Nicholson Tower, in the northwest corner near the president's office, is where MacSween always sat—a place cherished, feared and respected. One of my former professors and a friend, Neil MacKinnon, a Canadian historian, confessed in good humour that you were always a bit nervous around MacSween as you never knew when he would pull up a book in your field that you hadn't read, but which he had recently devoured. MacSween never showed off his learning, and he wasn't, as some have maintained, a scholar-as-gunslinger, ready to shoot you down at a moment's notice; rather, he simply wished to share his reading and knowledge, to get the word out on what was good, to talk, in fact. When his close friends, his colleagues and proteges, were around, the air was electric with humour and wit.

Sitting down for coffee with Pat Walsh, Sheldon Currie, Jim Taylor, Kevin O'Brien, and Philip Milner, MacSween began his gentle banter, then, halfway through our coffee, George Sanderson arrived and asked was it true that I had met Borges? Before I could say yes, MacSween interrupted: "You can't have met Borges, I just told my class he was dead."[5]

He was still living in MacIsaac House at the time, and most of his books were now divided between his office in Nicholson Hall and his residence. It is difficult to describe the nature and size of this library—it was constantly growing and moving about, but MacSween knew, or seemed to know, where almost every book was located. In 1984 I brought the Irish critic, poet and biographer of Samuel Beckett, Anthony Cronin, to have lunch with MacSween in his rooms. Cronin was suitably impressed by the library, but he was dumbstruck when MacSween said "Yes, I have X." "You have a copy of X!" Cronin replied in astonishment. "I have them all," said MacSween. X was a short-run "little" magazine that Cronin had edited out of London in the 1950s.

In his later years, many writers, both foreign and domestic, came to visit him in his rooms, and their surprise to find such a cosmopolitan sensibility hidden away in a small Nova Scotia town, using the title "Father" (he's a priest!) was always overwhelming. The English poet, translator and editor, Michael Hulse, remembered one of these visits in a poem entitled

"Celebration," a work he later published as a tribute to MacSween, not long after his death:

> It was a room like Plato's Cave
> from which a man could easily emerge
> large with generous intent
> to see the day as if it were the first.
> The first he'd seen that morning anyway.
>
> I told him Chesterton declared
> that lying long abed
> would be the perfect way to live
> provided you'd a coloured pencil
> long enough to draw on the ceiling.
> Of course he agreed and guffawed,
> and paid me back by teaching me
> the Gaelic for pullet shit.
> *Not* (he insisted) *chicken shit*
> *No.* (A canny grin.) *Pullet shit.*
>
> Funny, to remember
> that once in cold October
> when the snow first powdered filigree
> and fretwork in a wooden town
> as white as a wedding, a man
> who married light and dark
> could make his mark on me for life
> by teaching me talk of pullet shit.

Fig. 53 MacSween celebrating Mass in Ontario, 1984. Courtesy Stewart Donovan.

Fig. 54 MacSween with his brother George and Sister Catherine, 1984. Courtesy Stewart Donovan.

IN the spring of 1983 I began what was to be the first of six road trips to Toronto with MacSween. Like Pat Walsh and Mick MacKinnon (father and son) before me, I was participating in a tradition MacSween had more or less kept up since the early sixties—his "going down the road" to visit family, friends and alumni in Ontario. Fr. MacSween always made these journeys around the first or second week of May, and they were timed liked this so he could miss both the graduation and the priests' retreat; but they were also planned early to avoid what he saw as Toronto's infamous heat. He generally stayed for a week and then, on the Sunday of the visit, his Cape Breton family and friends would gather for a dinner party that was always preceded by a Mass, celebrated by MacSween himself in their living room.

Both his sister Catherine and brother George—like so many Cape Bretoners and Atlantic Canadians—had been living in Toronto for many years. Catherine had a gruff exterior, but she was in fact a very gentle and humorous soul. She shuffled about in her slippers making jokes with the other women and men in her housing complex, clearly cherished for her personal warmth and good spirits; although her eyes continually blazed behind her thick glasses, she would be dead early in the new year. Her brother, George, a tall man who looked in extraordinarily good shape for his age, was an engineer by training and still enthusiastic about inventions he would like to build or test (when I first met him he was talking about a prototype golf club for improving your swing). Like Catherine, George now lived alone in his own apartment, he had been separated from his wife for some time, but he had friends and relatives who constantly came and went.

After visiting with his sister and brother, MacSween then went to meet some of his former students—almost always women—with whom he kept in contact through correspondence. Some lived in downtown Toronto and one in Orillia, a town north of Toronto, known by many Canadians as the birthplace of Stephen Leacock. MacSween remembered this student fondly because of the great love she had shown for the poetry of Philip Larkin, one of his favourite writers in his later years.

Not long after this first trip to Toronto, I suggested to MacSween that he vacation with us in my home village of Ingonish at the northern tip of Cape Breton. He leapt at the idea of spending some time near the sea again as he had not been "down north," as it is sometimes called, in many years. He immediately booked a cabin near the beach for himself and his friends, Marg and Ray Drohan. Margaret Drohan, the reader will recall, was the woman MacSween had first met and helped as a young girl when he was a curate in New Waterford in the 1940s. The days MacSween spent in Ingonish brought his now faraway youth back to him, and he spoke longingly and nostalgically of friends and families he had once known—most of whom were now long since dead.

It was at about this time, too, that a different past would be brought to MacSween's attention: the horror story of sexual abuse at Mount Cashel, a Catholic orphanage run by the Christian Brothers in St. John's, Newfoundland, was first making its grim headlines.

Fig. 55 Marg and Ray Drohan. Courtesy Stewart Donovan.

MacSween knew that some of his colleagues had had affairs with women and he knew, too, that there were gay men who had put themselves in positions of danger and had to be given "help," as he put it. When Daniel Petrie's film, *The Bay Boy*, was first released, MacSween said that he was told that "Danny put in the sex" in order to sell the film. The sex he referred to was homosexual in nature, as opposed to the pedophilia of Mount Cashel, and it was pretty tame by mid-1980 standards. Later, MacSween acknowledged that Petrie had been right after all—and prophetic—and that the scene was both revealing and compassionate in its presentation. Mount Cashel and the Church's reactionary response to it—its failure to immediately acknowledge responsibility—would leave MacSween in a rage at the institution to which he had dedicated so much of his life. The rage would eventually lead to one of his most powerful and tragic poems, "Jerome," in which the fourth and fifth stanza single out his "heritage" and indict his Church:

> I have emerged from my den
> chains clinging to my limbs
> not the chains of church and state
> but the invisible bonds
> of my heritage
> the corruption of my time
> the animality of my nature
> the leaden things
> of my personal being

I should like to scratch
    the body of the church
    as a woman scours out a pot
    so that the genuine metal
    shines from within
I should like to throw the scrapings away
    as worthless
    as a waste of time to linger over
    as a blind for the shining core

Louis Dudek has called this poem, and these stanzas in particular, "a passionate and overwhelming confession, of faith, of despair, of radical return."[6] It is, of course, all these things and more.

Beginning in October of 1983 MacSween developed a very severe case of arthritis in his hip, he had had attacks before, but this time he was unable to bend over, and had great difficulty in doing the simplest of things, such as putting on his shoes and socks. He refused, predictably, to see a doctor, dismissing them with contempt: "There's nothing they can do but give you painkillers." Accompanying this predictable (but almost pathological) fear of doctors, was the added dread of surgery for a possible hip replacement. Stoically—some would say stubbornly and foolishly—he suffered for several months until the condition eased and eventually improved.

He continued, of course, to write poetry, reviews and essays for *TAR*, as well as edit its poetry manuscripts—still by far its most numerous submissions. He kept in contact too with his fellow nuns and priests on the faculty by eating lunch in what was then called the priest's dining room in Morrison Hall. Having their own dining room was one of the few perks these men were given, especially the older priests, whose salary was never more than a pittance. Even so, there were still some faculty members who envied them this privilege, envying the treatment as regal. MacSween's salary at the end of his career peaked at fifteen thousand dollars before tax. He received room and board of course—the noisy "zoo" residence of MacIsaac House, and the perk of an up-market "all you can eat" cafeteria food. Still, he never complained. It is clear that these men and women were taken advantage of in their old and middle age, teaching at institutions of higher learning that denied them a living wage, when monies for that purpose had been clearly available from provincial and federal resources. These professor-priests were not Jesuits, that is, they did not have a vow of poverty, though most of them, as it turned out, lived a life of one regardless. (The conditions for the teaching and labouring nuns of course was even worse.)

MacSween was still teaching at the age of sixty-nine, but his skin was becoming thin: a former student, Oliva Dube, recalled one difficult morning class:

> Just before the Christmas break we were to do 'Bartleby the Scrivener' by Melville. Father went through the first three rows asking if they had read the story. No one had. He then got angry at us for not wanting to read this masterpiece and he said, 'No, I won't say that. No. You're a, you're a bunch of shits. Now get out. No? Well, I'm leaving then.' Then he left.[7]

Olivia Dube also remembered that of the seventy or more students in the class not many were doing the required reading, and MacSween was having a hard time with their indifference. It could be argued of course that MacSween had now lived long enough to see Marshall McLuhan's prophecy come true, but he was unable to fully accept the fact that the Gutenberg Galaxy was under siege to the same extent as his beloved Ecclesia. It would be wrong to say that Professor MacSween did not have faith in the institution he had spent so much of his life in: though he constantly railed against the university, he still believed in it, always hoped that it could be made better. As far back as 1972, he had meditated and written on the state of modern education, most significantly in his impassioned review of Ivan Illich's *Deschooling Society*:

> The school system in itself is a gigantic corporation, dwarfing all others, designed to produce not learning, not scholarship, not the life of the imagination, but simply mindless uniformity. It does not exist for the benefit of students, but for the benefit primarily of those who administer it. For example, a teacher who is not accredited, even if he is the most brilliant member of his profession, loses his job. He loses it not because he defrauds his students but because he puts in danger his colleagues who have gained their rank not through talent for the most part but through drudging accreditation. The hungry students look up and are not fed.[8]

Prophetically, perhaps, 1984—George Orwell's once ominous but now domesticated and benign date—would be MacSween's final year in the classroom. His leave-taking, his exit—after more than forty years in the university—should have had something accustomed and ceremonious about it, to quote Yeats. Instead, and perhaps more typically, MacSween left his English department and his university fighting one last battle—it was a fight in which he would suffer both defeat and, as many of his friends and colleagues saw it, betrayal and humiliation. The battle, over a hiring in the English department, occurred when MacSween was asked by Pat Walsh to lend his support to Pat's candidate. When MacSween arrived at the department meeting to give his opinion and to vote, he was told he had no legal right to be there. According to Pat Walsh, MacSween had asked the Dean if he could participate, but the Dean had made a mistake: "He assumed that because of Father's status and long-time service that he naturally would still be a voting member of the department." It was the last time MacSween would see his department colleagues together, and the two friends whom he felt had betrayed him, one a former student, were no longer a part of his circle; his contact with them ended for good. He retired formally from the university in the following spring without pageantry: there was no party, no speeches, no gifts, no ceremony and no acknowledgement from the institution or department that he had spent more than forty years in as student, professor and priest.

By the summer of 1985, MacSween's health was in serious decline. He suffered, as do many chronically overweight people, from apnea, a condition which prevents the person from getting into deep sleep. In his last years, he avoided his bed almost entirely, choosing instead to sleep sitting up on his sofa or in a chair. He still feared doctors and never went to see them, so his condition went undiagnosed. Had it been, he might very well have lived longer—he certainly would have had a better quality of life in his final years. His constant waking in the night, his inability to sleep, meant he watched television—too tired to read, he surfed channels. The next day at lunch with his colleagues, his head, understandably, was full of the shows he had watched. Some of his colleagues were astonished at what he as watching, others were bewildered and still others, annoyed. Like so many retired people, he came to spend much time alone, long hours awake at night, no doubt often lonely. Like most of us, he hungered for human contact, and when that was not available the voice and image emanating from the blue light would have to do.

Still, it is surprising (and somewhat comic perhaps) that MacSween became addicted, even for a brief period, to day-time soap operas. Former students and friends alike were caught off guard by this obsession with the box: one former student, a medical doctor who was also keen on writing, drove the three hours from Halifax to spend the day with his retired mentor discussing, he hoped and expected, literature, writing and ideas. What he got instead, as he told George Sanderson, was an hour-long summary of the soft drink wars between Pepsi and Coke. Not just the soaps, then, but naturally enough the ads (the soap itself, or soft drink in this case) drew him in. McLuhan's sleeping giant, the cyclops as he christened it, had the retired polymath well in hand. MacSween's addiction to the soaps lasted for about two years—the period immediately after his complete retirement. Although he clearly had more free time, the loss of the day-to-day contact with the classroom—his students, colleagues and friends—came at a price he may not have reckoned.

The 1984-85 academic year, then, was a crucial time for MacSween, one that witnessed his complete break from the university and from *The Antigonish Review*; it was also, more fortunately, the year in which he finally received some national recognition for his poetry. Less happily, but predictably at this point in his life, MacSween's friends and family began, inevitably, to pass on. It was, as Martin Amis famously wrote, time to stop saying hi and start saying goodbye. On August 29 I went to visit him in his rooms, and when he answered the door his eyes were red—he tried to make a joke: "My sister just died, I suppose you had something to do with it." Then his eyes filled, again. Two weeks later he showed me a poem he'd written for her, it would appear in *Called From Darkness,* his last collection of poems; it is simply entitled "spring"; there is no reference to his sister:

> after aching and rage
> >   my heart like a stone
> is crouched in its cage
> >   of cold winter alone
>
> i had counted the days
> >   as the sun grew alive
> till my heart in the rays
> >   of its light would revive
>
> then the end of the wane
> >   of my sorrow would pass
> i would creep from my grave
> >   like a flower from the grass
>
> and the spring came like gold
> >   inspiring to song
> but my heart had been cold
> >   in the winter too long
>
> so my heart sang no word
> >   and shall never again
> like a child or a bird
> >   forever—amen

Catherine was the last of his sisters and he said, more than once over the weeks and months that followed, "I've only George left in Ontario now."

Later in the year, MacSween received more news about his writing: Fred Cogswell, the former editor of the *Fiddlehead* had included one of his stories in *The Atlantic Anthology* and more importantly perhaps, George Sanderson had brought out what would be his final collection of poems, *Called From Darkness*. The book was relatively well received in the Maritimes: Richard Lemm reviewed it favourably in *The Atlantic Provinces Book Review*: "R. J. MacSween is not a household name in Atlantic writing. Yet his devoted work over many years makes him a worthy figure in the region's literary tradition.... His latest poetry collection ... displays a graceful voice and wisdom that should not go unrecognized."[9] It was Louis Dudek, however, who first got MacSween national attention in a review he published in *The Globe and Mail* in June of 1985. The review was short, but the passages Dudek quoted were excellent and he was exuberant, fulsome in his praise. Always modest about his writing, MacSween was not untouched by this acknowledgement of his talent as an artist, his pleasure at the recognition is evident in a letter he wrote to his niece Dolores in September: "I take for granted that I sent you my last book—*Called From Darkness*. Tell me right away if I failed to do so. It got a very good review in *The Globe and Mail*—I intended to send that also. How about it? If I failed, send me a post card and I'll make it up."[10]

There is little doubt that *Called From Darkness* was his most eloquent collection to date. Dudek acknowledged the power of the verse, beginning with one of the most prophetic poems ever to be published in Canada, "the shrine":

In 1984, in his fourth and last book of poetry, *Called From Darkness*, R. J. MacSween wrote some prophetic words:

> people turn away
> from the magnet of former times
> the shrine of Lenin
> will be deserted
> as though the Russians
> had become weary

> it will happen suddenly....

I was struck by this prophecy when I first read it in the spring of 1985 (Gorbachev only took office in March, 1985), because I myself had made a similar statement, two years earlier.... Now, when Lenin's statue has been toppled in many parts of Russia, and the shrine in Moscow itself is likely to be removed or deserted, these predictions stand out as astonishing acts of foresight.[11]

With his characteristic insight and honesty, Dudek goes on to discover that MacSween's predictions were in fact several years before his own—"the shrine" appeared in 1980 in volume 43 of *TAR*. Other poems singled out by Dudek in the collection include, "because," "the unexplored," "surveillance," "just born" and "where are they gone." As in the earlier volumes, the familiar themes are here, but the voice is even more urgent, more insistent on spiritual awakening and accountability. So, in "once in the garden,"

> the heart longs to walk back
> into the womb that bore us
> to escape the misery of our race
> to forget the miles we traverse
> before death

The poem ends with a "seductive voice/ calling us to repeat / our gruesome history." "because" is a poem that also calls us all to account—the poet himself included. Here is the third stanza:

> I understand why someone
> suddenly hurls his precious books
> into a canyon
> without waiting for the sound they make
> far below
> or why someone smashes
> the rituals and sacred art
> that coil around some ancient good

Called From Darkness is about healing and understanding; it is also about the beginning of MacSween's own preparation for the "distinguished thing," as the master, Henry James, once defined death:

> because these things stand in the way
> they hinder his steps
> they clutter his mind
> but especially because there is
> so little time

It is easy, here, to see MacSween moving towards his great poem "Jerome" which he eventually publishes in the spring of 1986. Above all else, the poems in *Called From Darkness* bear witness to a healing and a letting go—they are poems about making an ending, an exit, with dignity, grace and some hard-earned enlightenment. The writer confirms this directly in the title poem of the collection:

> truth hides in the shadow
> effaced forever
> unless called from darkness
> into the bright sun
>
> we could spend our lives
> in shame and degradation
> unless we find the secret
> crouched within the forest
>
> maturity discovers
> the trembling fawn
> the frightened fawn
> motionless among the ferns

There is only one poem in the *Called From Darkness* collection that seems out of place, that appears to belong to an earlier time: it is called "celebration" and it opens with a priest saying Mass to a few souls. In his last years, I went with MacSween several times to the Mount St. Bernard Chapel where he had said Mass for almost forty years, and still did so on occasion. The sad and elegant chapel was all but deserted; empty except for a few lonely nuns, it had the feeling, if not the appearance of the chapel perilous of Eliot's Wasteland, where only the wind was at home. One Sunday morning there was no one but myself and one aged and frail beadswoman in the congregation:

> in wintry cold in lonely celebration
> the altar calls its votaries
> to sing of paradise
>
> the room small
> dingy from the years' neglect
> and the simple aging of wood....

"celebration" is a poem, in the end, that tries to celebrate the Church as a cultural and political institution when its time, at least in the west, seems all but done. The poem moves backward to the Roman Empire and further still to "the breathing of troglodytes," "and the animals of Bethlehem." It is no longer possible to link—in the contemporary world at least—the words "dignity" and "Empire." Although MacSween may have written this poem for his fellow religious, for those who'd "kept the faith" in political and cultural terms, throughout the good and bad times, few of these were his family or friends. These things were dear to his heart and he spoke of them often:

> There's no surety anymore that people will keep their religion. When my father's brother John James, when he went out to Winnipeg, to become a policeman, my father took him aside and warned him to go to church. But there was no trouble with him, he went. He wouldn't have to warn him. Very Catholic all my father's family were. They could travel anywhere and keep the faith. And Dr. Nicholson, too, although one of them was very wild, but he wouldn't divorce his wife although they broke up. And the oldest of whom I'm called after, he married an Irish Catholic woman down in the States. That generation would hang on to the faith. I met that Rod's wife once, aunt May—and tough on the faith—according to my father she drove the boys out of the church.

Given what we now know of both modern Ireland's and Boston's struggle with the church, we sympathize deeply with the independent Aunt May and her early Magdalene sisters. But we must always remember, too, that MacSween looked at the institution from the inside—it was family—and he felt for his fellow religious as genuine brothers and sisters—in all their loneliness and neglect. MacSween also wrote "celebration," one imagines, because he knew deep down that an angry and righteous tide was welling up and about to break over them all—guilty and innocent alike. Ironically, and sadly, the faith kept by many of his co-religious was political," and the political—as MacSween knew in his deeper self—could not sustain them. In poems like "learning," "surfaces," "so long denied," "the unexplored" and "surveillance," this deeper self of the poet overrides the sentimental, if well-intentioned and compassionate, priest:

> we should like to hide ourselves
> not from God
> but from ourselves
>
> we had thought the final days
> upon us
> but the final days are our
> time of truth
> we unlearn the lessons

Call From Darkness

so painfully acquired
and limp into understanding
of the mystery of life

we lift our heads like dogs
who sense an enemy
in the distance

we fear the revelation
of an avalanche
of old error
in the primary school
of our last days
(from "learning")

sometimes we descend
to the catacombs
empty these long years
there we find the rodents
prospering in nests
made from our cast-off robes
and there the spider strings his web
among our sacred emblems
thrown away
(from "surfaces")

the aged think that life in general
is deserving of tears
every day they feel within
a smother of sorrow
they try to preserve
a semblance of dignity
before the staring world
(from "so long denied")

there is always regret
at so much death
where life should reign
our greatest joy is a fraction
of what our lives should be
(from "the unexplored")

the world a museum
its modern age spinning on its weird way

into the future of might and maybe
surveillance always
beyond the edge of things
all settled and defined
as from white light
love falls
(from "surveillance")

There is a scene in the 1995 Academy Award-winning Netherlands/
Belgium film, *Antonia's Line*, directed by Marleen Gorris, where a severe
middle-aged priest, has finally had enough, in the words of Sheldon
Currie, of "the heavy handed rituals of the Catholic Church."[12] The priest
flees from his church, pulls off his robes, and runs through "the glory of
the open fields" in his long white underwear. He returns later, marries and
has many children with a loving and sensual wife. It is a wonderful (and,
yes, romantic) moment, that is by turns comic, liberating and satiric. The
ex-priest has been called from darkness in a more dramatic way than the
speaker in MacSween's poems, one that is perhaps easier for us, who live so
comfortably in the modern secular state, to comprehend. But while Gorris
and others like her celebrate the end of this old paradigm of patriarchy,
it is well to remember Terry Eagleton's warning about being on guard,
about the dangers of speaking of a post-religious age at a time when ugly
fundamentalisms lurk around corners and prey upon the lives of peas-
ant farmers and office cleaners who have been abused and disregarded
by uncontrolled capital and greed. Few people were better placed than
MacSween to know that culture could never replace religion as the most
resourceful symbolic form human history has known.

IN September of 1985, MacSween wrote once again to his niece Dolores.
He talks about his brother George who has had another stroke and about
his own health:

> *I've had some trouble: a very sore hip (ok now) and an awful flu last year. I
> feel much better now. I think I'm taking better care of myself than I used to.
> This year I'm not teaching at all and so I get up late every morning. That's a
> break. I never used to get enough rest and was always sleepy. I believe that
> my sore hip was the result of exhaustion.*

He doesn't say of course that he can now take a nap whenever he wishes
to, or that he is still not sleeping through the night. He does confess,
however, to not being as productive in his writing as he was, but he has
learned to let this go, as with so much else: "I thought I should write a

great deal more since I am completely retired now. So far I haven't. I feel just as keen as ever but I haven't the same compulsion to write, feeling that it's up to others now." He then goes on to reminisce about his vacation in Ingonish:

> *It was very good to be living by the ocean again. The water was cold—but of course I don't swim at all now. Once the whole bay before me was alive with fish—I have never seen the like. I was told it was pollock chasing caplin. For a while I could see fish leaping from the water everywhere—over the whole bay. (If you've been there you would know how wide the bay is.) It's said that the pioneers saw that phenomenon all the time—even in the brooks and lakes. A man came down to the shore while I was watching and, by casting, caught about six fish. His wife took them to their cabin in a plastic bag. If you're here next year early in July you may find me there—if I'm not in Antigonish, OK?*

MacSween was seventy years old when he wrote this letter and in the five years since he retired from *TAR* he has been extraordinarily productive, especially given his poor health. Besides writing enough poetry for his collection, he has published numerous reviews and three major essays on David Jones, Evelyn Waugh and Roy Campbell, the South African poet he had met in his youth. Because he no longer had an office on campus, he spent part of the working day in his beloved library, sometimes down in the room which stored many of his books, but mostly upstairs with his friends on the library staff. Though his life was now quiet, people continued to

Fig. 56 Celebrating Mass in Ingonish, 1985. Courtesy Stewart Donovan.

drop in on him, including Alistair MacLeod on his way to Inverness each summer, and John MacEachern, his nephew, on his way from Glace Bay to the Nova Scotia Legislature, where he eventually became Minister of Education. In a memoir he published shortly after MacSween's death, MacEachern recalled some of the meetings he had had with his uncle:

> I asked him what was the best book he ever read. He replied after more than a moment's hesitation that it was Chesterton's *Orthodoxy*. I asked him what was the greatest age of literature and he responded that it was the Shakespearean era and, when I asked why, he said that it was because of Shakespeare having lived then. I asked him how long it would take to become a scholar and he replied that it would take at least three weeks. And how long to become a mystic I asked. Even longer than three weeks he answered.[13]

In March of 1986 I brought the Irish novelist, Francis Stuart, to St. FX as part of a Maritime university tour. MacSween was intrigued and read several of his novels before he arrived. Stuart had fought on the Republican side during the Irish Civil War and was interned by the Irish Free State. Prior to his involvement in the Revolution, he had met and married Iseult Gonne, the Irish artist and daughter of Maude Gonne, the famous beauty, actress, patriot and subject of many of W. B. Yeats's famous love poems. It was through Maude Gonne that Stuart eventually became close friends with Yeats who was instrumental in establishing his early career. MacSween had lunch for us in his rooms and he spoke about his meeting with Tony Cronin, Stuart's close friend, and as with Cronin both men hit it off by agreeing, with much laughter, that they didn't like Yeats's poetry very much. The evening went well and MacSween was extremely pleased to meet this legendary figure from Ireland, not least of all because of the literary figures Stuart had known and met, among them François Mauriac and one of MacSween's heroes, G. K. Chesterton. Stuart told MacSween about a prize Yeats had given him for his first book of poems, "He crowned me with a wreath of laurel in a somewhat ridiculous ceremony." Chesterton was there and Stuart had spoken to him: "But, you see, it was in a fashionable tea shop in Dublin and Chesterton kept making these jokes, his huge frame shaking with laughter, and I could see that this didn't suit Yeats, so being very young and having just been crowned by Yeats, I thought I had better keep quiet."[14] MacSween's eyes lit up at the anecdote, especially at the mention of the great English Catholic apologist.

Coincidentally, at the time of his meeting with Stuart, MacSween was rereading much of Chesterton's output for an essay he would publish in a summer issue of *TAR*. That essay, as with so many of his critical pieces, throws light both on its subject and on MacSween's own life, ideas and beliefs:

> Chesterton returns again and again to the solid worth of the poor, and to their unerring sense of what is sane and healthy in life.... Here Chesterton reveals his weird ability to look beneath the surface of things. He said that the man who leaves home for far adventure is actually running away from the greater adventure of the family. His street is too exciting. His neighbours are too exciting. The true adventure is at home.... The glory of England (and its empire) had obscured the fact that it existed at the expense of the poor. In spite of his admiration for England (and it was very great), he felt that the rich had robbed the people not only of their property but also of their liberty.... He is always wholly himself, faults and all—he speaks to us, he jokes with us, and—alas!—he often makes flourishes for us: it is the flourishes which are most annoying, but they are there and a small price to pay for the keen mind that accompanies them. He is a talker, as most journalists are, and therein lies the secret of his lasting power. In his work a voice is always speaking. It escapes at moments, but it always returns. It is seldom a solemn voice; it is always vivacious, it is always kindly, it is always wise.... They are not just essays; they are essays elevated by genius into true literature. Nowhere else can one find so much life, so much talk, so many jokes, so many startling ideas, so many errors set right, so great a joy in life, so great a love of men and women.[15]

In May of 1986, MacSween prepared once again for his regular trip to Toronto and Ottawa; it would be our fourth road trip together. His brother George, after much suffering, had died during the winter, and as we left Antigonish he began, sadly and lovingly, to talk of him:

> He was the best looking boy in Glace Bay. He was tall and slender then, strongly built but not big, a wonderful face and his hair was so thick, curly hair. But there was a bit of instability in him. Nobody in the house was so affable as George, but that little trace of irritability if things didn't go right. It would come out of him suddenly. And he would also argue sometimes when he was wrong, he could be pretty awful.

MacSween also remembered, with more than a little regret, the argument he had had with his brother years ago on a trip to Toronto. "We were driving along and George was raving about engineers. He'd point at a bridge and say look at that engineering marvel and look at these roads and so on. Well, by the time we got to Fredericton I'd had enough. So I said, 'you are our servants.' Well, he got furious!" A year later, MacSween recalled, Pat Walsh was in Toronto and he saw George, "and do you know what he said? Rod thinks we're his servants." It was still on his mind!

On this particular trip, after much cajoling, I persuaded MacSween to let me record him on the journey. He resisted at first, saying that he had nothing important to say and that his life was not worth writing about anyway, mostly because he had done nothing but "sit at home on my bum." I had been prepared for this so mentioned what he had written about the letters of the Welsh poet and painter David Jones:

> His outer life was uneventful, but it contains one great moment which exhilarated his spirit and placed its mark upon him forever.... It must not be thought that this artist lived the life of action: in fact he was close to being a recluse.... He never married, ordinarily he lived in small apartments cluttered with the odds and ends that gather in an artist's life. He must have been alone often and in need of a friend's presence. And they came to his door, for indeed he had wonderful friends....[16]

MacSween, of course, responded that he was no David Jones, but he eventually surrendered to being recorded and soon forgot that the machine was on. Many of the topics we covered concerned his own childhood and youth, and after this trip I gave him a copy of Patrick Kavanagh's autobiography, *The Green Fool*, in order to try and encourage him to write a similar memoir. In the last years of his life, he made good on this and wrote—with encouragement from Jacqueline Walsh, editor of *The Casket* newspaper—a series of weekly articles about his ancestors, childhood and youth.

Naturally, the car was always loaded with books. The then poetry editor of *TAR*, Peter Sanger, described how they often took over the vehicle: "They slid from small, splaying stacks when you opened the door. They would often travel in your lap, ostensibly to avoid being trampled, but actually to enable you to flip through them quickly to find out what newness Father had found which would never be noticed or reviewed by anyone else in Canada, let alone the Maritimes." When we travelled he always liked to bring an anthology of poetry so he (and those of us travelling with him) could look something up or, more often than not, read a poem out loud. He had a brilliant capacity to recall whole poems—not that he deliberately sat down and memorized them—rather, he had taught them so often over the years that they seemed to naturally rest in his great memory. His favorite text in later years seems to have been Oscar William's *Little Treasury of Modern Poetry*. Although Ezra Pound was his favourite poet to study, in his later years—and on these trips in particular—he argued passionately for the lyric tradition, the tradition of song. He believed, in fact, despite the epic tradition of the *Iliad* and the *Odyssey*, that the lyric had a stronger and more lasting impact than the long poem. This was something his hero, Pound, despite *The Cantos*, also believed. When Tennyson came up, for instance, only the lyrics seem to survive, hidden though they were amid long narratives like Maud:

> Come into the garden, Maud,
>   For the black bat, night has flown;
> Come into the garden, Maud,
>   I am here at the gate alone;
> And the woodbine spices are wafted abroad,
>   And the musk of the rose is blown.
>
> There has fallen a splendid tear
>   From the passion- flower at the gate.
> I'm coming, my dove, my dear;
>   I'm coming my own, my fate
> Was there ever so airy a tread
>   My heart would hear it and beat
> Had it lain a century dead

When he finished he said, "I'm not sure if I got those right, it's been a long time." He hadn't got it quite right, but he was close enough after thirty years or so since he had taught it. Others he liked to quote from included the all-but-forgotten Ralph Hodgson poem, "Time You Old Gypsy Man,"

> Time you old gypsy man
>   will you not stay
>   put up your caravans
>   just for one day....

There were many others that stretched back and forth in time, one of his favourites from the 17th century was George Herbert's "Virtue":

> Sweet day, so cool, so calm, so bright,
> The bridal of the earth and sky:
> The dew shall weep thy fall tonight;
>   For thou must die. . .

It may seem strange to readers of his own poetry, that MacSween would have such a love for these simple but classical sounds, the cadences and music of verse, especially when his own poetry was so deliberately prose-like, so austere in its rhythms and chaste in its diction and final effect.

Naturally, other subjects besides poetry surfaced: there was, as always, his beloved Church. Still defensive and ever optimistic about its position in the west (though some of this was a posture), he genuinely hoped for its revival. When I pointed out that the Christian existentialist writers of the 20th century believed that Christianity would only survive now in small groups, he would have none of it: "You have to have an organization of some kind, human beings cannot get on without it. If you leave it with books, with small groups, it will disappear. The church wanted to include everybody, according to Christ. He did not want an elite. You have to have an organization." When I asked him bluntly if the Church would disappear he was defiant, eloquent and, as always, humorous:

No, it won't disappear. "Behold, I am with you all days, even to the end of the earth." It has to adjust to this age and the age is moving so fast that we're making a poor job. One dumb bell in a key spot can last say seventy years. The holy people are very important, but the day-by-day slogging will be done by the [priest's name] of this world. He's just in the wrong place, if he hadn't been elected beyond his capabilities, he'd be an ordinary fellow, doing good, preaching well. You've got to have a lot of those fellows because the elite can never go around. It must be a very flexible organization and it's not.

He then goes on to explain how the Church might be reformed. Many of his suggestions are by turns practical, literary, naive and utopian, but they were always delivered with wit, humour and insight. My brother Alvin was with me on this trip so he had more than an audience of one, and he loved an audience—it brought out his wit and humour like nothing else:

If I were starting to reform them I'd start with the miters and crosiers and all the paraphernalia of the bishop. The masses have been stream-lined, but it needs a little bit of elevation now. The canon of the Mass is beautifully done. We need better singing, singing is the thing that everybody likes doing, and you have to get your composers and every-body else going. I bought that new hymn book from England and a lot of the hymns are written by modern composers. Get Michelangelo in here to do the back of a church. Okay, Michael, what do you think? We have to get more of that rapport with the artist and so on. We have to get the priest, but especially the bishop, because he has more of the trappings of ancient times than anyone, get him down to the simple things. Get rid of the bishop's palaces, every one, get rid of them! Put him in an apartment somewhere, teach him humility. If you put a fel-low in a palace you get a terrific bureaucracy, put him in an apartment you get almost nothing. The thing almost creates the rest of it. Take the mitre off the bishop and he becomes a sensible guy. Put the mitre on him an he's a nitwit. Bertolt Brecht, that play, *Galileo*, where the Pope is getting ready to give it to him, and in the beginning he is all right, but as the vestments come on him he gets stricter and stricter, until, finally, he allows them to show Galileo the instruments of torture. It's true—those things bring on the rest. If a bishop sat down in his chair with a t-shirt on he'd never show the instruments of torture to Galileo. But put him down there with all kinds of things on—with a mitre on his head and a crosier in his hand—and by God he'd crush you like an ant, or an uncle. Get rid of all that stuff!

On matters such as divorce, birth control, celibacy and female clergy:

We'll force the bishops to keep a steady propaganda against the Pope. Set commissions up to study these things and follow what the commissions say. Put a good theologian on it. But you have to start with those externals because they lead people in false ways of thinking. They were all right when they were dealing with barbarians and pagans and so on. The Pope should set up committees of learned men to teach us things we've lost. To try to get the people to know what a mystic is. Like that Michael Hulse, he told me he was a fallen away Catholic and I asked what's wrong? And he said, "Oh, I've got objections to the church." And I said you have no reasonable ones. "Oh, yes, I have," he said and I said what are they and Doug Smith interrupted us. But I'm sure he couldn't have given us any. What he would speak to me about would be those externals and politics. Those are not the Church. And I said you'd better start reading the mystics. And he said what are they? or who are they? Why is Michael Hulse, who is thirty, why should I have to tell Michael Hulse that? He reads voraciously. I started with Julian of Norwich and John of the Cross's poetry and he looked at me as though I were introducing Arabic. But we have to use writers and artists more, because they're the people who are alive. People who study codfish in the Atlantic, they're not alive. [The dig was at my brother, Alvin, in the backseat whose Masters thesis in history at UNB had been on the Maritime Fisherman's Co-Op.] They will probably pick an Italian Pope, who will be tolerant.

MacSween finishes his defence of the Church siding, as it were, with Edmund Burke rather than Tom Paine when he insists that "the real revolution is not worth anything, it breaks things up and causes animosities. It will be changed by a bunch of conservatives from within who are frightened." At the end of his long and passionate defence, however, it is not the Gospels or rituals that he evokes and remembers, but rather the role the Church has played in matters of social justice:

When they asked Christ if he were the Messiah he said several things, but the last was: "And the poor have the gospel preached to them." That's how you know the Messiah is here. Whenever a saint has been tested to be somebody he has always been a man of the poor. Paul Claudel, when he was over in China, got a letter from Jacques Rivere who had been a Catholic who had left the Church, and he started writing to Claudel to get guidance. Claudel started to guide him, telling him what he should do, like reading the Bible and going to church, and doing this and that, but at the end he says, "But above all give alms to the poor." Above all! Ahead of prayer, ahead of Mass, ahead of everything! Give to the poor!

And so we drove on through Northern New Brunswick, then past the elegant silver spires of the north shore into the cold Québécois evening light, passing Kamouraska: "I forced my way through Kamouraska in English. I didn't enjoy it at all, the movie was better. I read another one, and again I had the same trouble. I had to force my way through it. Geoffrey Hill translated one of her [Gabrielle Roy] poems in *Agenda*." From literature, the conversation changed to sport, and so passing a local golf course brought back the game he had loved and the heroes of his youth:

> When I was in high school in the early 30s I went down to the movies one day and they had a short on golf and Bobby Jones. He would tee up somewhere, say over the water, and the camera would focus on the green and the balls would be dropping all around the pin. Just like rain all around the pin. And then he would go to a sand trap and the balls would come out all around the pin. God! you never saw anything so beautiful in your life! It's an amazing game, I'm glad I learned to play.

As we travelled along the St. Lawrence river with its busy shipping lanes, discussion of my six-year-old son's fascination with the *Titanic* surfaced. He had shown MacSween his model when we passed through Fredericton. The ship leads to the movie (the first one) which leads to E. J. Pratt's poem, a natural enough progression:

> It would be great if you could get that movie for him. I like the movie for itself and when it scrapes the iceberg, and you know it's going to be finished, but you can't help but be just as interested as though you didn't know. Pratt's got a tremendous facility. He was a great friend of Sister Doyle's.[17] I doubt if he was an agnostic. I saw him on television twice. What a delight! Could you get those things for your class? What a delightful man!

From E. J. Pratt we moved to television, his loves and hates:

> Look, I can't stand *MASH*. The very sound of the music gets me. Some
> of them have such lovely themes like the one Bob Newhart has. *Hills
> Street Blues* is good, *St. Elsewhere* is the same, if I take the time to
> watch it—I often skip it. I still watch *Cheers*, oh, I love it. It's wonder-
> ful. I don't think I've missed more than two of them. Oh, its a dandy,
> especially the girl Shelley and the little Jewish girl. And I love the
> music for *Cheers*. I like that whole introduction, it's very nostalgic.

When asked about other shows of interest, he insisted on the quality of
Star Trek:

> It's beautifully put together. I don't like it when they return in time
> to the earth. I like those that show imagination. I never saw a show
> with so many good examples of imagination as *Star Trek*. Some of the
> plots just stun you, they're so good. Rodenberry said he was saved a
> lot of trouble by not having money. He would simplify a plot, set, and
> clothes because he didn't have enough money. But he has a great mind,
> he wrote many of those. What they are good at is adventures. The best
> one I ever saw was a battle between the Clingon captain and Kirk. I
> feel like calling my friends up when it's on.

We always tried to make Drummondville our first overnight stop, so
Mississauga would be in afternoon striking distance the following day.
On this trip, MacSween had just finished reading Maynard Mack's biography of the 18th-century poet Alexander Pope, and he was preparing to
review it for *TAR*. So as we travelled down the 401 toward Kingston in
the 1985 Pontiac Bonneville, we time shifted and set our minds for the
18th century. MacSween always spoke as if all the ages—especially the
ones that mattered to him most, the ones he felt passionate about—were
contemporaneous with our own:

> I feel that Maynard Mack plays down his Catholicism a little too
> much. See, when Swift asked him to turn Protestant, and Bishop
> Atterbury asked him to turn too (the letters are preserved), he already,
> in the beginning of the book there, makes a play with his answer to
> Swift. He gives them very smooth answers, he doesn't want to offend
> them, but he's not going to turn Protestant and that's the important
> thing. Everything was in favor of him turning Protestant. He could so
> easily have done it, his father and mother were both dead when Swift
> wrote to him, and also when Atterbury wrote to him. These were close
> personal friends, but he gave them very smooth answers, he didn't
> want to say keep your damned religion. So he said to Atterbury, when
> I was young I read all the books of controversy on both sides and I
> was one thing with one book, and one thing with another book, so I

decided the best thing to do was to stay with your own religion. And you see this was in the air at that time, you didn't disturb what you had. But, nevertheless, behind it all is I'm not turning. And I think he was much more Catholic than they say.

MacSween's identification with Alexander Pope, his belief in the words and messages of the mystics and his defense and hopes for his Church as a fallible, human institution, all proclaim and occupy different aspects of what, throughout this biography, I have called his Catholic cultural nationalism. It might appear, in these recorded conversations, that all of these concerns seem to have more or less equal weight, equal billing, but this is not the case. MacSween could discuss and engage both high culture and popular culture—both entered his life and he enjoyed both—but there is little doubt about where he placed the higher value. He knew, of course, that there was a price to pay for engaging high culture, but he also knew that we were being entertained to death. He worried about the loss of traditional culture and the culture represented by his church—his poems constantly address this theme. He eventually came to an understanding of cultural studies and cultural theory without actually directly engaging these thinkers (though Terry Eagleton's career was followed from the very beginning, because of his Catholic and literary concerns).

Although MacSween took stances, postures and positions, for the Church-as-institution, he also knew that faith—and his own faith in particular—was rooted in something transcendent, something he found expressed in his beloved mystics. Still, as we have seen, he did believe in Ecclesia, in religion as culture, in eschatology—the grandest narrative of them all. And he held publicly to all of this, even as the faith of his childhood and youth lay wrecked, broken and abandoned about him. In many respects, of course, his profession of professor sheltered him: for all his protestations about the importance of the public intellectual, his scorn for elites, mercifully he was spared the onslaught of the day-to-day world in his old age. In this regard the ivory tower more than fulfilled its clichéd expectation. His last years were spent in the parish of the mind and heart.

Going down the road, then, there was something endearing, sad and otherworldly about MacSween's passionate defence of, for example, Alexander Pope, this long-dead-fellow-Catholic; and this was felt all the more keenly as we entered the huge sprawl of the secular city, the modern Gomorrah whose spires were not those of Chartres, Notre Dame, Cologne or Santiago de Compostella, but rather the commercial Mecca of Eatons, Skydome and CN Tower. We hated Toronto. We loved Toronto. After all, we were Cape Bretoners and this was our home away from home. The Jays were looking good (they were on their way to World Series status) and the traffic had not yet reached the levels of Cronenberg's *Crash*—though it was bad enough. When we arrived at Mick MacKinnon's, MacSween settled in around his family and friends and the stories and laughter would begin. During the day, in the quiet hours, he sat outside reading, always reading, pen in hand to mark the passages of importance. Besides a half-dozen or so books, he always read the latest literary magazines, and on this trip I recall him quoting from an issue of a little known poetry magazine from England called *Agenda*.[18]

On Sunday, his family and friends gathered for dinner and a Mass,[19] then, as usual on our journey home, we stopped in Ottawa where we visited his niece Jessie Sutherland and her family; we also visited David Conrad who then taught classics at Ashbury College. MacSween had published some of David's poetry in early issues of *TAR*, and he was keen to meet a young classics scholar fresh from studies in Greece and archeological digs in North Africa, mostly Tunisia. Their great debate at the time was whether or not the Roman Empire would have lasted had it not moved to the east; MacSween always insisted that it would have:

> They no longer regarded the empire as theirs, only the east was theirs.
> If they could have kept it easily, they would have, nobody likes to lose a

Fig. 57 MacSween with his brother George at a party at Michael MacKinnon's in Toronto. Courtesy Stewart Donovan.

part of the empire. But their real care was for the Greek part, once they
began speaking Greek. Justinian could still speak Latin, he was the last
Emperor who could, but after him that was it—it became all Greek.
Over in the east, the empire got smaller and smaller and David tried
to dismiss the fact that Justinian conquered Italy because it only lasted
twelve years. It shows the ineffectual grip that Constantinople had on
the rest of the empire. They conquered a big chunk of Spain and lost it
almost immediately. They conquered North Africa, held it with a garri-
son. The people didn't want them. The people were speaking Latin and
they were speaking Greek. Justinian had tried to conquer the whole
empire again and make it one, and he took chunks here and there and
softened his part of the empire by putting everything into the army,
but useless. It took the Arabs almost a hundred years to conquer North
Africa, especially near Tunis. Think of what the Romans could do,
sending in excursions and cutting off their shipping and all that—from
Rome, Constantinople is too far away. The future lay with the big areas
that were speaking Latin. You could always rely on them and they
loved Rome. All the break-up David talked about all happened after
they moved to Constantinople. Under one emperor again, with their
various fortresses along the Rhine and the Danube, they could still
hold out; and from the centre point which was Italy, they could send
armies in any direction, and across the sea. Over on the other side,
Constantinople had no boundaries. Look at it today.

The topic is interesting insofar as it highlights MacSween's lifelong interest in the classics, but it also has something ethereal and (though he
would groan at the word) academic about it. MacSween always regarded
and discussed the Roman Empire as others might discuss science fiction or fantasy literature; the battles of the empire were no more real to
him—contained no more blood or suffering—than those of *The Lord of
the Rings* or *Star Trek*. And it was not the connection with the Roman
church that sparked his interest, but rather the passageway back to his
boyhood and youth—when he first absorbed this world of empires and
battles from the land of black and white heroes and villains, Romans and
Visigoths, Celts and Vandals. Of course he was aware of the difference
between history and fantasy, and he wrote about the brutal realism of this
world in several poems, including "Tamerlane,"[20] the last stanza of which
recognizes the price of empire:

no Tamerlane is caught by time
every age hears the clangor
of his steed's hoofs
on the stones

> in the evenings fathers tremble
>> at the news from Turkestan
>> from an early age Tamerlanes know
> their work
>> the ordering and arranging
>> of mankind
> and with what cruelty
>> they act out the libretto
>> of their destiny

When we were leaving Ottawa, after a visit with his niece, Jessie, he remarked out of the blue and simply that: "It's a strange world, you know, that everybody has to die." He then went on to speak about his clan and family:

> They're a very nice family, those MacSweens in Ironville (Rod, Danny, Sister Gregory) but they were not powerful like our family, our family was like a vortex. George would talk to me about that golf club about ten years before he built it. (Pause) Eunice was one of the sweetest girls I ever met. I'll get Father Kehoe to go over with me. I told him I didn't want to say the mass, but I'd help the parish priest. Murdoch is seventy-six. Just five years older. It is a terrible waste, but what can you do. (pause) The king of Saxony was a Catholic and he commissioned the Mass from Bach. There were three or four Breughels and the elder was certainly a Catholic, but the most famous one was one of the younger ones.

The Eunice referred to is his nephew Jimmy's wife, who died of cancer while still in her early forties.[21] MacSween wrote of her and other matters in a letter to his niece Dolores in June of 1986:

> *She was very warm and friendly—and so young that her death seems an unfair thing (although it isn't). Don't try too hard to grasp my poetry. If you want to, a browse once in a while is the best way to grow into them. It can be done—and it's a good thing to conquer something difficult. I've done it often myself, because none of this comes easy. I've often had to work for years to assimilate a given writer. After a while you reach a boundary beyond which all is smooth—the mind gets trained first as any animal may be trained. Whatever is within the scope of that training will then become easy. If the attempt to conquer is not made, then the boundary becomes a wall beyond which you cannot develop. (Am I making things worse?) You yourself write very well and therefore have the essential ability to pass beyond into the area of facility. That's all. I'm living quietly, finding each day busy enough. In July I go to Ingonish for five days. Last year I stayed there for 10 days, but now I'm on pension. Beyond this I shall try to write*

and live. The enclosed magazine has a poem that you might like. Scientists think the universe began with a Big Bang. I imagine God as a great gambler setting off the Big Bang. Of course he would know (and a gambler would not) whatever would follow. So—imagine! Best wishes to you, to your husband and to the children! All kind of love!

His poem "the gamble" continues his long involvement and debate with the scientists; here is the opening stanza:

> when we are overwhelmed by sorrow
> or by the sheer drabness of every day
> the thought comes
> this great experiment of God's
> the universe sent spinning
> within his being
> like a ball into an enormous room

Another poem in that same volume he sent Dolores is entitled "a summer day" and was written in Ingonish as he relaxed by the ocean; its last stanza echoes something of the great equanimity he was approaching about his life and coming death, even while he raged at the world around him:

> the sun is warm like an animal
> embracing the body
> the water too is warm
> lazily lapping the shore
> satiated with its wealth
> of darting fish and seaweed
> it is the present and the past
> the harvest of life concentrated
> in a moment
> and contentedly lingering
> without thought of an ending

MacSween was writing his greatest poems at this time and he continued to do so until his death. In 1985 he published his "confessional" masterpiece "Jerome":

> now that I've reached the end
> I speak openly to others
> why should I not speak openly
> to myself

sitting all alone
        in preparation for my last journey
        I am like Jerome
        his lion glowering behind him
all the monsters of fancy
        peer from the surrounding darkness
        to see the spectacle of my fall....

There is little doubt that he spoke openly to others: it was, for instance, increasingly difficult to spend time with him at lunch in the priests' dining room as he would speak up and out loud if he heard someone saying what he considered nonsense about education, the Church, politics or—especially—sexual abuse. He was vitriolic if he heard any of his fellow priests trying to justify or sanitize what he saw as the destruction of children's lives and the betrayal of his vocation. There was, at the time, a feeling among the clergy and religious of being under siege, especially post-Mount Cashel. Fr. Kehoe, his good friend, looked out for him and helped him move to his new residence, a small apartment complex built primarily for retired priests. Kehoe was well known as the head of sports at St. FX and he described to his friend Rod how he was verbally attacked one evening at a basketball banquet in Halifax—told to take his collar off to shouts of Mount Cashel. MacSween felt sorry for his friend but said that it was not unexpected, and his fellow clergy should not be all that surprised at the public outcry, which he felt could have been much worse, given the nature of the crimes. Rod's brother Mike, and some of the other older priests in the Xavier apartments in Sydney, also spoke about being afraid to go out for walks for fear of being attacked or beaten up. Their fears were unfounded but this, apparently, was how they felt.

One of the poems MacSween published in 1986 was the anti-war poem, "in the quiet fields":

what cold heart in our days
     could start a war
     to set the tanks rolling
        the bombs falling
     to make the cities shake
        with the vibration of planes
     to say yes to the red-eyed hawks
        with their curled hands....

The poem echoes his earlier and more haunting "angel wings" from the spring of 1985. He said he wrote this poem after reading through a whole issue of Amnesty International's World Watch Report on Human Rights violations. Years earlier, MacSween had founded a chapter of the organization in Antigonish:

> if you were an angel
> > and flew over all the world
> > how you would cry
> > > at our scenes of torture

The poem then goes on to describe the various acts of torture taking place on the planet, "the lonely the beaten the starved," "the prairies of death." The last two stanzas end with the narrator taking off the beautiful wings of the angel:

> then you would return
> > to your starting point
> > heavy with the sorrow
> > > of a million helpless souls
> you would remove your wings
> > as a termite   its flight done
> > removes its useless wings
> > and tunnels into the earth again
>
> you would spread your wings
> > on the ground
> > where they would wink and flicker
> > like a peacock's tail
> > with emerald and sapphire
>
> then you would ask God
> > never to give you wings again

In July he spent five days in Ingonish; though shorter than his other visits, he got to meet Terry Whalen of St. Mary's University. MacSween was impressed by Terry and greatly admired the work he had done on *The Atlantic Provinces Book Review*: "It's amazing how he finds the time to put it out." Terry was also completing a book on Philip Larkin, one of MacSween's favourite poets in his later years.[22]

When the fall term began at my own university, I got a rare letter from him:

I am in hospital at present, and will be for another week, I think. I am suffering from angina and the medics are trying to ameliorate it to some extent. I've had the pain for about 10 years and it is much worse now (no worse than when you were here) I'm in no distress. In fact, I feel like a malingerer. Guests who come to see me look much worse off than I do—but I guess I'm the one in danger. Ken [Donovan], Barbara & Co. dropped in for a few moments. I haven't gone to see them since you left here, and so I was very glad to see them. I thought of Ken yesterday as I was reading a book on Rome. The author, about page 50 said that the average soldier signed up for 25 years. Then about page 30 he said that the population had reached a death age of 30 (going into the old error again!). Then he said that a boy could join at 15, serve for 20 (he pulled down his first figure by five points), and then die at age 35. He doesn't explain that the State used to give its veterans land for farming all over the Empire. (I think the world is populated by a bunch of shits!). How's that? Give my best to Denise and Hugo. Don't <u>think</u> of coming to see me. I am <u>not</u> sick.

No one knew that he had been suffering from angina for so long, even though it came as no surprise to those who knew him, given his size and general health. The doctors gave him nitroglycerine pills to ease his pain, but there is little doubt that the attack of angina hit him hard. In November (1986), Mary Lou O'Reilly did a feature on him in *The Casket* newspaper for his fiftieth anniversary as a St. FX graduate. When I saw the photo I was shocked by how much he had aged; he is seated with a picture of the class of 1936 in his hands, while Sister Kathleen Gorman, a fellow alumna, in great health, looks on.[23]

His angina attack meant that he would have to slow down his pace even more; others were slowing down too; his brother Mike would undergo a hip operation and retire to a home in Sydney. MacSween continued to visit his close friends, the Sandersons, every Sunday for dinner and they, in turn, would drop in to see him on a regular basis, as did other friends, colleagues and students. George Sanderson also brought writers to see him, some of whom were connected with *TAR*—Bruce Powe, the Toronto novelist and critic, and Michael Hulse from England among them. To get out of the apartment he continued to go to lunch in the priests' dining room

Fig. 58 With sister Kathleen Gorman class of 1936. Courtesy The Casket.

and from there he would go to the library to visit with staff members such as Kevin MacNeil. It is sad that his small office on campus was taken from him; he would have enjoyed meeting with students, but St. FX was no different from many other universities in this matter; Fred Cogswell at UNB, Louis Dudek and Hugh MacLennan at McGill all, eventually, had their offices taken from them.

In the fall of 1987 St. Thomas University awarded Honourary degrees to Gus Martin, Chair of Anglo-Irish Literature and Drama at University College Dublin, and the Irish Ambassador to Canada, Sean Gaynor. We organized a small conference to coincide with the convocation and invited scholars from Atlantic Canada and Montreal to give talks. MacSween drove up with Pat Walsh for the weekend; Gus Martin had been Pat's mentor at University College Dublin and he remained a close friend. MacSween stayed with my family in our apartment where he read a copy of David Adams Richards' novel *Blood Ties*, a book we had left on his bedside table. In the morning he had read most of the novel which he praised highly. He was especially impressed by the scene where the old people are fed baby food, "Boy! It comes to us all, eh?" was his remark. I reminded him that this was the writer whose career he helped give a boost to by publishing his first short story. "Is this the same fellow?" (When he went home he raved about Richards to the Sandersons, saying what a fine writer the young man had become.) Although he did not attend any of the talks or ceremonies, he did come to a dinner party hosted by an ex-priest and an ex-nun who were now husband and wife, Patricia and Hilarion Coughlan, and whose beautiful home overlooked the Saint John River. MacSween, predictably, was the proverbial life of the party and greatly impressed the Ambassador, his wife and the scholars—when he and Pat Walsh were leaving, Michael Kenneally from Montreal, one of Canada's leading Irish scholars, remarked of MacSween: "It was great to sit at the feet of a master."

In the spring of 1987, MacSween published a holocaust poem entitled, "crime":

> one awful thought haunts us
> when we pause for breath
> the crime inflicted upon an innocent people
> the pawns of history
> shuttled about from left to right
> then placed at the crossroads

a focus for violence
then blamed for their very presence
at that scene of murder....

That winter (1988) he also received his first letter from Louis Dudek:

I have wanted to write to you to say how much I have been moved by your poetry in the current Antigonish Review. It is what Pound called "straight as the Greeks," a poetry surprisingly effective through plain statement unadorned with imagery or metaphor (well, there are some, but one feels most strongly the pure statement). You prove again that all our theorizing is futile and the only requirement is to write a poem. It is a mystery deep from the human soul, for which one must always be grateful. You are unquestionably one of the best poets writing in Canada, and this must eventually be acknowledged....

That same winter MacSween published two poems "Adam" and the overtly Christian "when time ceases"; he also completed his long awaited essay on Gerard Manley Hopkins:

In dealing with G. M. Hopkins, we are always haunted by the question: What course would English poetry have taken had he been published early, say in the lifetime of Alfred Tennyson? It is obvious to us now that some kind of revolution was in the making, but it was delayed until the coming of Pound and Eliot, when Hopkins had been dead for some years. When the first edition of his poetry appeared in 1918, Eliot and Pound for the most part ignored it. It had come too late to be part of their heritage. Their, almost complete, silence in regard to Hopkins seems to be deliberate avoidance, a refusal to spend time on a mislaid ancestor.[24]

After a discussion of Hopkins's verse, his sprung rhythm and inscape, MacSween then describes his life: though he avoids Hopkins's sexuality—something he knew and acknowledged in conversation—there is much compassion in the description of the lonely English Jesuit among the Irish: "Probably some of Hopkins' trouble was the result of overwork on his delicate constitution. There were also his isolation in Ireland and his feeling that his life was drifting. Few writers have been so alone. The Jesuits around him were friends, but not one of them supplied the comradeship he needed."

That summer MacSween published a poem entitled "flying" and his long review essay on Maynard Mack's biography of Alexander Pope was finally completed. He knew that not many of his readers had sympathy for this poetry, or for the long dead figure from the distant past:

We look at Pope from across the chasm which was the Romantic Movement. Only by an effort of sympathy are we able to live within this poetry, to feel its intensity, to love its masterful technique and aristocratic tone. Wordsworth, the herald and philosopher of the Romantic Age, asked poets to base their work upon the conversation of the people. Pope took for granted that he was to base his upon the fine diction, the fine manners, the fine artistic sensibility of a highly educated elite, the aristocracy of the 18th century. He succeeded very well—but the age he represented was passing away, perhaps never to return. [25]

In these last years his niece Dolores and her family made one more visit from out west:

The last time I was there with Father Rod they were moving out his books. And I said are they going to name a library for you? And he said "Well, after I'm dead, not while I'm alive." And he said they named Nicholson Hall after Doc Pat died. He sounded like he might have hoped so, but if they were going to do it, it wouldn't be while he was still alive. When we were leaving he said, "Well, all the others are gone so come and give me a nice kiss." I said, oh, I don't think so. It seemed so strange. This is just when the priests were starting to be taken to court for molesting children. Mount Cashel had come out and two schoolmates of mine, the Richard twins had been charged. That was horrifying to me because I graduated with their sister and they were just ahead of us in school. All of that was just so shocking. And I was saying to Father Rod you know that I'm grateful that this is coming out and we have to face it and we're not to lose our faith over it. But we have to clean up, and these people deserve to be heard and so on. And I said, you know we were always taught that priests were asexual and he said "Oh! NO!" He was horrified that I had said that. And I said, but they were supposed to be to us. And he was just like "Oh how can you say that!" And I said, well, because that's what I was taught, that the nuns had no ears and never went to the bathroom. And the priests were supposed to be different too. We were never taught that they were human.

Fig. 59 MacSween with his niece Dolores and her two children, Glen and Heather. Courtesy Dolores Crawford.

IN January of 1988 MacSween again received national recognition through the support of Louis Dudek. The Montreal poet and critic had been asked by a literary editor at *The Globe and Mail* to name someone in Canada who was an expert on Ezra Pound: without hesitation, Dudek gave him the poet-priests' number. MacSween wrote a full-length review of John Tytell's *The Solitary Volcano* for the Saturday edition.[26] In March of that same year I brought the Irish poet Paul Durcan to St. FX as part of a Canadian university tour. MacSween told me he had read that Durcan was anti-Catholic. I told him, "He's anticlerical, but no more so than yourself." They got on famously when they met, though MacSween was not feeling well: he had had a bad case of the flu and his angina was steadily getting worse. He was also suffering from depression. Over lunch he spoke about people who commit suicide and told a story he had read about a man jumping from a building: "Boy, some days I understand how he feels." Durcan was fascinated by the man, by the way he spoke, "even the cadences of his voice." He was not attracted to MacSween's poetry, however, at least not to the *Called From Darkness* collection. His criticism was that he had paid such a price himself, personally, for his own verse, that he found it hard to relate to a poetry of ideas, a poetry where the personal element seemed absent or repressed. It is a severe criticism. Durcan's close friend, Francis Stuart, on the other hand, greatly admired MacSween's verse and wondered why it was not better known. When we were leaving St. FX, Paul asked me if "the man had any faith left." It was a fair and understandable question coming from an Irish poet who knew more than a little about the oppressive orthodoxy of the ultramontane Irish church, a church almost identical to that of old Quebec.

The spring of 1988 was to be our last trip to Toronto together. As in previous years, I drove to Antigonish to pick him up and we stayed in Fredericton. My partner at the time, Frances MacDonald, came on the trip with us, and besides enjoying her company we had the added comfort of having a registered nurse along for the trip. His health was poor and he was taking heavy doses of nitroglycerine and other medications. Those family and friends we met in Toronto felt that this might be the last time they saw him. We had spoken about the possibility of a trip to Spain, the one country he had ever expressed any interest in visiting: the old pilgrim routes to Santiago de Compostela, Gaudi's church of the Holy Family in Barcelona, the Roman ruins of Sagunta, the Prado and El Greco. His niece, Jessie, told him she would pay for his flight. He let the idea gently rock and wash over him like a warm wave, a pleasant pipe dream encouraged by all whom he told it to. "Yes, it would be good."

In the summer he continued to drive back and forth to Cape Breton, and he came to Ingonish for a few days as usual, but he spent most of his summer time now with Marg and Ray Drohan at their cottage in Bras d'Or just below the Seal Island bridge. Marg was, as always, very attentive to him and she recalled how he liked to sit in the kitchen singing old songs his mother had sung when she had prepared his supper. When he wasn't reading he spent much time in the past, recalling his boyhood and youth for the articles he was writing for *The Casket*.

Besides his pieces for *The Casket*, he was still publishing poetry and reviews: in *TAR* 73 he published a short essay on Evelyn Waugh's only historical novel, *Helena*. It is an interesting essay and highlights MacSween's own fascination with history. He did not enjoy historical novels especially, unless they had some kind of peculiar twist or were connected somehow with the present. I remember mentioning the novels of the Irish writer John Banville who had written books on Kepler and Copernicus. MacSween then mentioned his own favorite writer of historical novels:

> Have you read any of Alfred Duggan's historical books? They are masterpieces, they will not die. He wrote one on the *Consorts of the King*, *The Wisdom of the Dove*, a book on the first three Caesars, if you see any of them you should buy them, most of mine are in the library now. I sold a lot of novels to the library one time, I got $600 for three hundred books. That was the end of that. I got rid of all those fine books, eh. I must have had ten of Duggan's. But he writes the most masterly of historical novels. Banville would have to be good to beat Duggan. There's nobody in Duggan's books that's unusual, they are all ordinary human beings. Duggan was published by Faber. Nice neat books.

In his essay on *Helena*, MacSween confesses that a "certain minimum knowledge of Roman history must be the reader's or else he will turn away from the most original of stories."[27] But he also acknowledges that Waugh's historical novel is not a dull tome of chronicled events:

> Most people expect an historical novel to be a very serious affair. Waugh had different ideas. There is a note of fun running through the novel and also a note of fantasy. Behind it all there are serious concerns, especially the love of the real and the practical, and also the fact of religion in the here and now. We imagine we are beginning a fairy tale when we are told that Helena is the daughter of Old King Coel of Colchester, England who possesses a three-piece orchestra.... Waugh's own historical sense is so keen that he is able to bring us back to the fourth century with ease. He makes a few strokes, a bit of conversation, the short description of

a house—and we find ourselves hobnobbing with a Roman emperor or his servants.

In the spring of 1989 we organized an international conference at St. Thomas University for the Canadian Association for Irish Studies. MacSween was driven up by my youngest brother Leo and stayed at my home. There were many writers and scholars from Ireland, Scotland, England, the United States and Canada. MacSween had already met many of them including Tony Cronin and Paul Durcan. We did not make our annual trip to Toronto that spring because his health could not stand the stress of the long drive, and of course he still refused to fly.

Despite his weakened condition, he was still writing and had finished another poem, "the stars and comets," and completed a review of Shusako Endo's novel *Scandal* for *TAR* 76:

> This latest novel by Shusako Endo has brought anxiety to some readers. There is a turmoil in it that is not characteristic of Japanese fiction in general. That fiction as presented to the West in translation is a fiction of meditation, of silence, of quietly advancing thought and emotion. This is true, for example, of Tanazaki and also of Kawabata. We could imagine that we are examining glassware for flaws; the flaws inevitably appear but we are in the midst of silence.

In many respects, MacSween's review of Endo is more of an indication as to where his mind was in these last years than the essays and reviews—as great as they are—that he wrote on Catholic writers. In writing poems like "celebration" and "when time ceases" and essays about Chesterton, Hopkins, Newman and J. F. Powers, he was, of course, being loyal, not deserting the ship, doing what Moses Coady long ago said he could do—be a tremendous Christian apologist. But I would argue that this is not the only place where his heart liked to be.

On that last trip to Toronto I brought up the figure of Joseph Campbell, whose series on myth was running on television at the time. MacSween slowly built up to a ferocious *ad hominem* attack on Campbell that ended with, "Then he sticks that big ugly face up there...." I burst out laughing and said "There's not much left of poor Campbell on the floor beneath your feet." He began to laugh and shake, as was his way, saying: "I was pretty hard on him, wasn't I?" He continued, "But why couldn't he have stayed in the Church? His objections don't make sense." I did not, needless to say, try to defend Campbell. MacSween greatly admired the Scots-American's common sense and his wide and diverse audience appeal—a scholar who could reach out to the general public, a man who could talk about ancient myths and religions and relate them to the audience of *Star Wars* at the same time. He also liked his approach to religions, how they fulfilled a deep human psychological need over the centuries. He admired, too, his attitude towards science, not unlike his own, especially as expressed in poems like "the gamble."

In August 1989, MacSween wrote one of his last letters to his niece, Dolores, where he remarked that "We're all getting dreadfully old. I'm fairly well myself—on a diet at last and very hopeful about it. Next time you go to embrace me, you'll miss me, I'm sure. (Don't believe it!)

Dolores phoned him many times after this; during her last conversation she told him about a trip she made that year to what was, then, still Yugoslavia:

> I went to Croatia as a nurse with a friend who has diminished lung capacity, her daughter had been and she had been cured of M.S. and she wanted to go in gratitude, but Air Canada wouldn't take her without a nurse with her so my daughter and I went. Father Mike was very upset, he does not believe in it because it has not been sanctioned by the Pope, and he doesn't believe in this Mary stuff anyway. But Father Rod was very pleased and he said, "Good for you." But that was the last time I talked to him.

In 1990 MacSween published his last two essays, one on J. F. Powers and one on Cardinal Newman. Powers is an American short story writer and novelist who used priests as his main characters:

> When Catholics wrote about priests, they tended to make them into heroes or saints. The heroes engage in shallow melodrama, the saints tend toward pious anemia. When J. F. Powers regards priests, he sees them as they really are—some are saints, some are rascals; but most of them are ordinary.... The question has to be raised as to the symbolic value of the group. Is it representative of anything? Do its various manifestations of life call to our life? Is it significant of good, or of evil? At first sight one is inclined to answer in the negative. Ordinarily the priestly life is remarkably low-key, it is ordinary of the ordinary.... But to Powers no mode of life is ordinary. He is well aware of the twisted nature of the heart of man. He is appalled at the mediocrity of this group. He sees the individuals as plants that have not burst into fruitful life. They have wasted their promise. They have surrendered to materialism or to petty tyranny, they have compromised with evil. Tragedies lie around them.

In the early summer of 1990 my brother Ken and MacSween went to visit Mary Gillis, his cousin, and a granddaughter of George and Catherine Nicholson. Ken was working on an essay about the role of the visual arts in Cape Breton and MacSween thought he should mention the work of Christine MacKinnon. Christine MacKinnon was MacSween's first cousin and she had once sketched a portrait of his grandfather, George Nicholson. It was through MacSween's instigation that this long forgotten artist, who had lost her hearing at the age of two, and who had been helped by Alexander Graham Bell, finally got her work published and acknowledged. More significantly for us, MacSween told my brother on this visit to Sydney that he had just written his last poem. It would be published in *TAR* 81-82 with his essay on Cardinal Newman. It is entitled "our treasures":

> do not watch the artist at his practice
> the weight of the world strikes home
>   when we meditate the imperfect
> the boy labouring at the piano
>   while his comrades shriek in the fields
>   is a sad example
> not because he is clumsy
>   but because he reveals too clearly
>   the imperfections of us all
>
>   let us go to the concert
>   where the polished artist completes
>   a series of sounds
>   that whirl in the air
>   around us
>   then go home happy
>   joying in the experience
>   of a finished thing
>   that laughs at the process
>   that produced it
>   the stops and starts
>   the sour notes the rhythmic breaks
>   the sweat and the ennui
>
>   they are all ours
>   the splendours and the miseries
>   they are our treasures
>   art that makes us sing
>   with our whole being
>   pain that makes us cry
>   against the limits of our life

In August I met him at the Englishtown ferry in Cape Breton and drove him to Ingonish; he was in great pain so he stayed only for one night;

the next day my father drove his car to Englishtown and I followed. At the ferry he took over, he was only going as far as Bras d'Or to see Marg and Ray Drohan. I got out of the car and, for the second time in my life, I hugged him—I knew in my heart that I would not see him again. I did speak to him on the telephone though, and two things I remember: we were discussing the great French sculptor, Rodin. I was praising him, MacSween brought up Michelangelo: "The Horned Moses shows a man who had led his people, who had *seen* God and talked with Him. Rodin could never have produced it." The second occurred when, leafing through one of the old anthologies he had given me, I commented approvingly on his harsh marginalia on Wordsworth. "I was young and stupid," he said. "No, take a look at his 'Extempore Effusion Upon The Death of James Hogg'. A poem written in his old age about the death of his friends. How hard it is on him to remain behind." It is indeed a powerful and sad poem. He quoted two stanzas from memory:

> Like clouds that rake the mountain summits,
> Or waves that own no curbing hand
> How fast has brother followed brother
> From sunshine to the sunless land!
>
> Yet I, whose lids from infant slumber
> Were earlier raised, remain to hear
> A timid voice, that asks in whispers,
> "Who next will drop and disappear?"

On October 9 he was down in Sydney visiting Marg and Ray Drohan when he took sick. He told Marg that he could no longer read, he had difficulty seeing the book. The old City Hospital was on strike at the time, but he was admitted. They soon said it was best if he went to his own doctor in Antigonish so Marg and Ray drove him to St. Martha's Hospital where he underwent tests, joking all the time with the nurses and creating much laughter. He died early in the morning on October 10; he was 75 years old. His close friend and colleague, Sister Margaret MacDonald had died the same day. Joe Coffey, a former student and fellow writer, drove up from Maine for the funeral, and when he saw the remains of his old professor and friend he voiced what many of us at the time were feeling—MacSween looked as if he'd fled his body in relief, in escape. There was no sign of the man we'd known.

*A*fterword

*I*n Margaret Atwood's novel, *The Blind Assassin,* a war memorial is un-
veiled in the fictional Ontario town of Ticonderoga on Remembrance Day
1928: after the bagpipes are played speeches are made, "many speeches,
and many prayers, because the ministers of every kind of church in town
had to be represented. Though there were no Catholics on the organizing
committee, even the Catholic priest was allowed to say a piece.[1] Atwood
reaches back here into Ontario's—and by extension English-speaking
Canada's—Protestant past. It was a past beset with cultural and political
imperialism, a place and a time when religion, politics and ethnicity had
much (but not everything) in common.

This is the era in which R. J. MacSween was born. MacSween was
a Canadian Catholic priest who also happened to be a writer of genuine
merit, and although his position in the Canadian literary canon is still
subject to some qualification, there can be little doubt that he deserves a
place in that tradition. MacSween's career, of course, is of interest for reasons other than strictly literary ones—even though those reasons are not
unconnected to his writing. I have maintained that MacSween's complete
poems record, among other things, an extraordinary spiritual journey—a
journey unique not only to our own country, but, I would argue, to what
was once known as the Catholic world. As a priest, living in Catholic
communities, much of his life was naturally predetermined, but while he
lived and worked amid the traditional limits of the Catholic attitudes
of his time and place, he himself always sought a personal freedom that
constantly challenged those limits. The Protestant, Anglo-Canadian attitudes and power structures, recorded by Margaret Atwood in her novel

and elsewhere, persisted in varying degrees of intensity for almost fifty years of MacSween's life. We remember, that in our country's centennial year, 1967, he is part of a panel with Eli Mandel and Fred Cogswell that awards the young Atwood a prize for her poetry. He is there, as they are, to be both a religious and a literary representative. The moment was symbolical, but we cannot make too much of it, as the paradigm, even then, had already shifted—the old Protestant ethos, as much as the Catholic one, had given way, not simply to the modern world, but to the secular one as well. The English poet Philip Larkin recorded that *annus mirabilis*, that year of wonder, as 1963, but whatever its exact date, the Christian era—as Canadians, and much of the western world had known it—had ended.

And yet, for almost fifty years Fr. Rod MacSween had lived and worked almost exclusively in an English speaking (as opposed to Anglo) Canadian Catholic world. During these years his Catholic identity—his religion, culture and politics—what I have termed a version of his "nationalism," was seen to be both formative and pervasive; it was also intensified by the simple—and at times overwhelming—fact that he was a priest. It is a truism that the vast majority of citizens, of his and earlier generations, were—culturally at least—Catholics first and Canadians nationals second. This fact would later prove problematic for MacSween, especially when he is confronted with a nascent and secular Canadian cultural nationalism.

Some who knew MacSween—his intelligence, wit, insight and vast knowledge—wished he'd been a different writer from the one he became. They wanted an artist who would record the culture that he and they had come from; they wanted someone who could capture forever the rhythms, sights, sufferings and joys of their region and their people—they wanted, in fact, an Alistair MacLeod. As we have seen, for many reasons, MacSween was incapable of this, but to say so does not lessen his achievement—and his achievement is considerable.

His life, perhaps, more than most lives, contained contradictions: the artist in him promoted Canadian creative writing, and so he was one of the first to teach it at a university in Canada; when he founded one of Canada's pre-eminent literary journals for creative writing he chose an Englishman (albeit a Catholic priest) to edit it; he insisted on publishing Atlantic Canadian and Canadian writers first and foremost, but he refused early on to establish a course in Canadian literature. He was a committed and, at times, culturally sectarian Catholic; and yet, he was also extremely critical of his Church, its hierarchy and its often benighted dogma.

At times, publicly, he often gave the impression of someone who was fierce, bluff and domineering; and yet those who knew him intimately, in his more private moments, found him to be a man of extraordinary gentleness, sensitivity and kindness. His own personal past, the world of his parents and siblings, was often fraught with violence and tragedy, so he constructed, as many people do, a different and a gentler heritage. We can hardly blame him for that. In his old age, he wrote about this lost and largely fictional world, and not the traumatic one he had known and was heir to.

Summing up such a complex person, such a diverse life has not been a simple task. Those colleagues, friends and students who knew MacSween intimately and intellectually, generally express unreserved awe at the power of his mind. George Sanderson, who knew him better on this level than most, has placed MacSween with McLuhan in his ability to talk and connect. The judgment seems right, but unlike McLuhan, MacSween kept himself hidden, most of his probes, insights and humour were not recorded. Instead, they linger on in the minds of those of us who knew him, and pop up now and again in his best essays, but there is a sense that MacSween the intellectual and wit, the professor as iconoclast, might not survive. And unlike the late—and greatly lamented—Louis Dudek, R. J. MacSween did not get, or try to get, his personality into his poetry until very late in the game. This does not lessen the poetry, the achievement, but it makes it different; if anything it could be argued that it enhances the tragic nature of the verse. MacSween's poetry is a powerfully public verse that at times strikes a deep emotional chord—especially when public and private worlds collide. This is especially true in those poems about his

Church and his faith. In the end, MacSween achieved a serene equanimity in the matter of his faith, and while his poetry may indeed record an often tragic journey, he himself seemed accepting and reconciled with the world as it was, even as he hoped and prayed for its betterment.

MacSween once wrote of a favourite writer that there was something "learned, oblique, and delicate about this giant of a man." In one of the photos of himself he sent to his nostalgia deprived niece, Dolores, in the 1970s, this delicacy is evident—made manifest and dominant—because the camera has captured something else, something masked while

Fig. 61 Gentle smile, MacSween in Cape Breton, 1972. Courtesy Dolores Crawford.

in crowds, but something revealed in private with students, family and friends—gentleness. I like to believe that he sent the photo to Dolores—chose it deliberately for her—because his niece was so much in need of gentleness. In need of an image of the MacSweens so counter, so different, from the one she had grown up with, from the one she had fled.

IN July of 1987 McSween was spending ten days with our family in Ingonish. I told him I was taking my mother to New Haven to get fresh codfish, and then we were going on to White Point to visit her nephew Richard. "Would you like to come?" He hadn't been in White Point since 1940 when he was a green seminarian. He was nervous and shy. "Will they remember me?" After some coaxing by my mother we left for the fishing village. White Point is one of the most spectacularly beautiful places on Cape Breton Island: it looks like a Newfoundland outport with the houses clustered upon the side of a hill, the outcrop of rocks run down to the sea—Aspy Bay. Across the bay Sugarloaf Mountain rises from the water like a perfect small-scale model of Mount Vesuvius. After introductions to my first cousin, who was married to one of the residents, the villagers begin to descend the hill in search of the young curate they had first met almost fifty years earlier when they were children. MacSween was greatly moved by the reunion, as were the men and women—no longer the girls and boys he had taught catechism to when he had first met them in that long gone and forgotten world.

Fig. 62 Whitepoint, Cape Breton 1987. Courtesy Stewart Donovan.

284

IN among MacSween's papers of the late 1960s there is a note that could serve as fitting epitaph to at least one side of his life and work: it concerns a young woman, a student

> *from NYU—books under her arms—last question: "My boy friend committed suicide 2 weeks ago. Other friends of mine have done the same. What's wrong? Then I said I'll go to the Writer's Congress. They'll tell me. But you've told me nothing!" Tears streaming down her face. "You've told me nothing!" And the rest was silence! They could have told her a great deal—but no one really listens. But she told us how much is expected from literature: it must be the handmaid of all wisdom, and it must walk in front of religion and philosophy into the unknown countries that stand at the edge of our minds.*[2]

Notes to Introduction

1. Dudek's first essay on MacSween appeared in the Canadian Jesuit publication, Compass and was later reprinted in Essays in Myth and Reality (1992).

2. Eagleton, After Theory, 81.

3. Ibid., 81.

4. Much of the discussion of religion, faith, intellectuals and artists that appears in this text comes from Terry Eagleton's After Theory and The Gate Keeper: A Memoir.

5. Eagleton, After Theory, 99

6. Ibid., 99-100.

7. In his collected essays, George Steiner discusses the nature of Catholic nationalism that arose in France during the Dreyfus Case. He also discusses Pèguy's formulation: "When we touch upon the relationship of race to nation, and the relationship of both to the concept of a religious faith, we pass from politique to mystique." According to Steiner, "There is a politics of mysticism, of the mystical, which has its own lineaments, its own logic, its own demands, but which moves outside the realm of consensus through debate, through vote, through political education, through the expounding of meliorist solutions." See "Totem and Taboo" in No Passion Spent, 230.

8. The author in conversation with Paul Durcan in Dublin, June 10, 1998.

9. Interview with Robert Hass, American Poet, 1996.

10. Eagleton, After Theory, 208.

Notes to Chapter I

1. Interview with R. J. MacSween, April 1986.

2. Interview with Mary MacLean Gillis, conducted by Ken Donovan, 14 January 1991.

3. Ibid.

4. See Hornsby, Nineteenth-Century Cape Breton.

5. Andrews, "Military Aid to the Civil Power" (MA thesis). Although the most infamous strike in Cape Breton's long mining history occurred in 1925, when the military was brought in and several miners were shot at and one killed, many other strikes had occurred in previous years. In 1909, for instance, many of Cape Breton's coal miners were involved in a long and bitter strike over pay and working conditions. The often desperate and 19th-century conditions that these miners and their families laboured and lived under has been well documented in history, song and folklore. The life of the great Cape Breton labour leader J. B. MacLachlan is probably the most famous instance of this.

6. Interview with R. J. MacSween, conducted by the author, April 1986; interview with Murdock MacSween, 8 December 1990; interview with Father Mike MacSween, 10 December 1990.

7. Interview with R. J. MacSween, April 1986.

8. Interview with Rod and Geraldine MacSween, April 1991.

9. The strike of 1909-10 was when the United Mine Workers of America first entered Nova Scotia.

10. R. J. MacSween, "North Sydney VI," The Casket, 13 June 1990, 3.

11. MacSween, "Ironville II," The Casket, March 1988, 14; rpt. TAR 87-88 (1991-92): 11-17.

12. MacSween, "Ironville," first published in The Casket, March 1988, 14; The Antigonish Review, 87-88 (1991-92): 13-14.

13. Ibid.

14. Doc Pat's Gaelic column in The Casket attracted a wide rural readership.

15. MacSween, "Ironville."

16. MacSween, letter to Dolores Crawford, October 1977, private papers.

17. MacSween, "Ironville."

18. Interview with Dolores Crawford conducted by the author, 8 December 1996.

19. A year earlier in the Edmonton Journal for Saturday, 8 December 1973, there was a feature article with the title "Small college town big in poetry: Magazine edited by poet-priest." The poet priest was Rev. R. J. MacSween. Ironically, Dolores Crawford does not recall seeing the article about her uncle at the time of publication.

20. Interview with John MacEachern August 1996.

21. The Antigonish Review 87-88 (1991-92): 15.

22. R. J. MacSween. Called From Darkness.

23. Hugh had gone to Winnipeg because his brother lived there and helped him obtain work.

24. "Sages and Wise Men," The Casket, 1988.

25. R. J. MacSween, "A View of D. H. Lawrence." The Antigonish Review 87-88 (1991-92): 146.

26. See Frank's biography of the legendary Cape Breton labour leader: J. B. McLachlan.

27. Forbes, The Maritime Rights Movement, 60.

28. Ibid.

29. Quoted by Frank in "Tradition and Culture in the Cape Breton Mining Community," in Donovan, Cape Breton at 200, 216.

30. Ibid., 209. In his biography of Pius XII, Hitler's Pope, Cornwell gives a highly readable and well-documented survey of both the Catholic Church's anti-modernist position and its stance on Communism.

31. Ibid., 210.

32. R. J. MacSween papers. This collection of papers is housed at the offices of The Antigonish Review. Herein after MacSween papers, TAR.

33. Interview with Dolores Crawford.

34. See his articles on Baron Corvo, et al. in The Antigonish Review.

35. Interview with Malcolm MacDonell, 5 July 1991. See also James Cameron's For the People.

36. Raymond MacLean, Bishop John Cameron.

37. Interview with Michael MacSween, 7 December 1990.

38. Nicholson Papers, RG5/11/1802.

39. James Taylor, "Interview with Alistair MacLeod," The Antigonish Review 87-88 (1991-92): 299.

Notes to Chapter II

1. MacSween, "Coming to Antigonish," The Casket, February 1988, 15.

2. Cameron, For the People, 205. Cameron's work was the first history of St. Francis Xavier University.

3. Ibid., 207.

4. Joe Marinelli remembers that Rod had bad eyes, and this was his real handicap. In his autobiographical notes written later MacSween recorded, "Could never see the ball, or the puck. Years later, glasses on, went over to look at the net."

5. Interview with John Hector MacGregor, 1991.

6. Interview with John Ross, 1991.

7. Interview with Malcolm MacDonnell, 1991.

8. In his autobiographical notes for this period MacSween recorded, "8. Fascination of history. 9. Then college—history and biography: taking books home for Christmas and summer holidays. Amazement of other boys, satisfaction of librarian, Miss MacDonald. 10. Reproof over The Complete Poe. Injustice, I thought. 11. Gerard Manley Hopkins. 12. Lives of Saints—St. Francis Xavier, St. John of the Cross, St. Francis of Assisi, St. Thomas More. 13. Belloc and Chesterton. Left College—history and literature."

9. The Canadian Catholic Church dealt with the crisis of sexual abuse among its clergy a decade earlier than its American counterpart. The last chapter of this biography records MacSween's own response to this crisis.

10. In the early 1960s MacSween made a trip to New York with his former student, Pat Walsh. They saw the Broadway production of The Night of the Iguana by Tennessee Williams. Two of the many memorable lines in the play are: "There are worse things than celibacy." / "Yes, death and lunacy."

11. In number 14 of his autobiographical notes MacSween recorded: "One-year home [after graduating from St. FX] a book a week even if the sky fell. 'Lust for Life', world of artists, music, etc."

12. Interview with Arthur Doyle, 1991.

13. Walsh, "R.J. MacSween in conversation with Patrick Walsh," St. FX Alumni News, 1980, 6-17; rpt. The Antigonish Review 87-88: 235-51. In the same interview MacSween noted that "the books I bought while I was in the Seminary, of course, were mostly theological or philosophical and, after I was ordained, I got in touch with a very fine book store in New York—the Gotham Book Mart."

14. MacSween papers, TAR.
15. Interview with Hugh MacDonald, 1991.
16. Interview with Father Joe Marinelli, 13 August 1992.
17. Readers have, of course, reminded me that sometimes a sausage is just a sausage.
18. Hugh A. MacDonald preserved the copy of this poem from his time in the seminary.
19. Letter to the author from B. M. Broderick, 1992.
20. "White Point, Victoria County," The Casket, March 1988, 20.
21. MacSween papers, TAR.
22. In autobiographical notes 16 & 17, the older MacSween remembered the Seminary years with some enthusiasm, "A New World!! Music, Fathers, Doctors: the wonder of it!! from the inside!!" MacSween papers, TAR.

Notes to Chapter III

1. Interview with Leona MacDonald, June 1991.
2. Letter from E. A. Kelly, 28 November 1942. MacSween papers, TAR.
3. Interview with Betty and Jack MacDonald, 1992.
4. "R. J. MacSween in conversation with Patrick Walsh," TAR 87-88 (1991-92): 235-51.
5. MacSween papers, TAR.
6. Interview with Kevin MacNeil, 31 July 1996. Peter Sanger, friend of Father MacSween's and poetry editor of TAR, discusses one of MacSween's early books, The Confessions of Saint Augustine, in his article, Truth Worth Telling, 315.
7. Interview with R. J. MacSween, May 1986.
8. See Brian Tennyson and Roger Sarty, Guardian of the Gulf.
9. MacSween papers, TAR.
10. Although some of the MacSween family were skeptical about George's "audience with the Pope" there is no reason to believe that he did not meet Pius XII. John Cornwell in his recent biography notes that many soldiers had audiences with the Pontiff, including one of Rod MacSween's favourite writers, Evelyn Waugh, who was a captain at the time of the liberation of Rome. See Cornwell.
11. Interview with Rev. Mike MacSween, 7 December 1990. Father Mike recalled that when his father got married he did not drink again because he felt it was no example for children. Pat left for overseas in 1944, his father got married in 1909.
12. Interview with Father Frank MacNeil, 1992.
13. Interview with Father MacSween, May, 1986.
14. Nicholson Papers, RG5/11/11291 and RG511/11292, PNP, STFXUA.
15. See Richard Kearney's interview with George Steiner, "Culture: the price you pay," in States of Mind and Terry Eagleton's "The End of English" and "The Crisis of Contemporary Culture" in The Eagleton Reader.
16. See Cameron, For The People.

17. Letter to Pat MacSween, 8 January 1945, PNPP, RG5/11/11288, STFUA.
18. Letter to Nicholson, 16 February 1945, PNPP, RG5/11/11289, STFUA.
19. R. J. MacSween, Furiously Wrinkled, 77.
20. Interview with Mary MacKinnon. At one point Mary chaired a meeting for the federal Liberal government minister, Judy LaMarsh.
21. Interview with Effie and Jim Duggan, 1992.
22. Interview with Kay Beaton, 1992.
23. Interview with Theresa (MacSween) Gallant, 1992.
24. Nicholson papers, RG5/11/11255.
25. Interview with Father Mike MacSween.
26. Interview with Pat Walsh, TAR 87-88 (1991-92): 235.
27. See Chapter 1, note 58. See also Edward Said, Culture and Imperialism, Terry Eagleton, Heathcliffe and the Great Hunger and Denis Donoghue, We Irish. All these critics have written on the close connection and interdependence that exists between culture and religion, culture and nationalism.
28. MacSween dated and signed all of his books as soon as he got them. A curiosity of this book is its wartime logo: an eagle screaming from the sky with a book in its talons and a banner in its mouth proclaiming: Books Are Weapons in the War of Words.
29. There are many biographies of Pound that describe his years in Italy; Humphrey Carpenter's A Serious Character: The life of Ezra Pound, is one of the more exhaustive (and exhausting) ones.
30. Cameron, 271.
31. Letter to Mary and Mick MacKinnon, private papers.
32. Nicholson Papers, RG5/11/11295.
33. R. J. MacSween in conversation with Patrick Walsh, Alumni News 1980, 7; rpt. TAR 87-88 (1991-92): 238.
34. Ibid., 235.
35. "Named to St. FX teaching staff," clipping among MacSween papers, TAR.
36. "Farewell Made to Parishioners," clipping among MacSween papers, TAR.

Notes to Chapter IV
1. Interview with Rev. Frank MacNeil. Father A. A. Johnston was the author of the monumental two-volume work, A History of the Catholic Church in Eastern Nova Scotia; Cf. Kathleen MacKenzie, Antigonish Diocese Priests and Bishops.
2. Interview with Michael MacSween, July 1991.
3. Interviews with Malcolm MacLellan and Malcolm MacDonell, July 1991.
4. Cameron, For the People, 270.
5. R. J. MacSween in conversation with Patrick Walsh, Alumni News (1980), 15; rpt. TAR 87-88 (1991-92): 236.
6. Interview with Jack MacDonald, July 1991.

7. R. J. MacSween in conversation with Patrick Walsh, Alumni News (1980), 15; rpt. TAR 87-88 (1991-92): 237.

8. Interview with Rod and Geraldine MacSween, October 1992.

9. Interview with Effie and Jim Duggan, October 1992.

10. R. J. MacSween in conversation with Patrick Walsh, Alumni News (1980), 16; rpt. TAR 87-88 (1991-92): 247.

11. Interview with Freeman Whitty, July 1991.

12. R. J. MacSween in conversation with Patrick Walsh, Alumni News, 17; rpt. TAR 87-88 (1991-92): 240.

13. Interview with Sr. Madeline Connolly, TAR 87-88 (1991-92): 288.

14. Interview with Katherine Chisholm, July 1991.

15. C. J. Fox, "R. J. MacSween: A Beacon," TAR 87-88 (1991-92): 290.

16. Nicholson papers, RG5/11/1130.

17. Letter to Mary and Michael MacKinnon, Private papers.

18. Cameron, For the People, 271.

19. Interview with Father Bauer, July 1991.

20. R. J. MacSween, letter to Nicholson, Nicholson papers, RG5/11/11260

21. Mike MacSween, letter to Dr. Nicholson, 28 July 1950, Nicholson papers, RG5/11/11260.

22. Nicholson Papers, RG5/11/11306.

23. Nicholson Papers. RG/11/11260 and RG5/11/11802.

24. See Dudek's letters from Ezra Pound in DK/Some Letters of Ezra Pound. See also Stewart Donovan, "The Critic As Artist," TAR 100 (1995): 39-55.

25. Nicholson Papers, RG5/11/11262.

26. Coady Papers, RG30/21/13826. Stepinac, like his more famous contemporary, Pius XII, is currently being considered for beatification in Rome. John Cornwell in his acclaimed biography, Hitler's Pope, makes many grim and substantiated observations and accusations against the man Coady and MacSween were defending.

27. Contemporary (Alumni News) 7, no. 2.

28. The Index is a list kept by the Vatican of proscribed, censured books. Galileo was on this index until a few years ago, when the ban on his excommunication was finally lifted.

29. MacSween, "Talking Bronco," TAR 50 (1982): 29.

30. Cameron, 303.

31. "Little University of the World," The Casket, 21 May 1953, 3.

32. MacSween papers, TAR.

33. Interview with Joe Marinelli, July 1991.

34. Interview with Murdock MacSween, July 1991.

35. MacSween, the forgotten world.

36. Cameron, 304.

37. Interview with John Young, September 1995.

Notes to Chapter V
1. Interview with MacSween, May 1986.
2. Interview with Helen Aboud and Agnes Cordeau, November 1994.
3. Donovan, "In Conversation with Sr. Margaret MacDonell," TAR 87-88 (1991-92): 293.
4. Kilmer, Dreams and Images.
5. Interview with Pat Walsh, October 1992.
6. "James Taylor interviews Alistair MacLeod," TAR 87-88 (1991-92): 299.
7. In Al Capp's Lil' Abner, Moonbeam McSwine is large, dirty and ignorant, so it's understandable that MacSween did not like the sobriquet.
8. "James Taylor interviews Alistair MacLeod," TAR 87-88 (1991-92): 300-301.
9. Interview with George Sanderson, 1992.
10. He did, however, write a poem for the great critic and man of letters, but it was never published. It is different from his other poems in that it singles out a famous literary person. It was written in October of 1971:

Sam Johnson
during Sam Johnson's life
 he walked in fear of death
he saw the shadow before
 the substance
from the hedges
 the corners of every room
had a busy spider

his health plagued him
even when good
 it threatened to be bad
now psychologists
 hold him in their hands
that mountain man
 heavy with judgment

he differs from us all
 only in his ability to speak
 and in his biographer
who is not afraid of death
 is a fool

but there are no fools

only those who cannot speak

or have no biographer

11. See MacSween's "Alexander Pope Under Attack" TAR 28 (1977): 95-105; rpt. TAR 87-88 (1991-92): 166. This is one of two major essays that MacSween would write on Pope.

12. Both of Pat's parents died when he was at St. FX and Fr. MacSween became like a second father to the young American. Pat had also been considering the priesthood:

So I was wrestling with that problem and the reason that it was big for me with my father having died was that my mother got heart trouble when I was born and she used to say, "You were the beginning of all my troubles and you're going to be the end of me." Heavy burdens. And she also said to me, "I could have died, you could have died, but I promised Jesus and his mother that if you and I were spared that I would do everything in my power to help you become a priest." My mother was Italian, and my Irish father, who was a great friend of priests all his life, told me that priests were very lonely guys, they need help. And wherever we went priests always came to the house. They always came and they could take off their shirts and have a beer, a game of cards, whatever—relax. My father made a point of being friendly with priests to give them some kind of human contact.

See also "Travels with Father MacSween" Alumni News (1991): 11-14.

13. Father McSween remembered that when Lyndon McIntyre approached him about getting into the course, he said he wanted to become a journalist. MacSween replied that this was not journalism; McIntyre persisted, however, saying, "No, but it will help." MacSween admired the persistence.

14. Macsween papers, TAR.

15. Ibid.

16. Interview with R. J. MacSween, April 1986.

17. Ibid.; interview with Margaret MacSween, October 1992.

18. Welton, Little Mosie from the Margaree. See also Cameron.

19. MacSween papers, TAR papers.

20. Interview with Hugh MacDonald.

Notes to Chapter VI

1. MacSween, "Cardinal Newman, Writer," TAR 81-82 (1990): 93-108; rpt. TAR 87-88 (1991-92): 193-208.

2. Dr. Hugh Somers and Rod MacSween were natural enemies for many reasons, not least their views on education. Somers insisted on accreditation, on PhDs in all areas including the arts—without exception. Somers also came from the middle-class of the town of Antigonish, and MacSween would not have disagreed with the sentiments expressed by Father Michael Gillis in a letter to Coady regarding Somers' vision for St. FX: "Is not Somers planning a similar enslavement of the unemployed and poorly employed to meet the demands of the sons of the so-called elite and

larger income class through the academic St. FX and Xavier College?" (Cameron, 315). If, however, a single reason for the animosity that existed between the two men were to be sought, it would have to lie in the fact that Somers was the driving force behind Doc Pat's exile at age 67 to the largest parish in Sydney. That MacSween was able to resist Somers's "suggestion" that he retire came from the fact that the popular teacher had amassed considerable support among the faculty and, more importantly, among the professor-priests for whom he had become a spokesman on issues of salaries, pensions and general living conditions. (Interview with MacSween, April 1986.)

3. Interview with Jackie Walsh, October 1992.

4. He also visited Jack and Betty MacDonald.

5. Sanderson eventually edited, with Frank MacDonald, a special issue of TAR dedicated to McLuhan's work. This issue was subsequently published as Marshall *McLuhan: The Man and His Message.* TAR 74-75 (1988).

6. In MacSween's notes he records this text as coming from a book entitled "European Paideuma given to Douglas Fox to publish."

7. MacSween, "Ezra Pound: a Personal Estimate," Contemporary (St. FX Alumni News) 1 no. 1; rpt. TAR 87-88 (1991-92): 134.

8. Interview with Gertrude Sanderson, October 1992.

9. Contemporary (Alumni News) 4 no. 1, 15 March 1966; rpt. Halifax Chronicle-Herald 30 March 1966,.

10. MacSween, Xaverian, 116.

11. Contemporary 6 no. 3, 3-4. In later life, MacSween always took pride in the fact that his fellow priests, his colleagues, had taken a stand against Humane Vitae. A newspaper clipping Fr. MacSween kept among his papers came from the Halifax Chronicle-Herald, 24 September 1968, and it announced: "Letter Sent to Bishop":

Fifty-five members of the faculty of St. Francis Xavier University here have sent a letter to the Canadian Catholic Conference of Bishops regarding birth control. In the letter to the conference meeting this week in Winnipeg, the faculty members, both lay and clerical, ask the bishops to interpret the Papal encyclical on birth control in such a way that the supremacy of the Christian's conscience on the regulation of birth be protected, and that the final judgment of the question of birth control be left to the couple.

The priests who took a stand against Humane Vitae included Fr. Gregory MacKinnon and Fr. Bernie MacDonald.

12. Eagleton, The Gate Keeper.

13. MacSween papers, TAR.

14. "Father MacSween: A Memoir," TAR 87-88 (1991-92): 258.

15. R. J. MacSween, "Morley Callaghan: Some Words in Praise and Criticism," Contemporary 3, no. 4, 4.

16. It is a debate on the fringe now, but it was very fashionable in America in the last two decades: the late Alan Bloom was seen as its leading apostle with his book

The Closing of the American Mind; other writers, with no particular axe to grind, also joined in the debate: see Robert Hughes's The Culture of Complaint.

17. R.J. MacSween, review of *The Novels of Hugh MacLennan*, by Robert H. Corcxburn. TAR 2, no. 1 (1971): 91-92.

18. R. J. MacSween, "Yeats and His Language," TAR 2, no. 2: 68-73.

19. Vince Pasaro, "Dragon Fiction," Harper's, September 1996, 71.

20. One of his favourite pastimes in old age was arguing whether or not the Roman Empire would have survived if the Emperor had not moved the capital to the East.

21. MacSween, the forgotten world, 76.

22. MacSween papers, TAR.

23. MacSween in conversation with Patrick Walsh.

24. R. J. MacSween, "Consider the Child," MacSween papers, TAR.

25. R. J. MacSween, "Should the University Be Abolished" and "The University is Going," MacSween papers, TAR.

26. George Sanderson who was a Features Editor for The Sun responded to the MacLennan article in the following letter dated March 1, 1969:

Dear Sir,

I read your feature "Universities must act or outraged public will" by Hugh MacLennan with some interest. However it was disappointing. It does not clarify the situation to refer to "neurotic forces" coming to the fore; the nametag does not enlighten! Enclosed is an article—"Should the University be Abolished"—by R. J. MacSween, professor of English at Saint Francis Xavier University. This article does help one to grasp, perhaps only dimly, the significance of the present student crisis. I send you this item for reprinting as I think the gravity of the crisis demands greater understanding.

27. The five Englishmen were Geoffrey Baker, Rev. Brocard Sewell, Angus Somerville, William Tierney and Derek Wood. Of the five hired only two would remain and establish permanent careers at St. FX. Some of these Englishmen—but by no means all—objected to MacSween continuing as Chair. Their reasons, according to Pat Walsh, were mixed: some of it was personality, but mostly it came down to MacSween's perspective on teaching and writing, his attitude and distinction between scholars and academics; there were, of course, other members of the department besides these Englishmen who did not belong to MacSween's camp and who, for reasons of their own, did not wish to see him continue as Chair.

28. In the English Department, at this time, MacSween had hired Pat Walsh, Sheldon Currie, Kevin O'Brien and James Taylor—all of whom were former students; later, on Kevin O'Brien's recommendation he would also lobby to get Philip Milner, an American Catholic, hired.

29. Currie, "Big Mac," St. FX Alumni News, Winter 1991, 43.

Notes to Chapter VII

1. MacSween, the forgotten world. All quotations are from this edition.

2. Interview with MacSween, May 1986.

3. Dudek, "In the Tragic Mode," in Paradise: Essays on Myth, Art and Reality, 115. I had the good fortune to get to know Louis Dudek as a friend in his old age, and we corresponded on MacSween until Louis' final illness before his death on March 22, 2001.

4. Eagleton, After Theory, 210.

5. When the late Philip Larkin's collected poems were published in 1988, MacSween remarked to me that he felt the publishers had done him a disservice. The effect of reading all of the poems together created what he felt was an air of unrelieved despair that Larkin himself would have recoiled from. The slim volumes published during his lifetime did not, MacSween believed, overwhelm the reader.

6. MacSween, review of Children of Albion: Poetry of the Underground in Britian, edited by Michael Horovitz. TAR 2, no. 2 (1971): 97. This would also apply to one of MacSween's other favourite poets, Philip Larkin see his "Church Going" in contrast with MacSween's "ecclesia."

7. MacSween, review of *Children of Albion: Poetry of the Underground in Britian*, edited by Michael Horovitz. TAR 1, no. 1 (1970): 115.

8. MacSween, "The Enigma of Hemingway: was it whistling in the dark?" Contemporary and Alumni News 2, no. 3 (1964): 2.

9. Eagleton, Heathcliff and the Great Hunger, PAGE.

10. Ibid., 258.

11. Derek Walcott, Collected Poems 1948-1984, 324.

12. Many of the poems in this first collection also evoke the notion of apocalypse. The apocalyptic and post-apocalyptic world is now part of the popular imagination: the Mad Max and Terminator films, Bladerunner and Waterworld are futuristic and often comic-book/superhero-style portrayals of life after the end of "civilization." In literature there have been many dystopias: H. G. Wells's The Time Machine, Aldous Huxley's Brave New World and George Orwell's 1984 all come to mind as does the work of our own Margaret Atwood, The Handmaid's Tale and, more recently, Oryx and Crake. Among the writers in English MacSween's poetry most closely resembles are figures like William Golding and Angela Carter: Golding's post-war, post-holocaust vision of human nature was one MacSween greatly admired and identified with. He had read all of the Englishman's novels and spoke highly of both their style and subject matter: the products of a "strange and fascinating mind." The fiction of Angela Carter was even closer in expression to MacSween's poetry. In novels such as Heroes and Villains, the post-apocalyptic world has arrived and is here to stay. Carter would eventually die at the relatively young age of 52, but not before she achieved fame and an almost cult-like status. MacSween knew her work well, though it was the man he hired, Father Brocard Sewell, and not MacSween himself, who eventually published one of her short stories in an early issue of The Antigonish Review.

13. And "the other" is, in the words of Michael Ondaatje's Sikh, the brown races of the world. In a central passage in The English Patient, the young sapper speaks for Ondaatje and all those who live in the shadow of empire:

I grew up with traditions from my country, but later, more often from your country.

Your fragile white island that with customs and manners and books and prefects and reason somehow converted the rest of the world. You stood for precise behaviour. I knew if I lifted a teacup with the wrong finger I'd be banished. If I tied the wrong kind of knot in a tie I was out. Was it just ships that gave you such power? Was it, as my brother said, because you had the histories and printing presses? You and then the Americans converted us.

MacSween would have recognized these sentiments and, especially towards the end of his life, he would have sympathized with many of them. I remember speaking to him, for example, when President Ronald Reagan gave the order to bomb Gadaffi's home and family in their tent in Libya. He had (somewhat sadly) spoken in defense of Reagan's White House early on; part of this was in support of the President as an actor (he did not like the contempt for actors that was being voiced at the time), but he also thought, in the beginning at least, that Reagan would do a good job. After the bombing he said simply that "it was the act of a cowboy."

14. Dudek, "Reeling poetry and decapitating books," The Globe and Mail, 8 June 1985. This review later appeared in Dudek's collection In Defense of Art, 241-43.

15. Dudek, "In the Tragic Mode and "Blighted Lives"; both of these essays appeared in Paradise.

16. Powe, A Climate Charged. These essays were originally commissioned by George Sanderson for The Antigonish Review.

17. Dudek's recognition of MacSween was not simply the act of a literary historian or a critic doing his job: there is a strong affinity between the two poets, both in their choice of subject matter and in their careers. Both professors of modern literature were highly influenced by the modern movement in poetry and prose, and both recognized the poet Ezra Pound as the central figure of that movement. Dudek sought Pound out in Washington and, later had a fruitful correspondence with him that he subsequently published. MacSween would spend half a lifetime teaching Pound's poetry, especially his Cantos. Other things the two poets had in common included their intense intellectual bent, their love of history and classical literature and, finally and not insignificantly, their Canadian Catholic heritage. This last fact is important insofar as it gave Dudek (a lapsed Catholic) the knowledge, sympathy and understanding necessary to appreciate more fully the world which MacSween, a Catholic priest, had come from.

Notes to Chapter VIII

1. Alumni News, Summer 1980.

2. Ibid.

3. Interview with Chris Connor, October 2000.

4. MacSween was rather proud that Muggeridge had acknowledged him. He liked the story of Fr. Gatto's: when at dinner in the priests' dining room with Fr. Edo Gatto a question came up about a particular writer and Muggeridge said, pointing to MacSween's table, "Ask that big fellow, he'll know."

5. These manuscripts were The King Was in His Counting House, retitled The Coordinator, a David Lodge style satire about life at St. FX; the essence of the story,

in MacSween's words: "How things fall apart when no strong hand rules"; I Went To The Rock (a love/murder story based partly on his brother Pat's life, in essence: the terrible struggle to survive in winter—all alone); The Adversaries, another love/murder story set in Antigonish, in essence: envy of a man of many gifts. All of these manuscripts are at the archives of The Antigonish Review.

6. Letter to Dolores Crawford, 9 December 1974.

7. Letter to Dolores Crawford, 21 October 1977.

8. Interview with Dolores Crawford, 8 December 1996.

9. Dolores eventually got to know Mike as well as—if not better than—her uncle Rod.

10. I include a letter of Dolores Crawford's to illustrate the ease and grace with which she wrote and how this helped to initially break the ice with her uncle:

Going through my dear daily missal you gave me oh so many years ago, I came across an old prayer card—a little worse for wear I'm afraid—and it is a commemorative card from your ordination and it seems you have just celebrated your 45th anniversary! Wow!! What an honour!!! I'm so sorry I didn't find the card sooner in order to acknowledge you on the occasion itself. Better late than never—here I am, an old bundle of rags, held together with chewing gum and binder twine, saying a hearty "Congratulations." Did you celebrate? I hope so!!! I had mentioned to you on the phone recently that my parish priest is leaving next month—in his place we are getting two priests—or should I say one pastor and one "Baby"—newly ordained—only two months old. Oh, my, everybody seems so young as I get older. However, it shall be interesting; the "baby's" name is Fr. Mike so it will at least have a familiar ring to it. I am joyous! Bill and the children have been away for three weeks on holidays—expected back tomorrow or Sunday. They went to the West coast, visiting relatives and Expo on the way to Vancouver Island where they rested by the sea for two weeks. I find it's no holiday for me if I go along and also we need the time apart. Heather and Glen need time with their dad, who is very busy and away a lot all the rest of the year. Glen and I need time apart; we are much too close at times—he'll be 12 in Aug. Time to separate and mum has to push the baby out of the nest. Also, going to the Pacific is only a poor substitute for the Atlantic, but even at that two weeks isn't long enough. So-o-o-o-o to make a long story longer, I remained home, utterly delighted in books, cats, solitude, music, T.V., redecorating, visiting, talking on the phone, not cooking meals and other wondrous, sundry, decadent meandering. I far better enjoyed doing "this" at home, rather than going off on my own to "be" in some strange place. I would have wasted about 1/3 of the time settling in and besides I did get a lot of things done here that needed doing. I had time to do some new things—I laid new tile in Glen's room and replaced wall sockets, first time for both, fixed three closet doors and painted two bedrooms. I just can't or won't (I'm not sure which) do that when everyone's here—then it's real work because I have to cook meals etc. Well, darlingest, I'm off to save lives and stamp out disease at "heaven's porch."

11. Cheng Chia's poems are in indeed lovely but sad. I include "Snow and "One more spring":

Notes

Snow
In tears of remembrance
I walk in the snow
the snows of your dreams

Had you but seen once
how the snows of one night
change the whole world

Had you but seen once
how soft the flakes
cover the pines

I would walk in the snow
in smiles of solace
the snows of your eternal dreams

One more spring
This body this firm flesh
this flow of silk black hair
and these strong white teeth—
the envy of the old man of the sea

This mind this fresh thought
this sea of unfathomed feelings
and these quick warm waves
the envy of the advocate at Naples

Could they all go in one season?

Scarcely dare I hope
for one more spring

12. R. J. MacSween to Dolores Crawford. Private papers.

13. Mary Lou O'Reilly, "Rev. R. J. MacSween: Priest, Teacher and Writer," The Casket, 4 November 1985, 11.

14. Other members of TAR who came and went during these years included William Tierney, E. Gatto, Charles Plummer, Jeffrey Baker and Philip Milner.

15. Walsh, "R. J. MacSween: In conversation with Patrick Walsh," TAR 87-88 (1991-92): 235-51.

16. Wyndham Lewis' Blast, Ezra Pound's Little Review, Marianne Moore's the Dial, Cyril Connolly's Horizon and Sean O'Faolain's The Bell all come to mind.

17. Walsh, TAR 87-88 (1991-92): 235-51.

18. Letter to Father Sewell, 2 February 1971. MacSween Papers, TAR.

19. Ibid.

20. Some of the books include Children of Albion: Poetry of the Underground; Thirst for Love by Yukio Mishima; Madly Singing in the Mountains (about Arthur Walley); Mrs. Eckdorf in O'Neill's Hotel by William Trevor; The Honeymoon Festival by Marian Engel; The Driver's Seat by Muriel Spark; Yeats and the Nineties; Belloc: A Biographical Anthology; The Life of Ezra Pound; An Anthology of Revolutionary Poetry.

21. MacLeod's poem is a Cape Breton elegy on his mother and her sister entitled: "Two Graves in Late November." Its tone and diction are what many might have expected from MacSween.

22. George's collaboration with MacSween was the most intimate of all the editors. His championing of McLuhan was responsible for much of the layout and eventual "look" of TAR.

23. MacSween, "Ivy Compton-Burnett: Merciless Understanding." TAR 7 (1971): 39-46.

24. MacSween, "Ivy Compton Burnett." TAR 24 (1975): 25-30.

25. Alumni News, 1980.

26. MacSween, "Evaluating Evelyn Waugh." TAR 25 (1976): 41-50.

27. Christopher Hitchens draws attention to this side of Waugh in his Unacknowledged Legislation: Writers in the Public Sphere, 133.

28. Mircea Eliade, "Ordeal by Labyrinth: Conversations with Claude-Henri Rocquet," TAR 51 (1982): 53-55.

29. MacSween, "Ezra Pound Under Attack." TAR 28 (1977): 95-105.

30. MacSween, review of Emir Rodriguez Monegal, Jorge Luis Borges: A Literary Biography, TAR 38 (1979): 107-108. 36; rpt. TAR 87-88 (1991-92): 216.

31. Dudek, "Blighted Lives: The Prose of R. J. MacSween." TAR 87-88 (1991-92): 266-72.

32. MacSween sent a copy of his stories to his niece Dolores telling her that the story came from his brother Pat.

33. MacSween, the burnt forest.

34. Dudek, "Blighted Lives." TAR 87-88 (1991-92): 266-72.

35. Interview with Msgr. Malcolm MacLellan, 1992. This side of MacSween, his support for his priest colleagues and his tenacity in fighting for their rights, was always acknowledged by his colleagues including the late Fathers Hogan, Kehoe and Gatto to mention a few. After all they had given to the institution, the community and the diocese, these men—who owned almost nothing—still had to fight for a living pension. We can imagine that MacSween's indignation would have been great.

36. Alumni News, 1980.

37. MacSween, review of Alexander Gladkov, Meetings with Pasternak. TAR 34 (1978).

Notes to Chapter IX

1. Alumni News, 1980, 4.
2. Interview with MacSween, 1986.
3. One of Bannon's many epigrams might be construed as homophobic, but I believe it is fairer to say that it was motivated by his Irishness:
> On a white horse rode William and Mary
> She was Queen and he was a Fairy
4. MacSween papers, TAR.
5. Donovan, "Breakfast with Borges." TAR 52 (1983): 67-70.
6. Dudek, Paradise.
7. Interview with Olivia Dube and Alvin Donovan, 1996. I should point out that both Olivia and Alvin read the story, and both graduated with first class honours, she in English and he in history.
8. MacSween, review of Ivan Ilich, Deschooling Society. TAR 8 (1972): 105-106; rpt. TAR 87-88 (1991-92): 207.
9. Richard Lemm, "R. J. MacSween's Poetry," The Atlantic Provinces Book Review, 15.
10. Letter to Dolores Crawford, private papers.
11. Dudek, "In the Tragic Mode," in Paradise, 100.
12. Sheldon Currie, a review of Ann-Marie MacDonald, Fall On Your Knees. TAR 113 (1998): 44.
13. John MacEachern, "Father Rod." TAR 87-88 (1991-92): 295-98.
14. Donovan, "Remembering Yeats," TAR 71-72 (1987-88): 57-62.
15. MacSween, "G.K.C.: The People's Journalist." TAR 87-88 (1991-92): 181.
16. MacSween, "The Letters of David Jones." TAR 49 (1982): 45-50.
17. Sister Doyle taught for many years in the St. FX English Department.
18. MacSween was always interested in small magazines and had subscriptions to many of them including Agenda:

I got Agenda from the very beginning. It was only like a leaflet first, eh, two or three pages, not even stapled, then it got bigger and bigger. Did you meet that Sargent fellow that was here a few years ago? He runs a poetry review in England. He mentioned how poor the poetry was in Agenda. He's right. And Father Sewell's old magazine The Aylesford Review, terrible poetry. So I had to agree with Sargent, although he was a little shit. That Sargent after he was here, I saw a review of 3 or 4 poetry books in the TLS, I think, and you should have seen what they did with him. They gave each book about a half a column and then they said, there is this awful book out by so-and-so Sargent and the less said the better. That's all, two lines. He is a poor poet, but full of himself. He received some decoration from the Queen about a year before. But was he ever full of himself and he was telling us what a great friend of T. S. Eliot's he was. I wasn't fussy about him.

19. An example of MacSween's humour and love of jokes occurred during this trip: My brother, Alvin, and I were relaxing, hiding in the basement rec-room drinking cold beer, smoking cigars and watching hockey (the playoffs were on) when a beautiful young woman in a tank top descended the stairs. She came up to us and shaking our hands said, "So, you're monks?" My brother had a half mouthful of beer which he partly sprayed over himself in suppressed laughter, I choked back on my cigar. Apparently, MacSween had informed the guests that he had brought a couple of monks from the nearby village of Monastery, where there is indeed an Augustinian Order.

20. MacSween, Called From Darkness, 41.

21. Both Father MacSween and his niece, Jessie Sutherland, related a comic story that happened at this time. After the funeral, all of the MacSween clan gathered back at Art and Jessie's hotel room. For some reason the conversation turned to a discussion of language and in particular obscene language. The ubiquitous word fuck came up and Father MacSween was asked about it. He spoke about its possible origins, about Philip Larkin's famous use of it in his famous poem, "This Be The Verse"; about the fact that it was overused, but he also, begrudgingly, acknowledged that it had its place, especially, it seemed, when people wished to express anger. The evening wore on and the conversation changed to other topics. After several hours MacSween got up to leave, his niece, Jessie, showed him to the door and then asked, with everyone waiting for a response, if they would see him tomorrow: the priest, door in hand, replied gently, "Fuck off" then closed the door. He immediately reopened it to grin into the room that had erupted in laughter.

22. Whalen, Philip Larkin and English Poetry.

23. MacSween's mind, however, was as strong as ever—as the following anecdote clearly illustrates: my brother Ken, (a professor at Cape Breton University and a staff historian at Fortress Louisbourg) had accepted an offer to give history lectures on board a special cruise ship that was coasting the eastern seaboard from New York to Greenland, with stops at places of historic or naturalistic interest. Other experts on board included naturalists, marine biologists, botanists, ornithologists and archaeologists. Fascinated by Greenland my brother took many slides and absorbed as much of the history as he could. On his return he invited MacSween to come to supper and told him that he had a slide show he wished him to see. The next day I received a call from MacSween in Antigonish: "Stewart, you would have been proud of me, though I was a miserable shit!" He then proceeded to tell me how Ken would put a beautiful slide on the screen say, of a monastery, and before he could "utter two words, I jumped in." Isn't that the monastery established by ... and so it was with every slide that came up. My brother Ken phoned me later that day and said simply, "Stewart (let me tell you!) I was impressed!" MacSween said "I got a bug on Greenland when I was nineteen and read everything I could find on it."

24. MacSween, "G. M. Hopkins: The Hidden Poet." TAR 71-72 (1988): 25-56.

25. MacSween, "The Pleasures of Pope" TAR 69-70 (1987): 29-88.

26. MacSween, "Wild Brilliant Genius" a review of *Ezra Pound: Solitary Outlaw* by John Tytell. The Globe and Mail, Saturday, 30 January 1988.

27. MacSween, "Helena: Waugh's Failure," TAR 73 (1988): 27-128; rpt. TAR 87-88 (1991-92): 201.

Notes to Afterword

1. Margaret Atwood, The Blind Assassin, 149.

2. MacSween papers, TAR.

*B*ibliography

Andrews, Ian. "Military Aid to the Civil Power: The Cape Breton Coal Strike of 1909-1910." (MA Thesis). University of New Brunswick, 1987.

Atwood, Margaret. *The Blind Assassin.* Toronto: McLellan and Stewart, 2000.

Bloom, Alan. *The Closing of the American Mind.* New York: Simon and Schuster, 1987.

Cameron, James. *For the People: A History of St. Francis Xavier University.* Montreal-Kingston: McGill-Queens University Press, 1996.

Carpenter, Humphrey. *A Serious Character: The life of Ezra Pound.* London: Faber, 1988.

Cogswell, Fred. "Father MacSween: A Memoir." *TAR* 87-88 (1991-92): 258.

Cornwell, John. *Hitler's Pope: The Secret History of Pius XII.* New York: Viking, 1999.

Currie, Sheldon. "Big Mac." *St. FX Alumni News* Winter (1991): 43.

———. A review of Ann-Marie MacDonald, *Fall on Your Knees. TAR* 113 (1998): 44.

Donovan, Ken. *Cape Breton at 200: Historical Essays in Honor of the Island's Bicentennial 1785 - 1985.* Sydney, NS: Cape Breton University Press.

Donovan, Stewart. "Remembering Yeats," *TAR* 71-72 (1987-88): 57-62.

———. "In Conversation with Sr. Margaret MacDonnell." *TAR* 87-88 (1991-92): 293.

———. "The Critic as Artist." *TAR* 100 (1995): 39.55.

Donoghue, Denis *We Irish:* essays on Irish literature and society. New York: Knopf, 1986.

Dudek, Louis, ed. *Dk-some letters of Ezra Pound* Montreeal: DC Books, 1974.

———. *In Defense of Art Critical Essays & Reviews.* Quarry Press, 1988.

———. "Blighted Lives: The Prose of R. J. MacSween." *TAR* 87-88 (1991-92): 266-72.

———. *Paradise: Essays in Myth, Art and Reality.* Montreal: Vehicule Press, 1992.

Eagleton, Terry. *Heathcliffe and the Great Hunger: Studies in Irish Culture.* London: Verso, 1995.

———. "The Crisis of Contemporary Culture." *The Eagleton Reader,* edited by Stephen Regan. Oxford: Blackwell, 1998.

———. "The End of English" in *The Eagleton Reader,* edited by Stephen Regan. Oxford: Blackwell, 1998.

———. *The Gate Keeper: A Memoir.* Penguin, 2001.

———. *After Theory.* Penguin, 2003.

Eliade, Mircea. "Ordeal by Labyrinth: Conversations with Claude-Henri Rocquet," *TAR* 51 (1982): 53-55.

Forbes, Ernest R. *The Maritime Rights Movement, 1919-1927: A Study in Canadian Regionalism.* Montreal: McGill-Queen's University Press, 1979.

Fox, C. J. "R. J. MacSween: A Beacon." *TAR* 87-88 (1991-92): 290

Frank, David. "Tradition and Culture in the Cape Breton Mining Community." In *Cape Breton at 200: Historical Essays in Honor of the Island's Bicentennial 1785 - 1985.* Sydney, NS: Cape Breton University Press, 1985.

———. *J. B. McLachlan: A Biography.* Toronto: J. Lorimer, 1999.

Hass, Robert. *American Poet.* 1996.

Five American poets : Robert Hass, John Matthias, James McMichael, John Peck, Robert Pinsky / with an introduction by Michael Schmidt. -- Publication info: Manchester : Carcanet New Press, 1979.

Hitchens, Christopher draws attention to this side of Waugh in his *Unacknowledged Legislation: Writers in the Public Sphere*: London, New York: Verso, 2000.

Hornsby, Stephen J. *Nineteenth-century Cape Breton: A Historical Geography.* Montreal: McGill-Queen's University Press, 1992

Hughes, Robert. *Culture of Complaint: The Fraying of America.* New York: Oxford University Press, 1993.

Johnston, A. A. *A History of the Catholic Church in Eastern Nova Scotia.* Antigonish, NS: St. Francis Xavier University Press.

Kearney, Richard. Culture: The Price You Pay. In *States of Mind: Dialogues With Contemporary Thinkers.* New York: New York University Press, 1995.

Kilmer, Joyce. *Dreams and Images:* an anthology of Catholic poets. New York: Boni and Liveright, 1926.

Lemm, Richard. "R. J. MacSween's Poetry. The Atlantic Provinces Book Review." May-June (1985).

MacEachern, John. "Father Rod." *TAR* 87-88 (1991-92): 295-98.

MacKenzie, Kathleen. *Antigonish Diocese Priests and Bishops.* Antigonish: The Casket Printing and Publishing, 1994.

MacLean, Raymond. *Bishop John Cameron: Piety and Politics.* Antigonish: The Casket Printing and Publishing, 1991.

MacSween papers. Offices of *The Antigonish Review.*

MacSween, R. J. "North Sydney VI," *The Casket*, 1988.

———. "Ironville II," *The Casket*, 1988.

———. "Ironville." The Antigonish Review, 87-88 (1991-92): 13-14.

———. *Called From Darkness.* Antigonish, NS: Tarlane Editions, 1984.

———. "Sages and Wise Men," *The Casket*, 1988.

———. "A View of D. H. Lawrence." *The Antigonish Review* 87-88 (1991-92): 146.

———. "G. M. Hopkins: The Hidden Poet." *TAR* 71-72 (1988): 25-56.

———. "The Pleasures of Pope" *TAR* 69-70 (1987): 29-88.

———. "*Helena*: Waugh's Failure," *TAR* 73 (1988): 27-128; rpt. *TAR* 87-88 (1991-92): 201.

———. "Wild Brilliant Genius" a review of *Ezra Pound: Solitary Outlaw* by John Tytell. *The Globe and Mail*, Saturday, 30 January 1988.

———. "A View of D. H. Lawrence: Prophet Preaching Liberation." *Contemporary* 6 no. 3 (1968), 3-4.

———. "G.K.C.: The People's Journalist." *TAR* 87-88 (1991-92): 181.

———. "The Letters of David Jones." *TAR* 49 (1982): 45-50.

———. Review of Alexander Gladkov, *Meetings with Pasternak. TAR* 34 (1978).

———. Review of Ivan Ilich, *Deschooling Society. TAR* 8 (1972): 105-106.

———. "The Enigma of Hemingway: was it whistling in the dark?" *Contemporary and Alumni News* 2, no. 3 (1964): 2.

———. "Ivy Compton-Burnett: Merciless Understanding." *TAR* 7 (1971): 39-46.

———. "Ivy Compton Burnett." *TAR* 24 (1975): 25-30.

———. "Evaluating Evelyn Waugh." *TAR* 25 (1976): 41-50.

———. "Ezra Pound Under Attack." *TAR* 28 (1977): 95-105.

———. Review of Emir Rodriguez Monegal, *Jorge Luis Borges: A Literary Biography*, *TAR* 38 (1979): 107-108. 36.

———. "Coming to Antigonish," *The Caskett*, 1988.

———. "White Point, Victoria County," *The Casket*, 1988.

———. *The burnt forest [and other stories]*. Antigonish, NS: Antigonish Press, 1975.

———. *Double shadows*. Antigonish, NS: Antigonish Press, 1973.

———. *The Confessions of Saint Augustine.*

———. *Truth Worth Telling.*

———. *Furiously Wrinkled*. Antigonish, NS: Antigonish Press, 1976.

———. *the forgotten world*. Antigonish, NS: Antigonish Press, 1971.

———. *TAR* 87-88 (1991-92): 91-92.

———. "Talking Bronco." *TAR* 50 (1982): 29.

———. "Alexander Pope Under Attack." *TAR* 28 (1977) 95-105.

———. "Ezra Pound: A Personal Estimate." *TAR* 87-88 (191-92): 134.

———. *Contemporary* (*Alumni News*) 4 no. 1 (1966); rpt. *Halifax Chronicle-Herald* 30 March 1966.

———. "Morley Callaghan: Some Words of Praise and Criticism." *Contemporary* 3, no. 4 (1965): 2.

Nicholson papers. St. FX University Archives.

O'Reilly, Mary Lou. "Rev. R. J. MacSween: Priest, Teacher and Writer." *The Casket*, 4 November 1985.

Pasaro, Vince. "Dragon Fiction." *Harper's* September (1996): 71.

Powe, Bruce W. *A Climate Charged*. Oakville, ON: Mosaic Press, 1984.

Said, Edward. *Culture and* Imperialism. New York: Knopf, 1993.

Sanger, Peter. Truth Worth Telling

Small college town big in poetry: Magazine edited by poet-priest. *Edmonton Journal*, Saturday, 8 December 1973.

St. FX Alumni News, 1980, 6-17; rpt. The Antigonish Review nos 87-88 (Fall-Winter 1991-92): 235-51.

Steiner, George. *No Passion Spent" Essays 19978-1995*. Yale University Press, 1996.

Taylor, James. "James Taylor Interviews Alistair MacLeod." *TAR* 87-88 (1991-92): 299.

Tennyson, Brian and Roger Sarty. *Guardian of the Gulf: Sydney, Cape Breton, and the Atlantic wars*. Toronto: University of Toronto Press, 2000.

Walcott, Derek *Collected Poems 1948-1984. Toronto:* Collins, 1986.

Walsh, Patrick. "R. J. MacSween in conversation with Patrick Walsh," *TAR* 87-88 (1991-92): 235-51.

———. "Travels with Father MacSween." *Alumni News* Winter (1991): 11-14.

Welton, Michael R. *Little Mosie from the Margaree: A Biography of Moses Michael Coady*. Toronto: Thompson, 2001.

Whalen, Terry A. *Philip Larkin and English Poetry*. Hampshire: MacMillan, 1986.

*I*ndex

Index for Poems